D1096490

WOLVERINE
PATCH

S.H.I.E.L.D.
DOSSIER
file no.
22-0209316

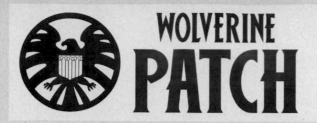

WOLVERINE PATCH

S.H.I.E.L.D.
DOSSIER
file no.
22-0209316

DOB: [redacted]
STATUS: [redacted]
SSN: [redacted]

SUBJECT:
Patch
A.K.A. Wolverine
A.K.A. Logan

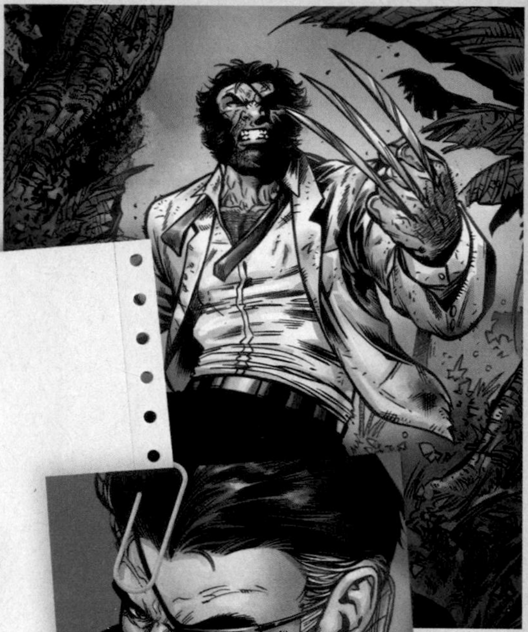

KNOWN ASSOCIATES:
WR
PR
IN
CO
LE
COV
ASS
EDI
SEN

File Amendment 202001

WRITER: Larry Hama
PENCILER: Andrea Di Vito
INKER: Le Beau Underwood

COLOR ARTIST: Sebastian Cheng
LETTERER: VC's Clayton Cowles
COVER ART: Geoff Shaw & Edgar Delgado
DOSSIER DESIGN: Nick Russell

ASSISTANT EDITOR: Drew Baumgartner
EDITOR: Mark Basso
SENIOR EDITOR: Jordan D. White

COLLECTION EDITOR: DANIEL KIRCHHOFFER
ASSISTANT MANAGING EDITOR: MAIA LOY
ASSOCIATE MANAGER, TALENT RELATIONS: LISA MONTALBANO
DIRECTOR, PRODUCTION & SPECIAL PROJECTS: JENNIFER GRÜNWALD
VP PRODUCTION & SPECIAL PROJECTS: JEFF YOUNGQUIST
BOOK DESIGNERS: SARAH SPADACCINI & NICK RUSSELL
SENIOR DESIGNER: JAY BOWEN
SVP PRINT, SALES & MARKETING: DAVID GABRIEL
EDITOR IN CHIEF: C.B. CEBULSKI

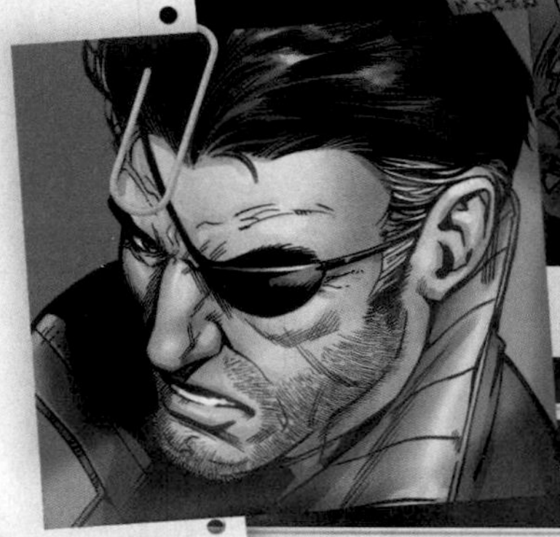

BRI

[redacted]

[redacted]nutant [redacted]

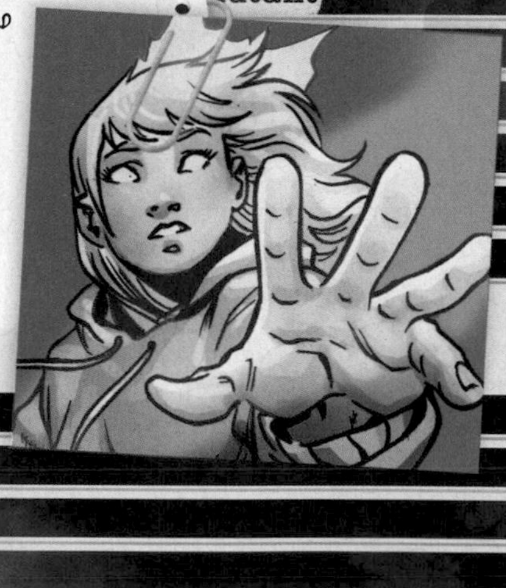

DESCRI

[redacted]d claws [redacted]ys aggressive behavior , and [redacted]

[redacted] and dangerous, [redacted]

WOLVERINE: PATCH. Contains material originally published in magazine form as WOLVERINE: PATCH (2022) #1-5. First printing 2022. ISBN 978-1-302-93206-0. Published by MARVEL WORLDWIDE, INC., subsidiary of MARVEL ENTERTAINMENT, LLC. OFFICE OF PUBLICATION: 1290 Avenue of the Americas, New York, NY 10104. **Printed in Canada.** KEVIN FEIGE, Chief Creativ Officer; DAN BUCKLEY, President, Marvel Entertainment; DAVID BOGART, Associate Publisher & SVP of Talent Affairs; TOM BREVOORT, VP, Executive Editor; NICK LOWE, Executive Editor, VP of Content, Digit Publishing; DAVID GABRIEL, VP of Print & Digital Publishing; SVEN LARSEN, VP of Licensed Publishing; MARK ANNUNZIATO, VP of Planning & Forecasting; JEFF YOUNGQUIST, VP of Production & Special Project ALEX MORALES, Director of Publishing Operations; DAN EDINGTON, Director of Editorial Operations; RICKEY PURDIN, Director of Talent Relations; JENNIFER GRÜNWALD, Director of Production & Special Project SUSAN CRESPI, Production Manager; STAN LEE, Chairman Emeritus. For information regarding advertising in Marvel Comics or on Marvel.com, please contact Vit DeBellis, Custom Solutions & Integrate Advertising Manager, at vdebellis@marvel.com. For Marvel subscription inquiries, please call 888-511-5480. **Manufactured between 9/9/2022 and 10/11/2022 by SOLISCO PRINTERS, SCOTT, QC, CANAD**

10 9 8 7 6 5 4 3 2 1

INTERNAL REVIEW ONLY

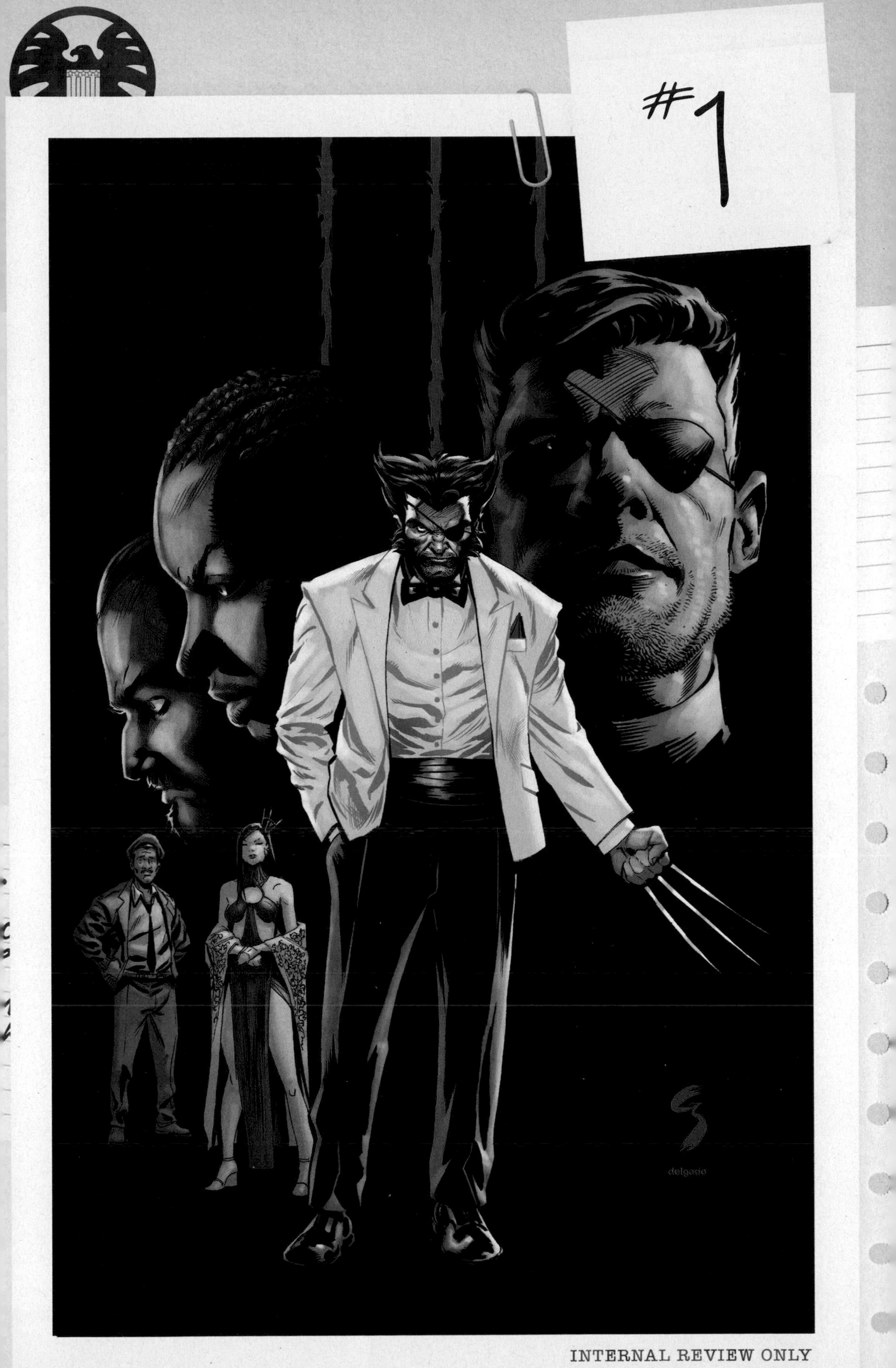
#1
delgado

INTERNAL REVIEW ONLY

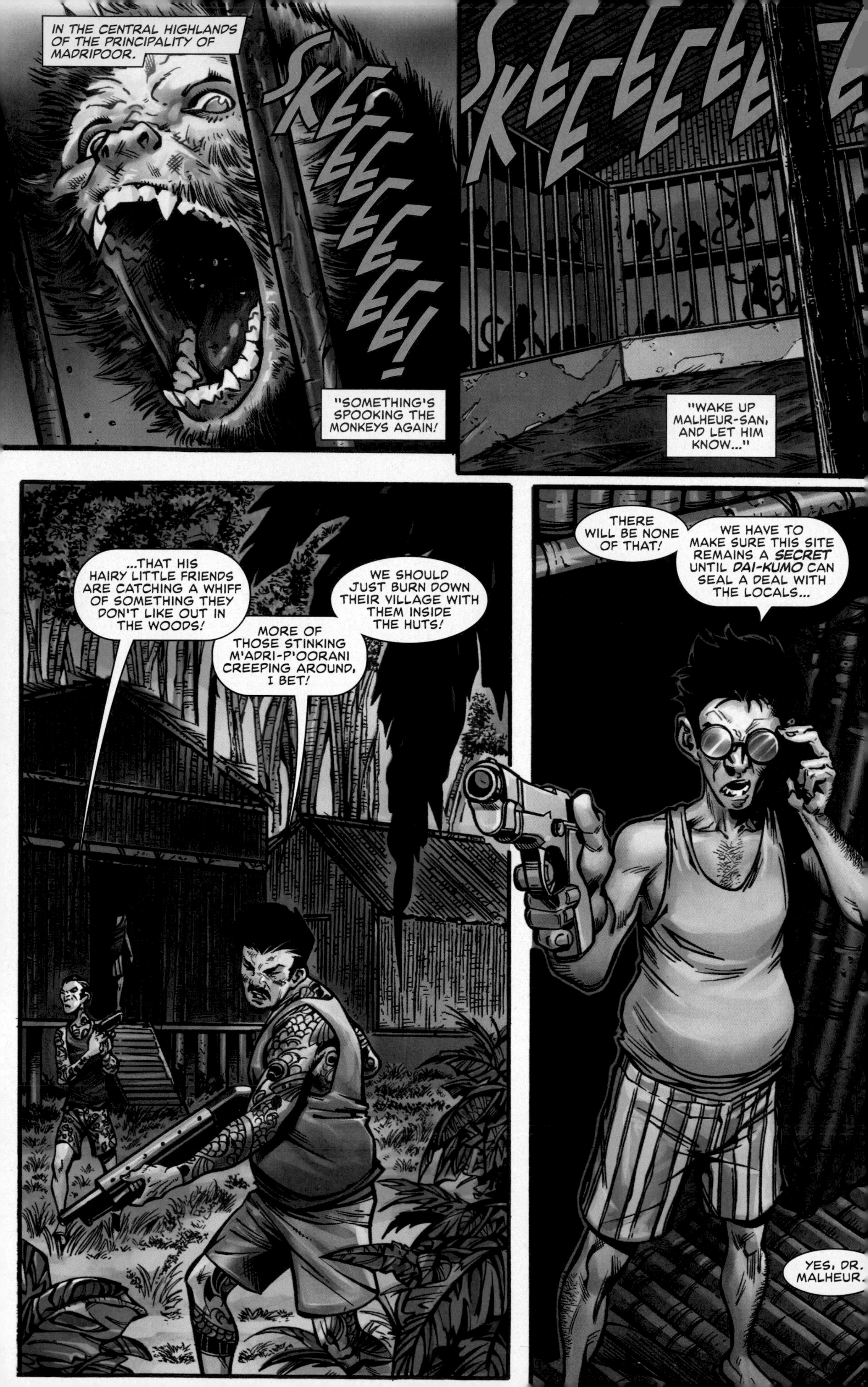

IN THE CENTRAL HIGHLANDS OF THE PRINCIPALITY OF MADRIPOOR.
SKEEEEEEEE!
"SOMETHING'S SPOOKING THE MONKEYS AGAIN!
SKEEEEEEEE
"WAKE UP MALHEUR-SAN, AND LET HIM KNOW..."
...THAT HIS HAIRY LITTLE FRIENDS ARE CATCHING A WHIFF OF SOMETHING THEY DON'T LIKE OUT IN THE WOODS!
MORE OF THOSE STINKING M'ADRI-P'OORANI CREEPING AROUND, I BET!
WE SHOULD JUST BURN DOWN THEIR VILLAGE WITH THEM INSIDE THE HUTS!
THERE WILL BE NONE OF THAT!
WE HAVE TO MAKE SURE THIS SITE REMAINS A SECRET UNTIL DAI-KUMO CAN SEAL A DEAL WITH THE LOCALS...
YES, DR. MALHEUR.

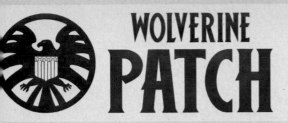

WOLVERINE PATCH

S.H.I.E.L.D. DOSSIER

file no. 22-0209316

DOB: [redacted]

STATUS: [redacted]

SSN: [redacted]

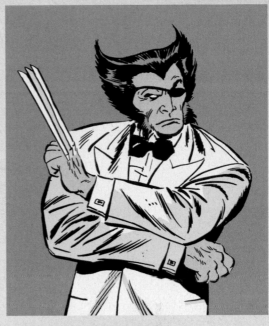

SUBJECT:

Patch
A.K.A. Wolverine
A.K.A. Logan

KNOWN ASSOCIATES:

Tyger Tiger
Archie Corrigan
(see dossiers)

BRIEF:

Formerly the X-Man known as WOLVERINE, subject has a mutant healing factor and retractable adamantium claws. Now living incognito in Madripoor. Base of operations seems to be the PRINCESS BAR, a nightspot he co-owns with TYGER TIGER. While he has proven a powerful ally, subject has a strong independent streak that may compromise S.H.I.E.L.D. interests in the region.

LAST KNOWN LOCATION:

[redacted]

RECOMMENDATION:

[redacted]

Tyger Tiger

- A.K.A. Jessán Hoan.
- Co-owner, with Patch, of the Princess Bar.
- More fingers in more pies than we'd like.

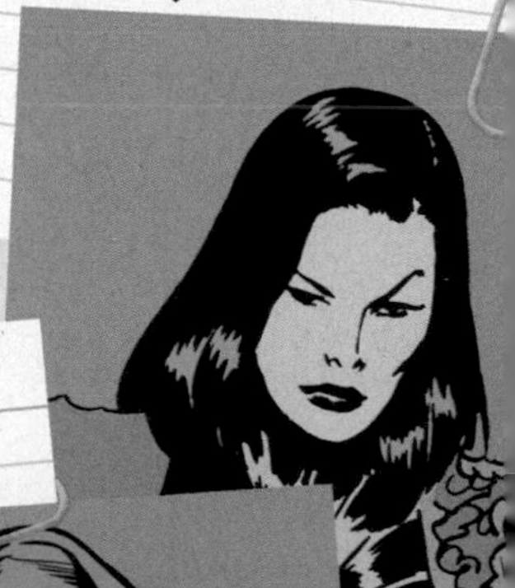

Archie Corrigan

- Local freighter pilot.
- Hangs around Princess Bar with Patch.

One to watch.

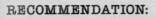

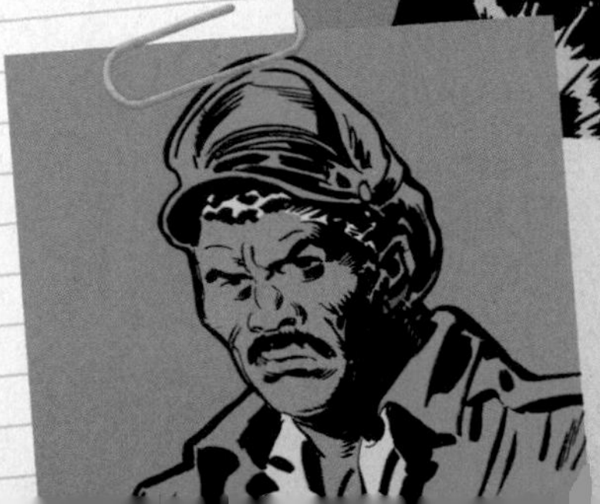

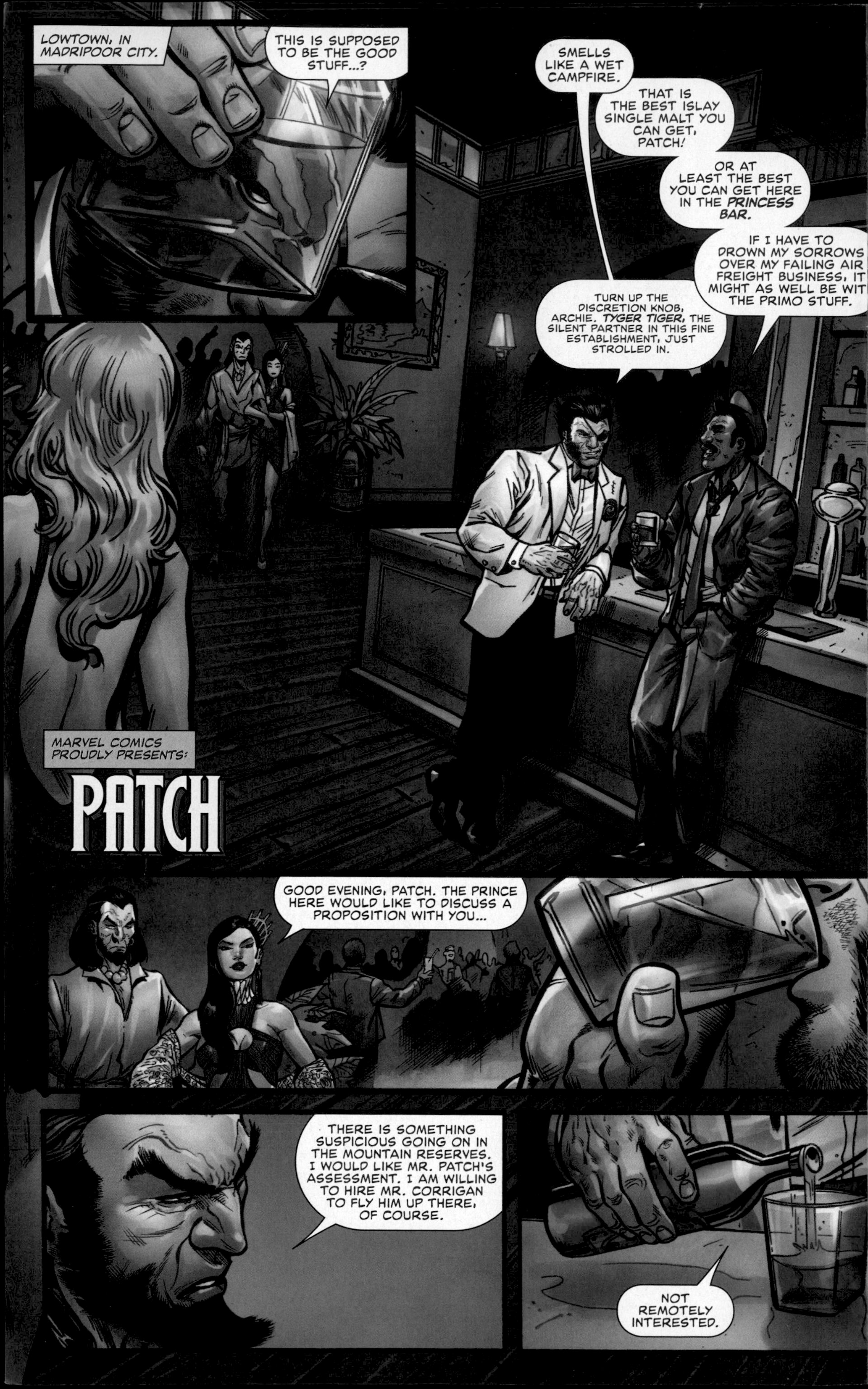
LOWTOWN, IN MADRIPOOR CITY.
THIS IS SUPPOSED TO BE THE GOOD STUFF...?
SMELLS LIKE A WET CAMPFIRE.
THAT IS THE BEST ISLAY SINGLE MALT YOU CAN GET, PATCH!
OR AT LEAST THE BEST YOU CAN GET HERE IN THE PRINCESS BAR.
IF I HAVE TO DROWN MY SORROWS OVER MY FAILING AIR FREIGHT BUSINESS, IT MIGHT AS WELL BE WIT THE PRIMO STUFF.
TURN UP THE DISCRETION KNOB, ARCHIE. TYGER TIGER, THE SILENT PARTNER IN THIS FINE ESTABLISHMENT, JUST STROLLED IN.
MARVEL COMICS PROUDLY PRESENTS:
PATCH
GOOD EVENING, PATCH. THE PRINCE HERE WOULD LIKE TO DISCUSS A PROPOSITION WITH YOU...
THERE IS SOMETHING SUSPICIOUS GOING ON IN THE MOUNTAIN RESERVES. I WOULD LIKE MR. PATCH'S ASSESSMENT. I AM WILLING TO HIRE MR. CORRIGAN TO FLY HIM UP THERE, OF COURSE.
NOT REMOTELY INTERESTED.

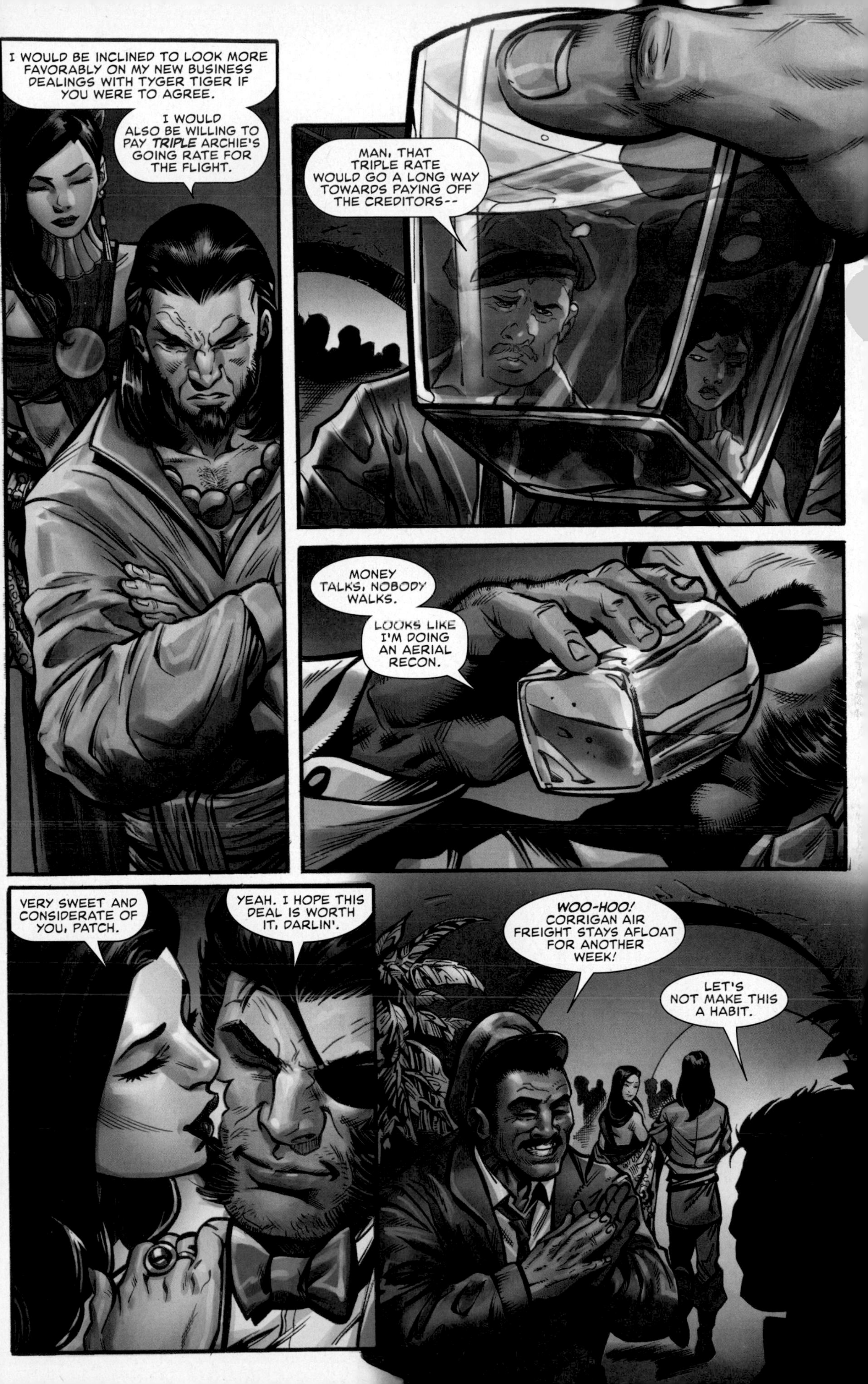
I WOULD BE INCLINED TO LOOK MORE FAVORABLY ON MY NEW BUSINESS DEALINGS WITH TYGER TIGER IF YOU WERE TO AGREE.
I WOULD ALSO BE WILLING TO PAY *TRIPLE* ARCHIE'S GOING RATE FOR THE FLIGHT.
MAN, THAT TRIPLE RATE WOULD GO A LONG WAY TOWARDS PAYING OFF THE CREDITORS--
MONEY TALKS, NOBODY WALKS.
LOOKS LIKE I'M DOING AN AERIAL RECON.
VERY SWEET AND CONSIDERATE OF YOU, PATCH.
YEAH. I HOPE THIS DEAL IS WORTH IT, DARLIN'.
WOO-HOO! CORRIGAN AIR FREIGHT STAYS AFLOAT FOR ANOTHER WEEK!
LET'S NOT MAKE THIS A HABIT.

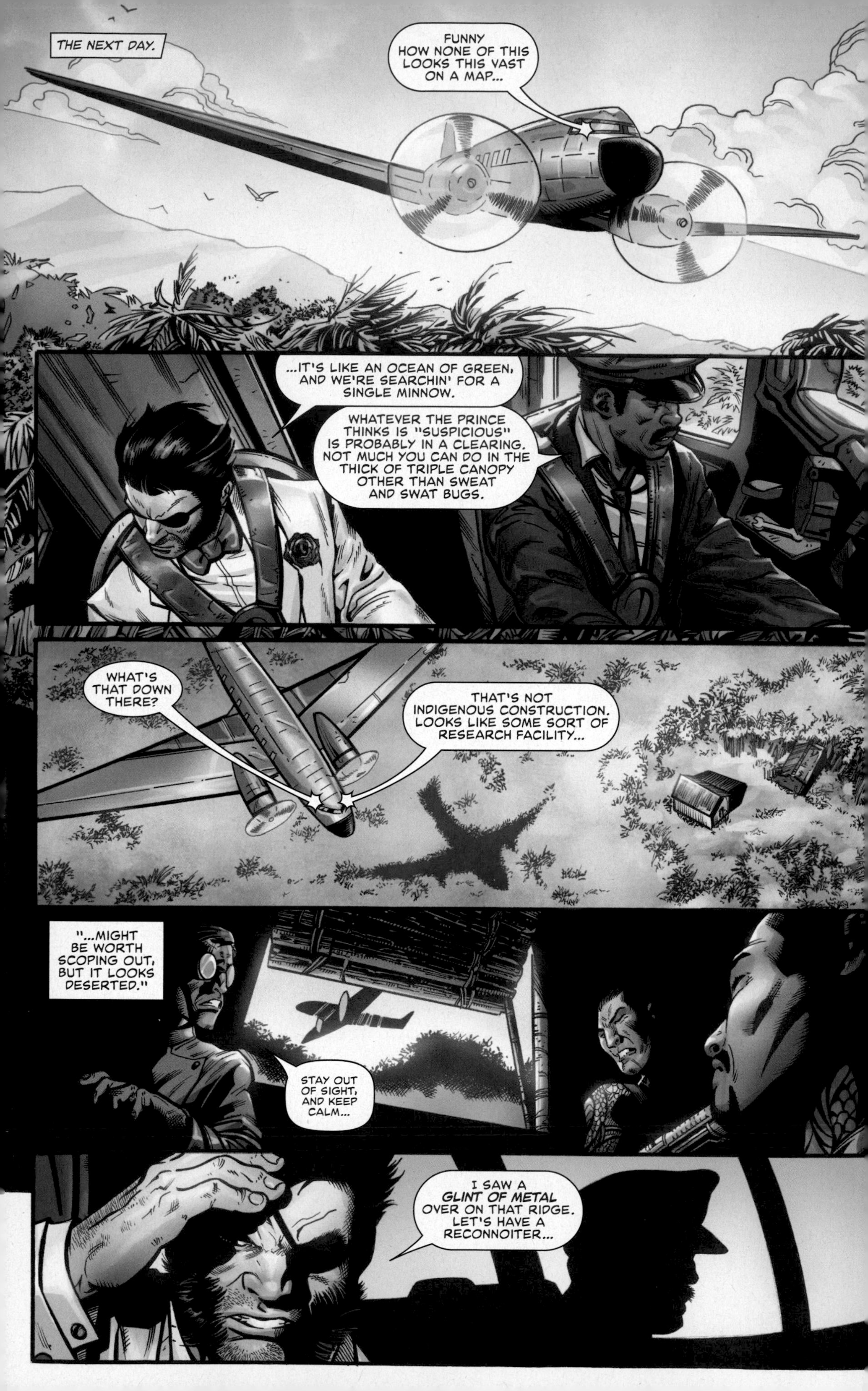
THE NEXT DAY.
FUNNY HOW NONE OF THIS LOOKS THIS VAST ON A MAP...
...IT'S LIKE AN OCEAN OF GREEN, AND WE'RE SEARCHIN' FOR A SINGLE MINNOW.
WHATEVER THE PRINCE THINKS IS "SUSPICIOUS" IS PROBABLY IN A CLEARING. NOT MUCH YOU CAN DO IN THE THICK OF TRIPLE CANOPY OTHER THAN SWEAT AND SWAT BUGS.
WHAT'S THAT DOWN THERE?
THAT'S NOT INDIGENOUS CONSTRUCTION. LOOKS LIKE SOME SORT OF RESEARCH FACILITY...
"...MIGHT BE WORTH SCOPING OUT, BUT IT LOOKS DESERTED."
STAY OUT OF SIGHT, AND KEEP CALM...
I SAW A GLINT OF METAL OVER ON THAT RIDGE. LET'S HAVE A RECONNOITER...

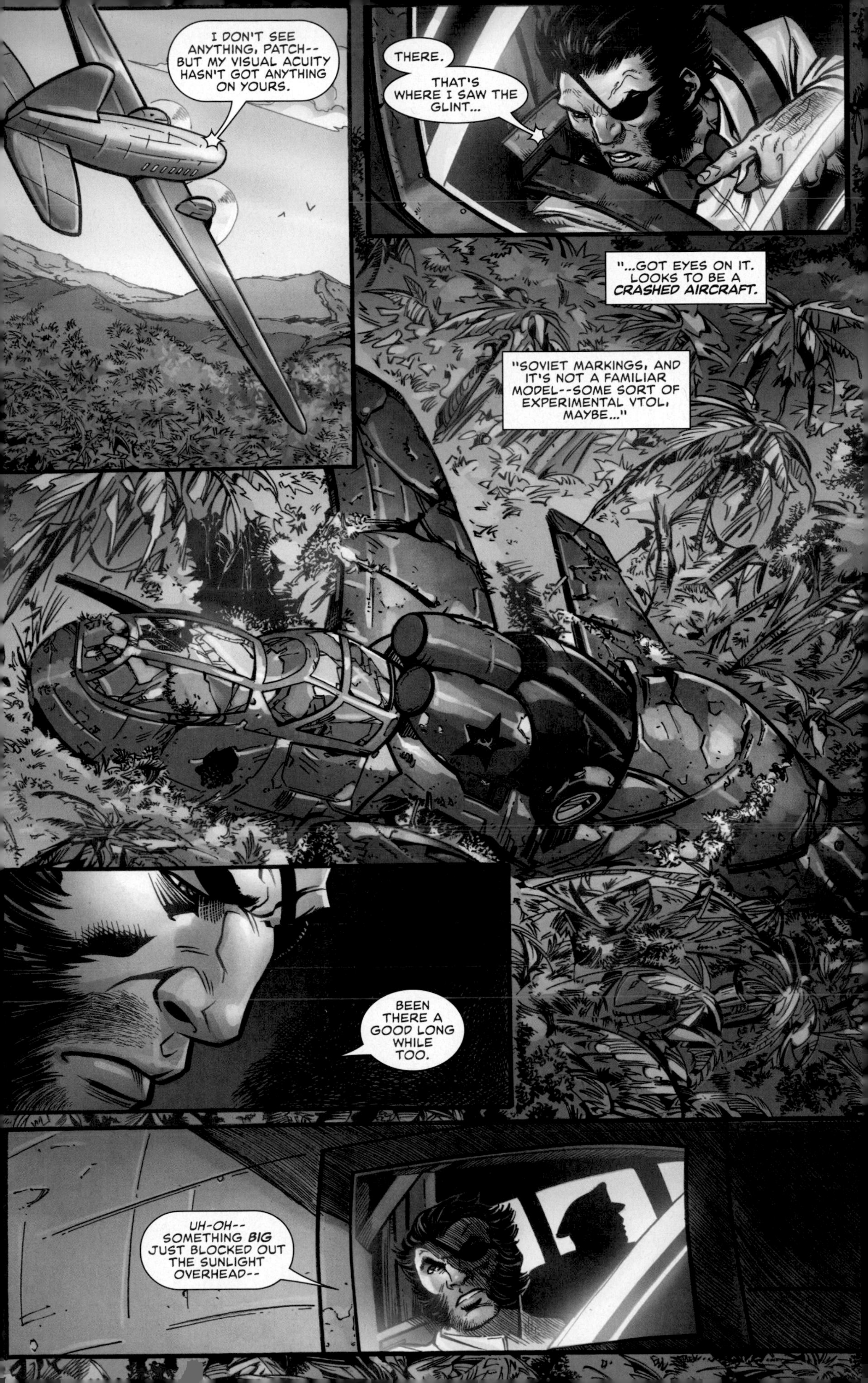
I DON'T SEE ANYTHING, PATCH--BUT MY VISUAL ACUITY HASN'T GOT ANYTHING ON YOURS.
THERE.
THAT'S WHERE I SAW THE GLINT...
"...GOT EYES ON IT. LOOKS TO BE A CRASHED AIRCRAFT.
"SOVIET MARKINGS, AND IT'S NOT A FAMILIAR MODEL--SOME SORT OF EXPERIMENTAL VTOL, MAYBE..."
BEEN THERE A GOOD LONG WHILE TOO.
UH-OH--SOMETHING BIG JUST BLOCKED OUT THE SUNLIGHT OVERHEAD--

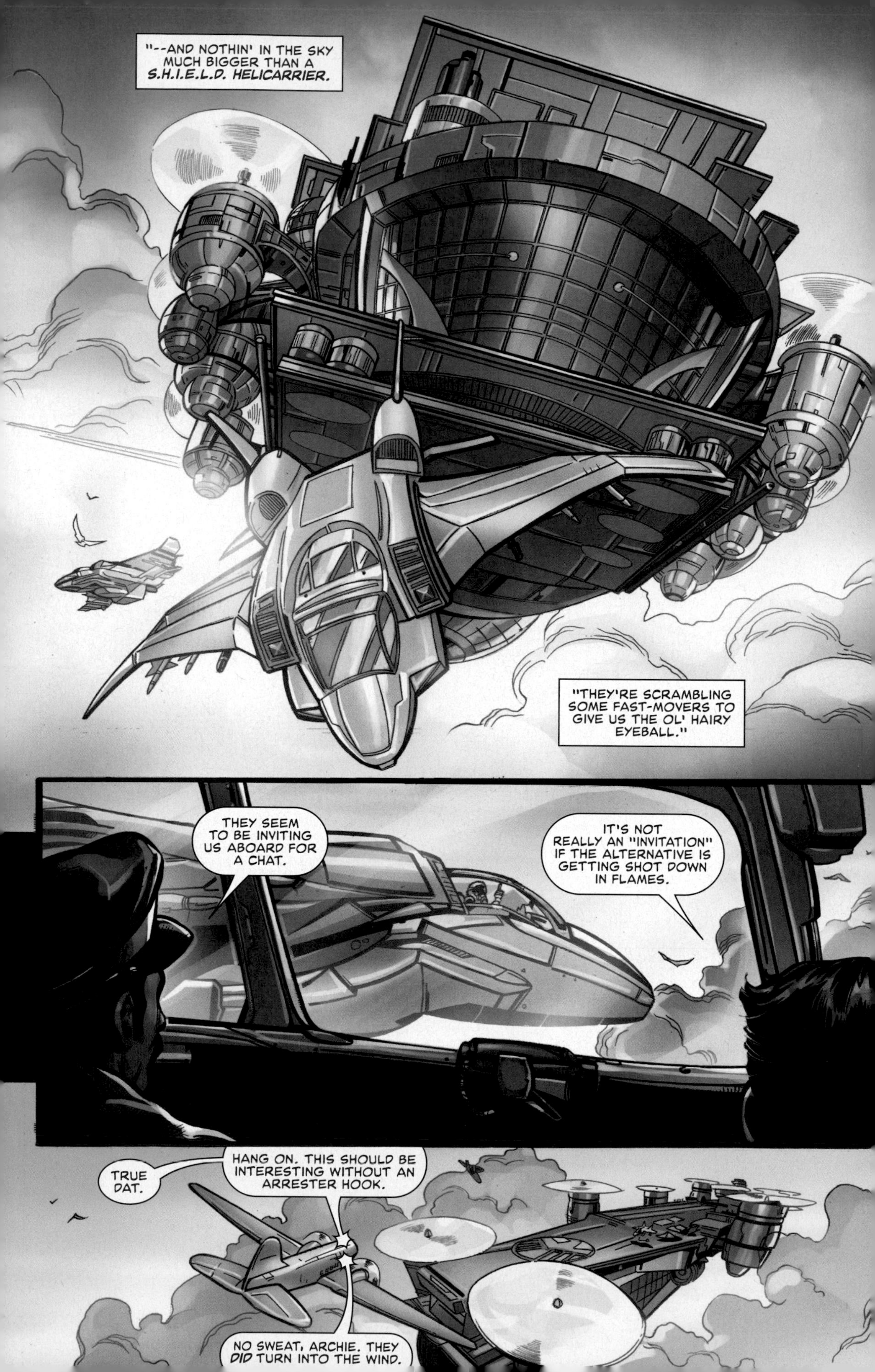
"--AND NOTHIN' IN THE SKY MUCH BIGGER THAN A S.H.I.E.L.D. HELICARRIER.
"THEY'RE SCRAMBLING SOME FAST-MOVERS TO GIVE US THE OL' HAIRY EYEBALL."
THEY SEEM TO BE INVITING US ABOARD FOR A CHAT.
IT'S NOT REALLY AN "INVITATION" IF THE ALTERNATIVE IS GETTING SHOT DOWN IN FLAMES.
TRUE DAT.
HANG ON. THIS SHOULD BE INTERESTING WITHOUT AN ARRESTER HOOK.
NO SWEAT, ARCHIE. THEY DID TURN INTO THE WIND.

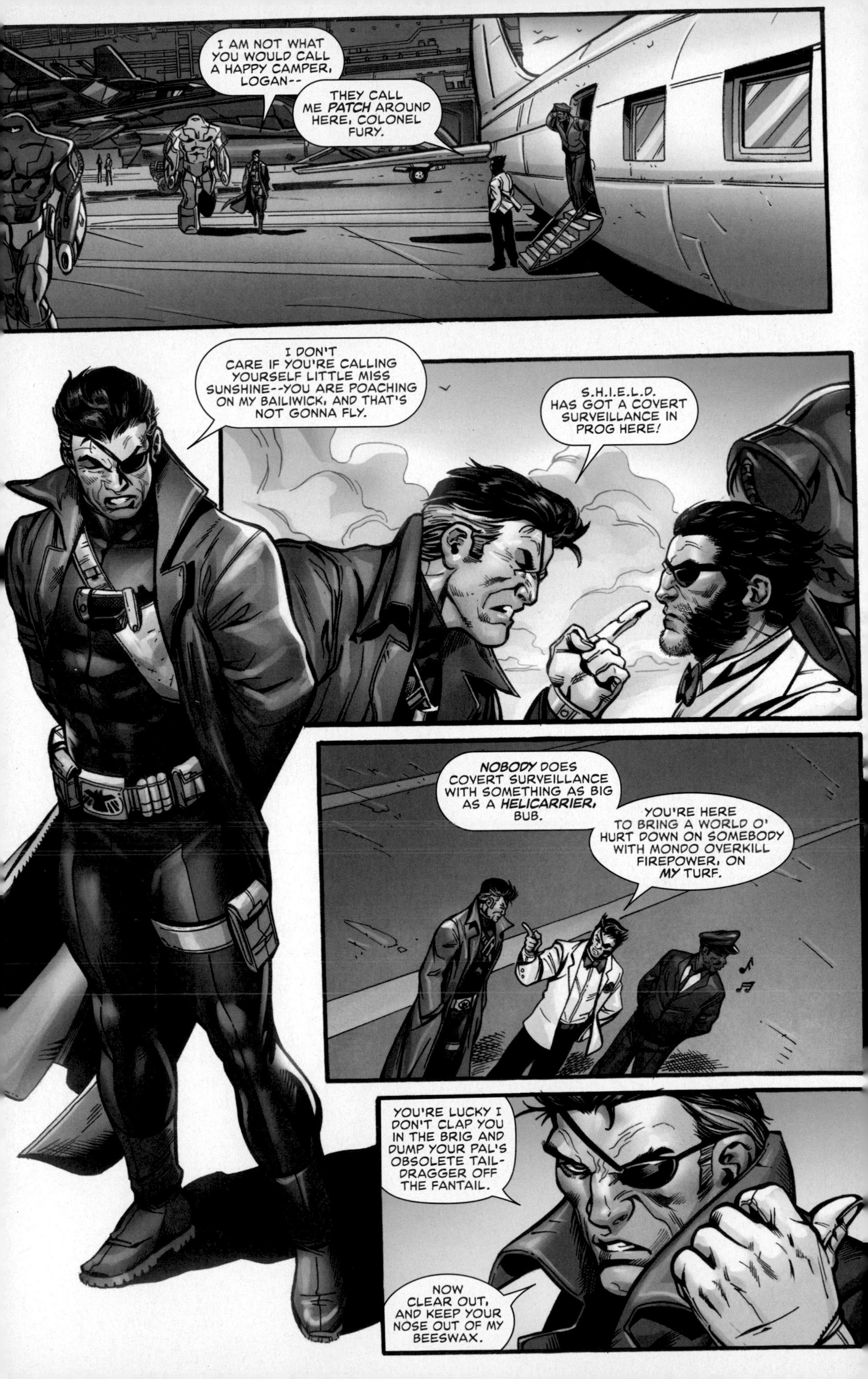

I AM NOT WHAT YOU WOULD CALL A HAPPY CAMPER, LOGAN--
THEY CALL ME *PATCH* AROUND HERE, COLONEL FURY.
I DON'T CARE IF YOU'RE CALLING YOURSELF LITTLE MISS SUNSHINE--YOU ARE POACHING ON MY BAILIWICK, AND THAT'S NOT GONNA FLY.
S.H.I.E.L.D. HAS GOT A COVERT SURVEILLANCE IN PROG HERE!
NOBODY DOES COVERT SURVEILLANCE WITH SOMETHING AS BIG AS A *HELICARRIER,* BUB.
YOU'RE HERE TO BRING A WORLD O' HURT DOWN ON SOMEBODY WITH MONDO OVERKILL FIREPOWER, ON *MY* TURF.
YOU'RE LUCKY I DON'T CLAP YOU IN THE BRIG AND DUMP YOUR PAL'S OBSOLETE TAIL-DRAGGER OFF THE FANTAIL.
NOW CLEAR OUT, AND KEEP YOUR NOSE OUT OF MY BEESWAX.

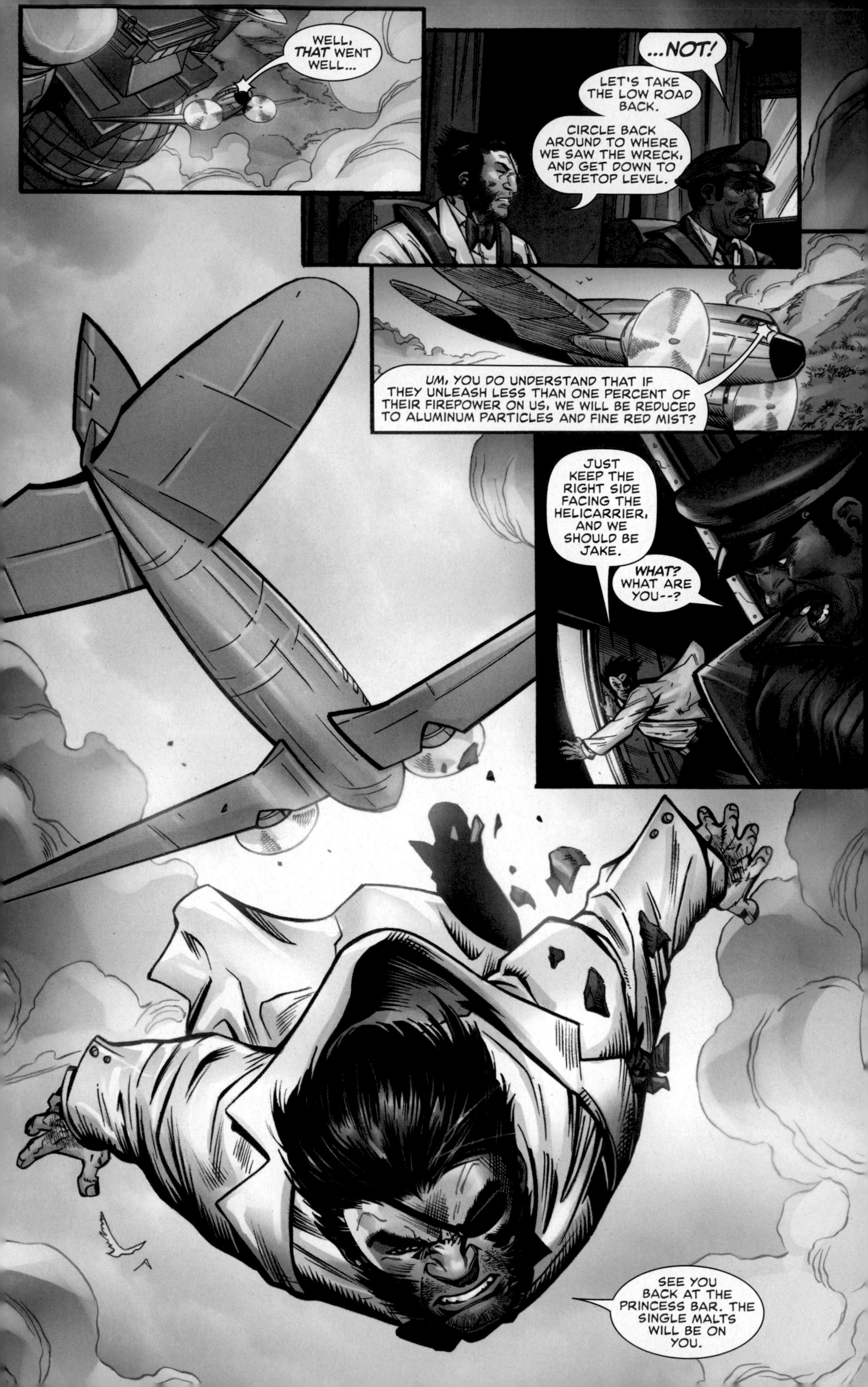
WELL, THAT WENT WELL...
...NOT!
LET'S TAKE THE LOW ROAD BACK.
CIRCLE BACK AROUND TO WHERE WE SAW THE WRECK, AND GET DOWN TO TREETOP LEVEL.
UM, YOU DO UNDERSTAND THAT IF THEY UNLEASH LESS THAN ONE PERCENT OF THEIR FIREPOWER ON US, WE WILL BE REDUCED TO ALUMINUM PARTICLES AND FINE RED MIST?
JUST KEEP THE RIGHT SIDE FACING THE HELICARRIER, AND WE SHOULD BE JAKE.
WHAT? WHAT ARE YOU--?
SEE YOU BACK AT THE PRINCESS BAR. THE SINGLE MALTS WILL BE ON YOU.

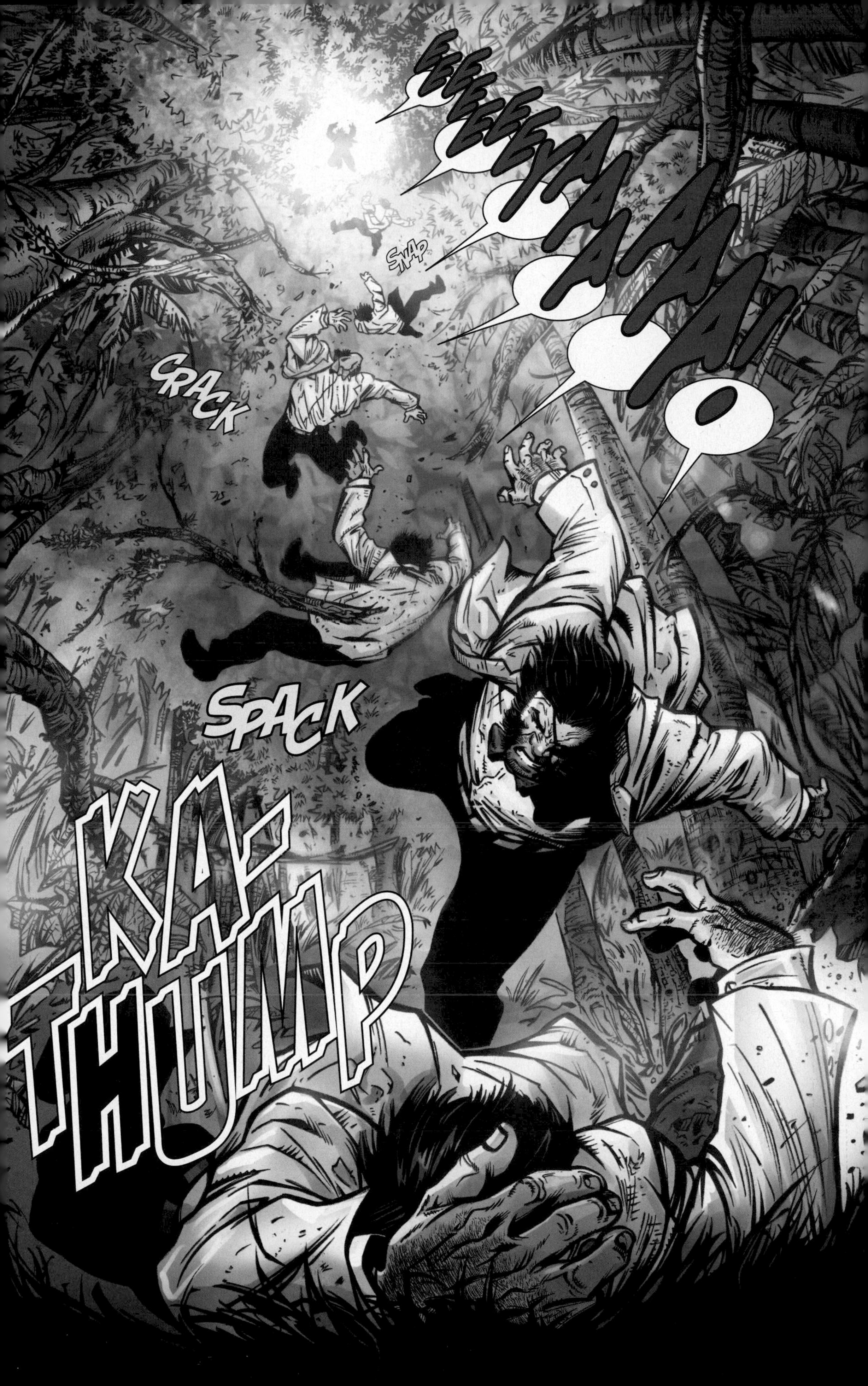
EEEEEEEEYAAAAAAAAAIIIIIOOOOOOO
SNAP
CRACK
SPACK
KA-THUMP

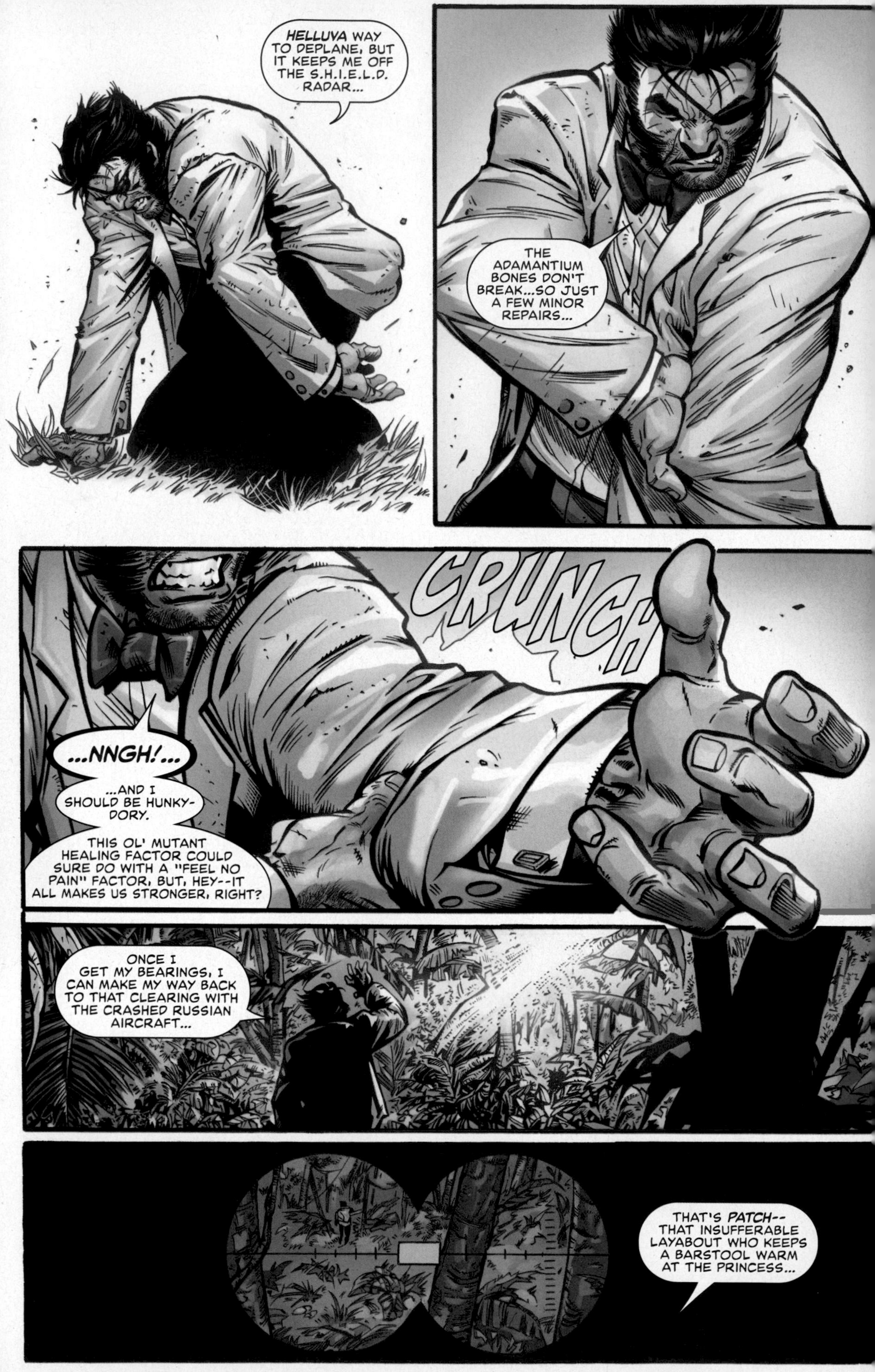
HELLUVA WAY TO DEPLANE, BUT IT KEEPS ME OFF THE S.H.I.E.L.D. RADAR...
THE ADAMANTIUM BONES DON'T BREAK...SO JUST A FEW MINOR REPAIRS...
CRUNCH
...NNGH!...
...AND I SHOULD BE HUNKY-DORY.
THIS OL' MUTANT HEALING FACTOR COULD SURE DO WITH A "FEEL NO PAIN" FACTOR, BUT, HEY--IT ALL MAKES US STRONGER, RIGHT?
ONCE I GET MY BEARINGS, I CAN MAKE MY WAY BACK TO THAT CLEARING WITH THE CRASHED RUSSIAN AIRCRAFT...
THAT'S PATCH--THAT INSUFFERABLE LAYABOUT WHO KEEPS A BARSTOOL WARM AT THE PRINCESS...

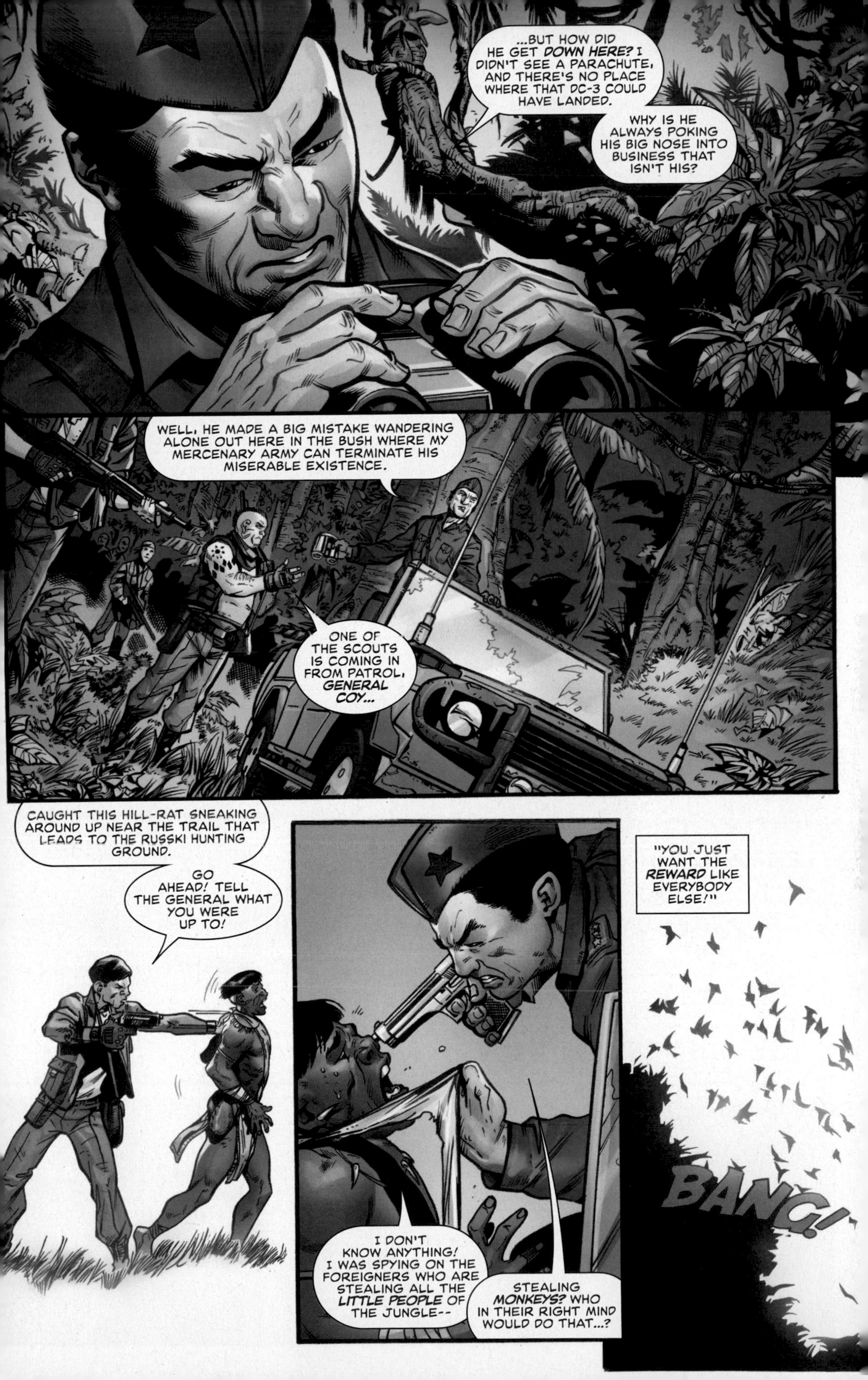
...BUT HOW DID HE GET DOWN HERE? I DIDN'T SEE A PARACHUTE, AND THERE'S NO PLACE WHERE THAT DC-3 COULD HAVE LANDED.
WHY IS HE ALWAYS POKING HIS BIG NOSE INTO BUSINESS THAT ISN'T HIS?
WELL, HE MADE A BIG MISTAKE WANDERING ALONE OUT HERE IN THE BUSH WHERE MY MERCENARY ARMY CAN TERMINATE HIS MISERABLE EXISTENCE.
ONE OF THE SCOUTS IS COMING IN FROM PATROL, GENERAL COY...
CAUGHT THIS HILL-RAT SNEAKING AROUND UP NEAR THE TRAIL THAT LEADS TO THE RUSSKI HUNTING GROUND.
GO AHEAD! TELL THE GENERAL WHAT YOU WERE UP TO!
I DON'T KNOW ANYTHING! I WAS SPYING ON THE FOREIGNERS WHO ARE STEALING ALL THE LITTLE PEOPLE OF THE JUNGLE--
STEALING MONKEYS? WHO IN THEIR RIGHT MIND WOULD DO THAT...?
"YOU JUST WANT THE REWARD LIKE EVERYBODY ELSE!"
BANG!

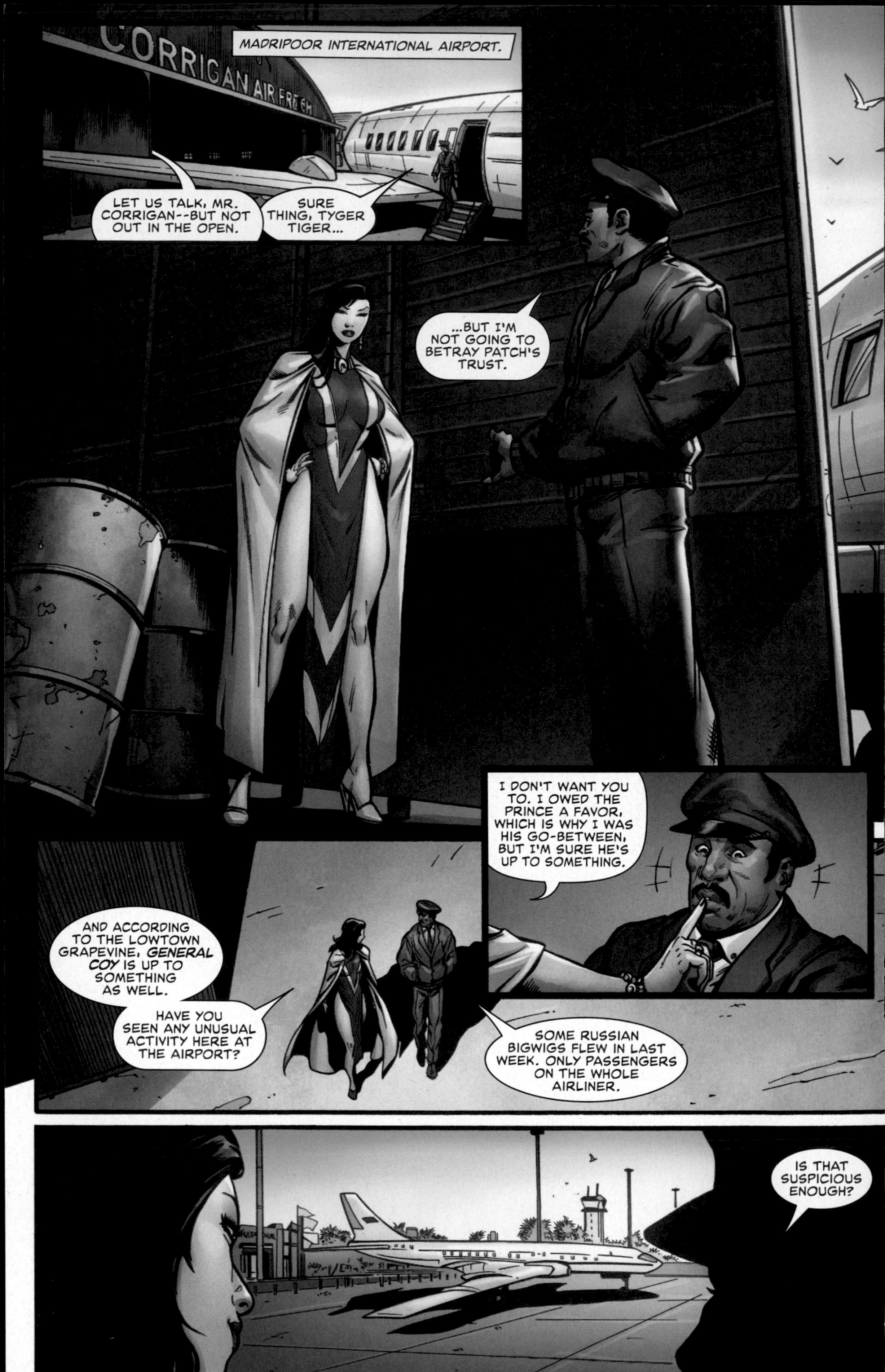
CORRIGAN AIR FREIGHT
MADRIPOOR INTERNATIONAL AIRPORT.
LET US TALK, MR. CORRIGAN--BUT NOT OUT IN THE OPEN.
SURE THING, TYGER TIGER...
...BUT I'M NOT GOING TO BETRAY PATCH'S TRUST.
I DON'T WANT YOU TO. I OWED THE PRINCE A FAVOR, WHICH IS WHY I WAS HIS GO-BETWEEN, BUT I'M SURE HE'S UP TO SOMETHING.
AND ACCORDING TO THE LOWTOWN GRAPEVINE, GENERAL COY IS UP TO SOMETHING AS WELL.
HAVE YOU SEEN ANY UNUSUAL ACTIVITY HERE AT THE AIRPORT?
SOME RUSSIAN BIGWIGS FLEW IN LAST WEEK. ONLY PASSENGERS ON THE WHOLE AIRLINER.
IS THAT SUSPICIOUS ENOUGH?

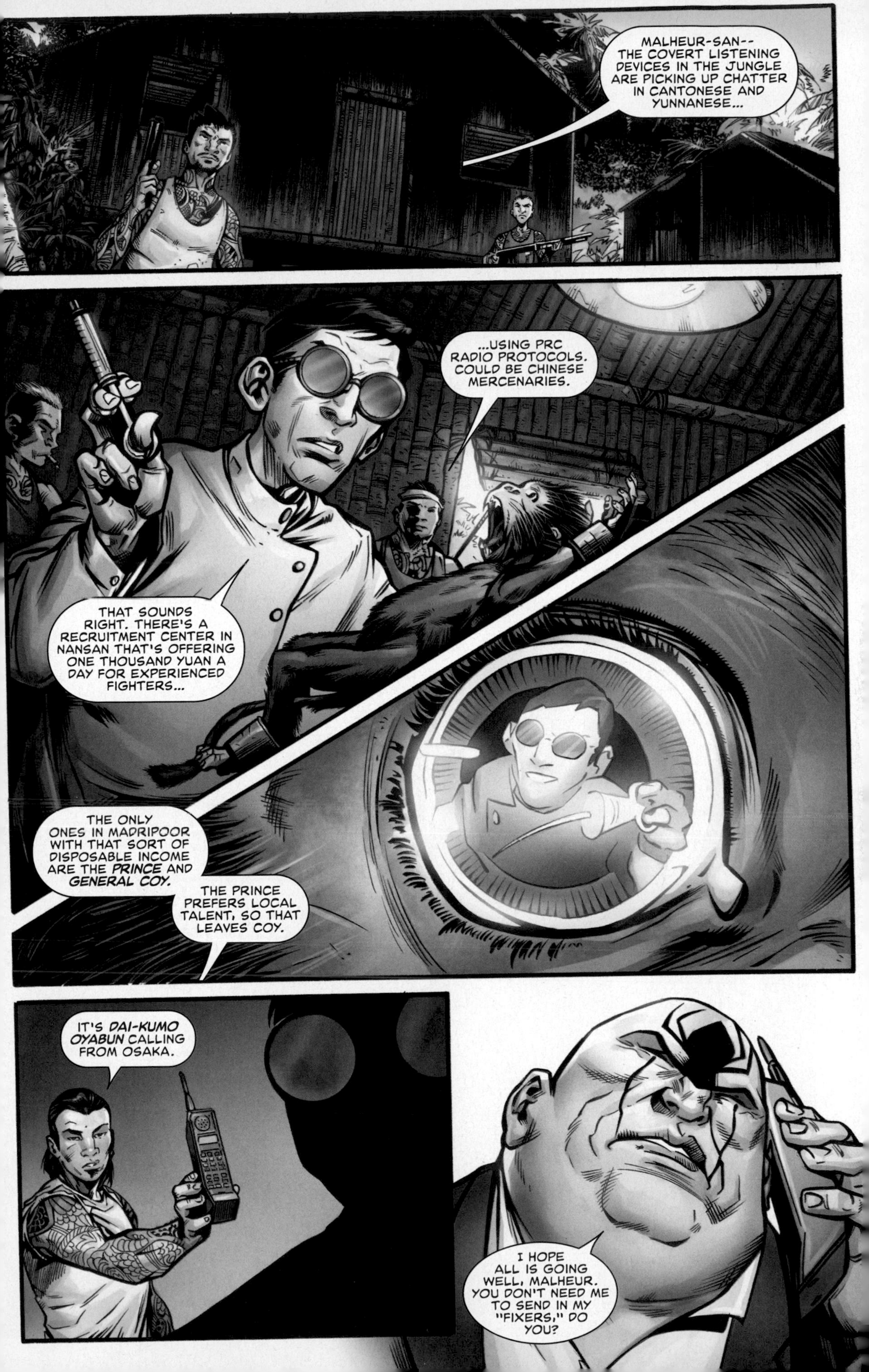
MALHEUR-SAN-- THE COVERT LISTENING DEVICES IN THE JUNGLE ARE PICKING UP CHATTER IN CANTONESE AND YUNNANESE...
...USING PRC RADIO PROTOCOLS. COULD BE CHINESE MERCENARIES.
THAT SOUNDS RIGHT. THERE'S A RECRUITMENT CENTER IN NANSAN THAT'S OFFERING ONE THOUSAND YUAN A DAY FOR EXPERIENCED FIGHTERS...
THE ONLY ONES IN MADRIPOOR WITH THAT SORT OF DISPOSABLE INCOME ARE THE *PRINCE* AND *GENERAL COY.*
THE PRINCE PREFERS LOCAL TALENT, SO THAT LEAVES COY.
IT'S *DAI-KUMO OYABUN* CALLING FROM OSAKA.
I HOPE ALL IS GOING WELL, MALHEUR. YOU DON'T NEED ME TO SEND IN MY "FIXERS," DO YOU?

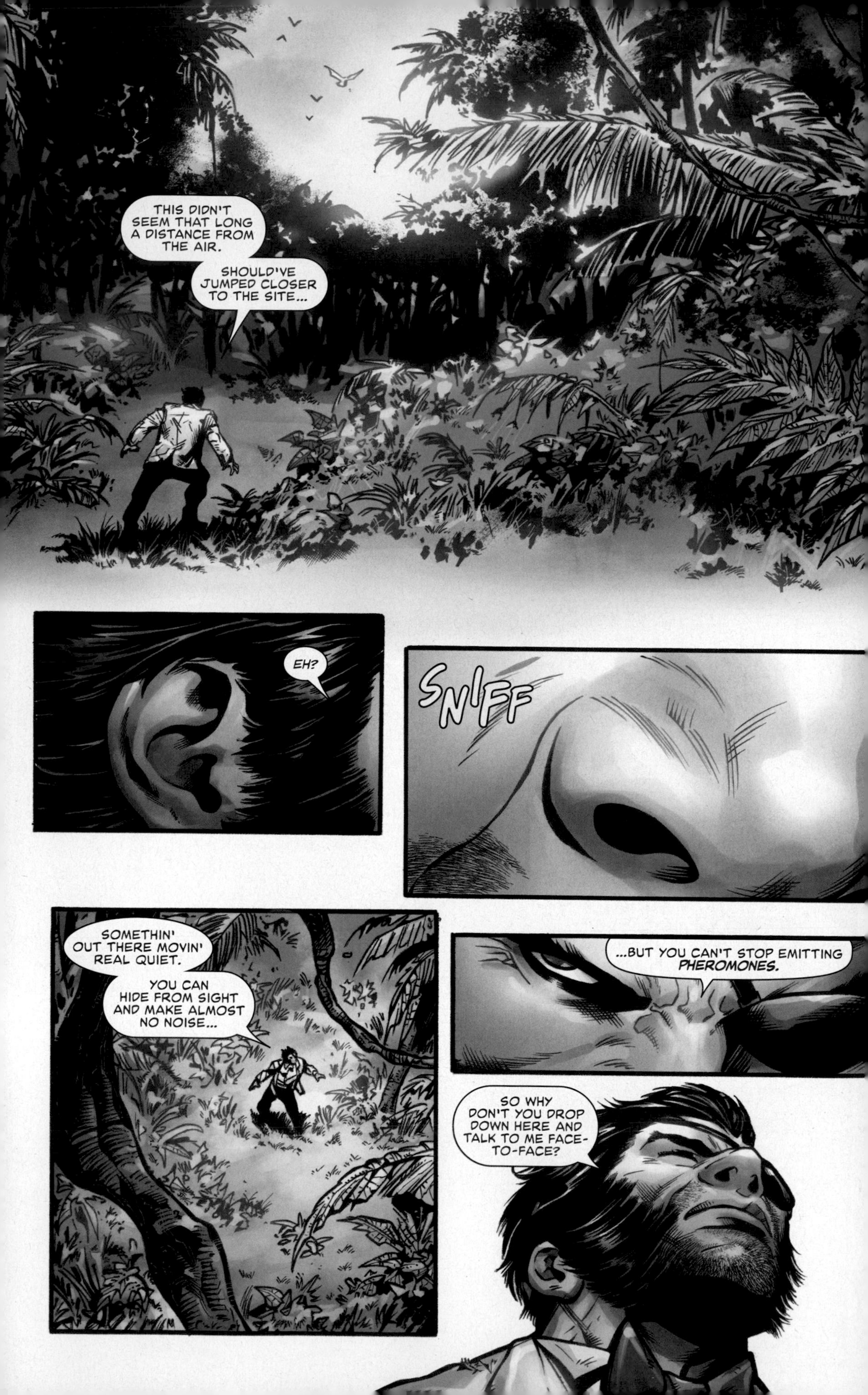
THIS DIDN'T SEEM THAT LONG A DISTANCE FROM THE AIR.
SHOULD'VE JUMPED CLOSER TO THE SITE...
EH?
SNIFF
SOMETHIN' OUT THERE MOVIN' REAL QUIET.
YOU CAN HIDE FROM SIGHT AND MAKE ALMOST NO NOISE...
...BUT YOU CAN'T STOP EMITTING *PHEROMONES.*
SO WHY DON'T YOU DROP DOWN HERE AND TALK TO ME FACE-TO-FACE?

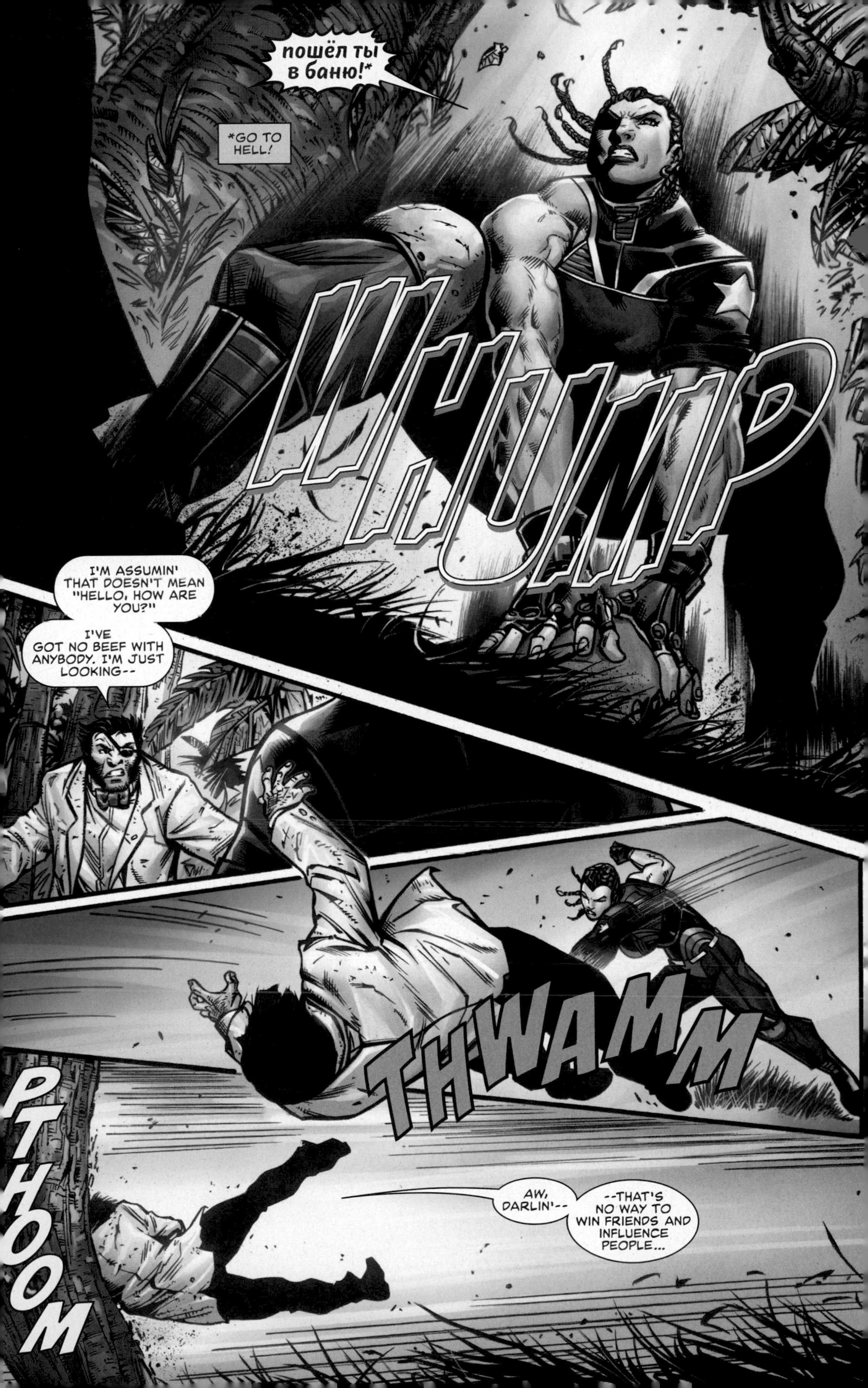
пошёл ты в баню!*
*GO TO HELL!
WHUMP
I'M ASSUMIN' THAT DOESN'T MEAN "HELLO, HOW ARE YOU?"
I'VE GOT NO BEEF WITH ANYBODY. I'M JUST LOOKING--
THWAMM
PTHOOM
AW, DARLIN'--
--THAT'S NO WAY TO WIN FRIENDS AND INFLUENCE PEOPLE...

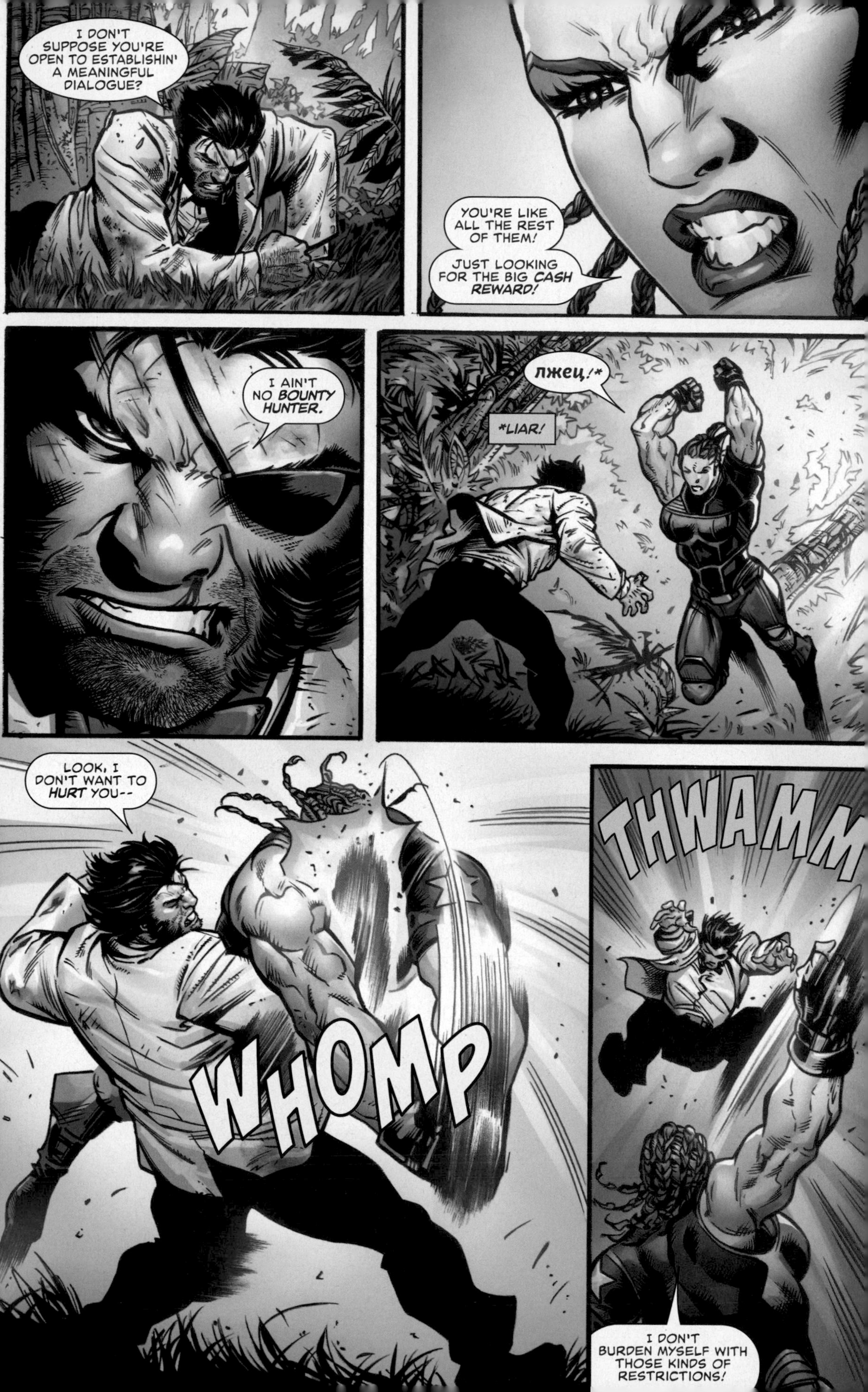
I DON'T SUPPOSE YOU'RE OPEN TO ESTABLISHIN' A MEANINGFUL DIALOGUE?
YOU'RE LIKE ALL THE REST OF THEM!
JUST LOOKING FOR THE BIG CASH REWARD!
I AIN'T NO BOUNTY HUNTER.
лжец!*
*LIAR!
LOOK, I DON'T WANT TO HURT YOU--
WHOMP
THWAMM
I DON'T BURDEN MYSELF WITH THOSE KINDS OF RESTRICTIONS!

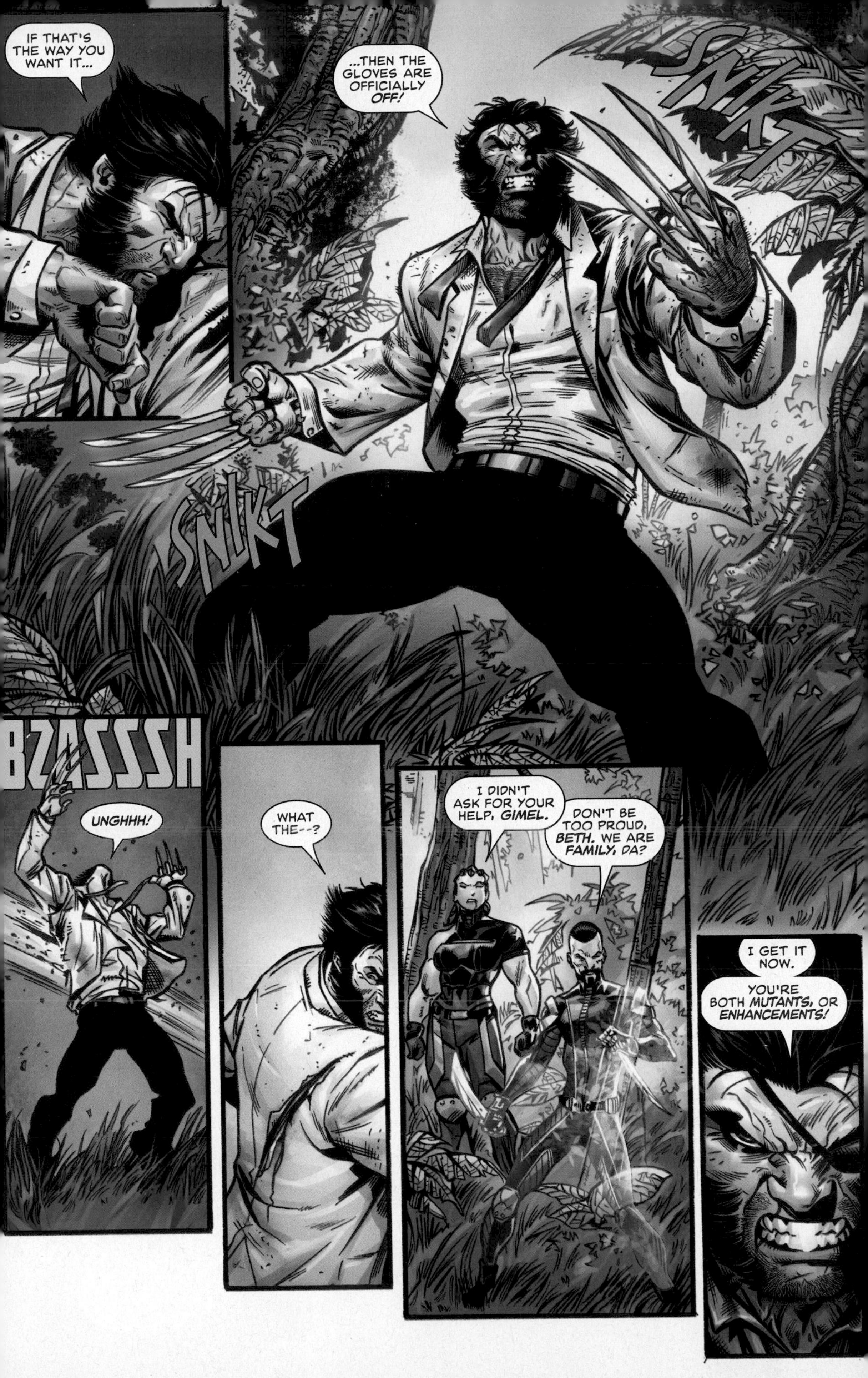
IF THAT'S THE WAY YOU WANT IT...
...THEN THE GLOVES ARE OFFICIALLY OFF!
SNIKT
SNIKT
BZASSSH
UNGHHH!
WHAT THE--?
I DIDN'T ASK FOR YOUR HELP, GIMEL.
DON'T BE TOO PROUD, BETH. WE ARE FAMILY, DA?
I GET IT NOW.
YOU'RE BOTH MUTANTS, OR ENHANCEMENTS!

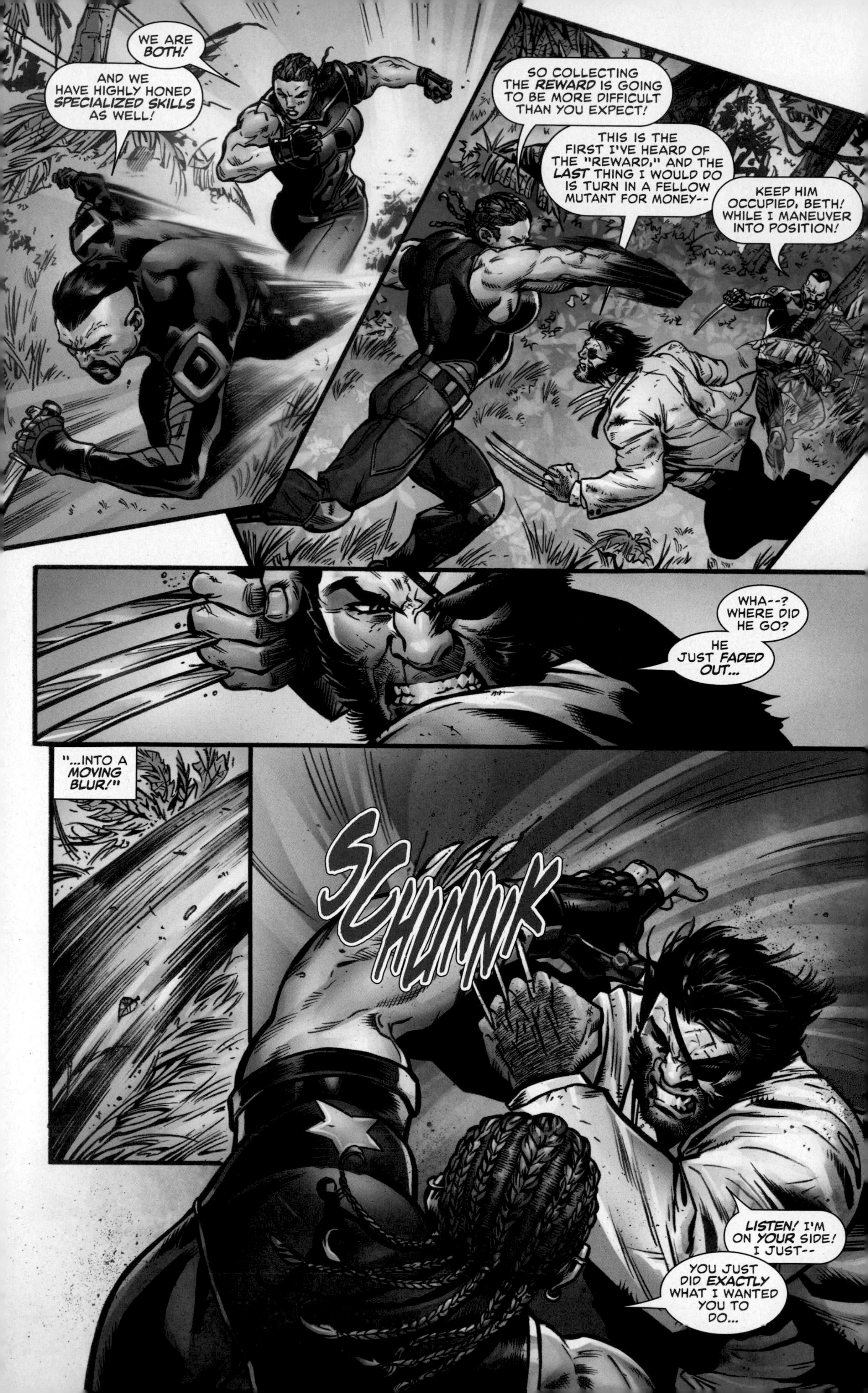
WE ARE BOTH!
AND WE HAVE HIGHLY HONED SPECIALIZED SKILLS AS WELL!
SO COLLECTING THE REWARD IS GOING TO BE MORE DIFFICULT THAN YOU EXPECT!
THIS IS THE FIRST I'VE HEARD OF THE "REWARD," AND THE LAST THING I WOULD DO IS TURN IN A FELLOW MUTANT FOR MONEY--
KEEP HIM OCCUPIED, BETH! WHILE I MANEUVER INTO POSITION!
WHA--? WHERE DID HE GO?
HE JUST FADED OUT...
"...INTO A MOVING BLUR!"
SCHUNNK
LISTEN! I'M ON YOUR SIDE! I JUST--
YOU JUST DID EXACTLY WHAT I WANTED YOU TO DO...

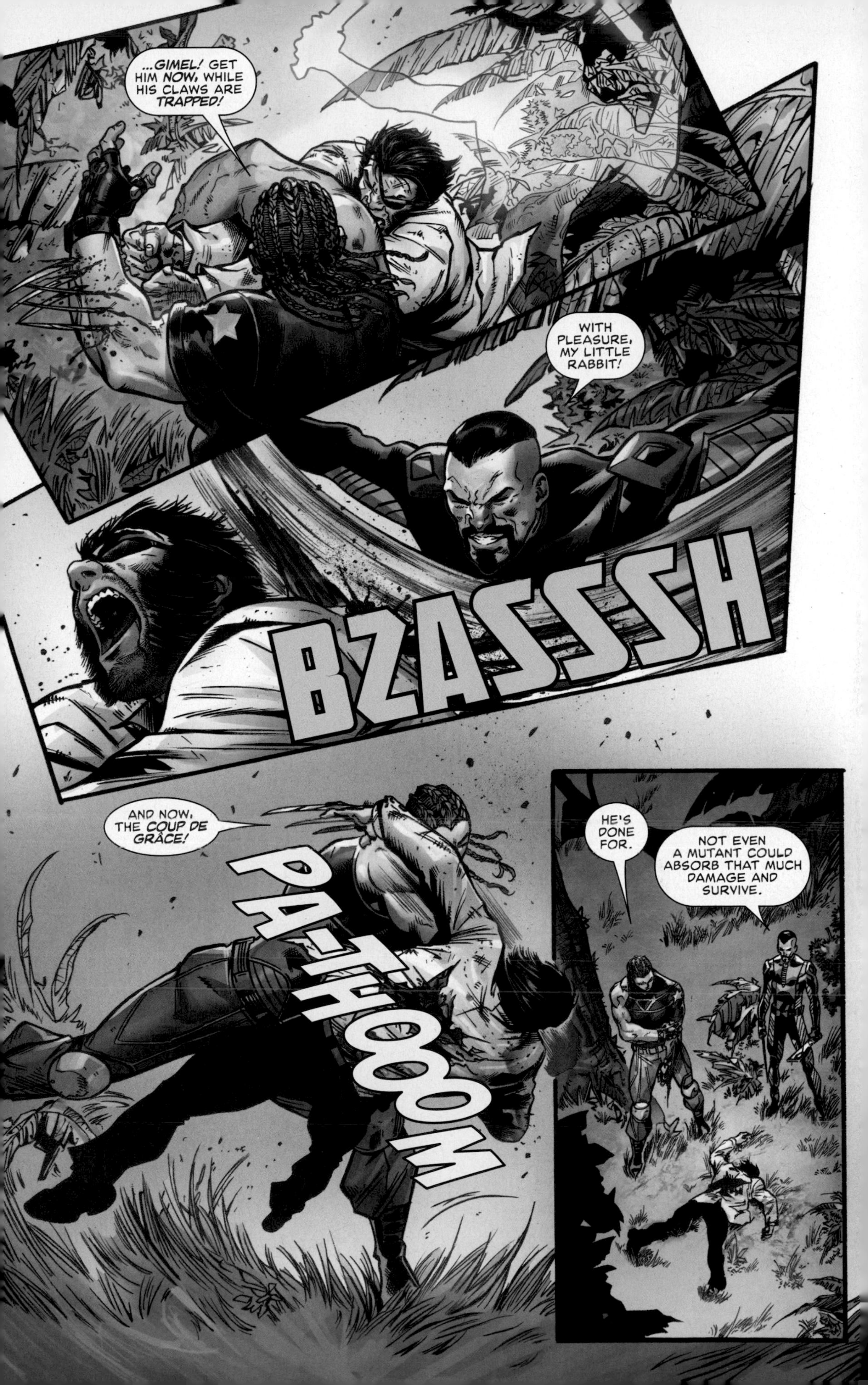
...GIMEL! GET HIM NOW, WHILE HIS CLAWS ARE TRAPPED!
WITH PLEASURE, MY LITTLE RABBIT!
BZASSSH
AND NOW, THE COUP DE GRÂCE!
PA-THOOOM
HE'S DONE FOR.
NOT EVEN A MUTANT COULD ABSORB THAT MUCH DAMAGE AND SURVIVE.

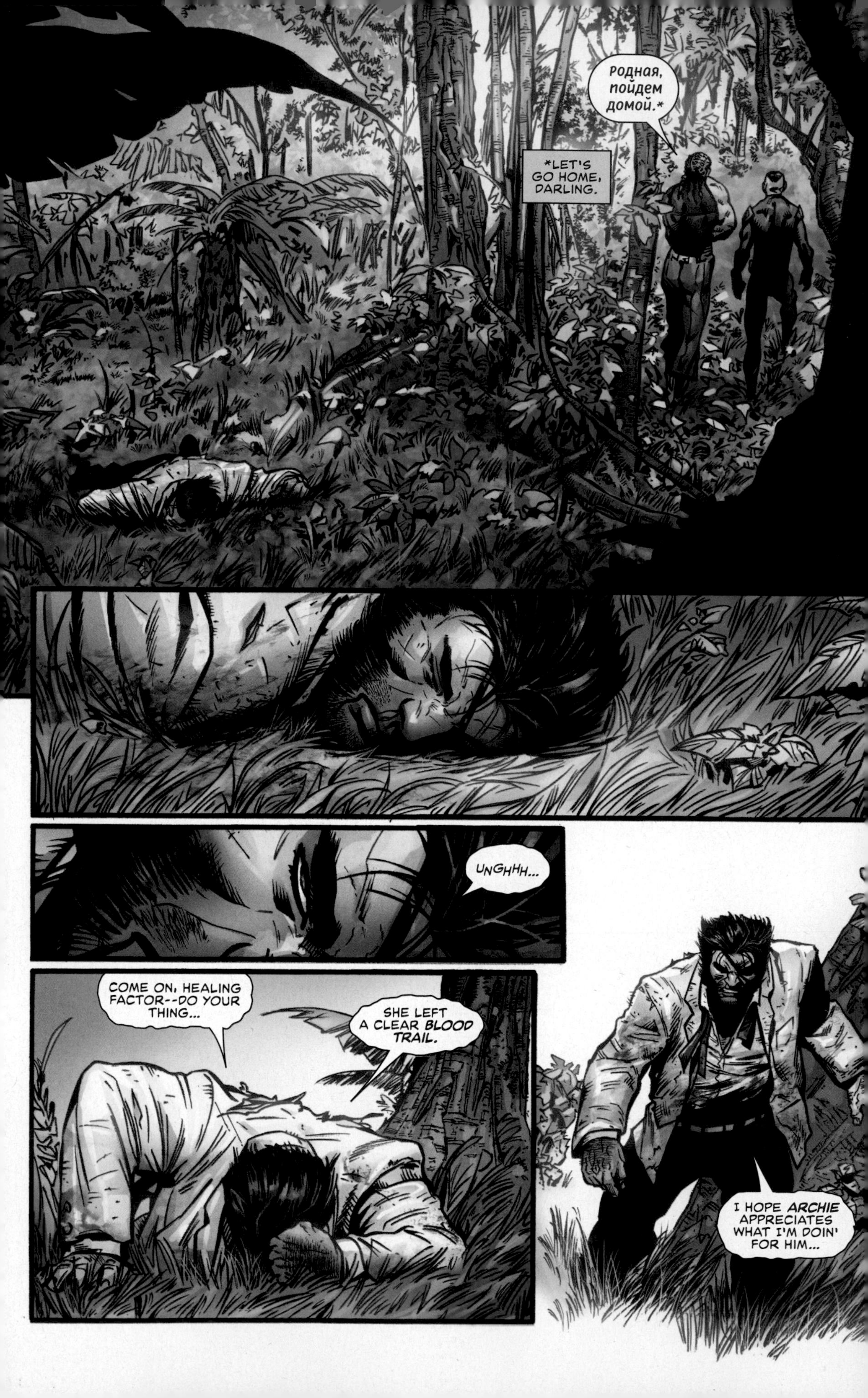
Родная, пойдем домой.*
*LET'S GO HOME, DARLING.
UNGHHH...
COME ON, HEALING FACTOR--DO YOUR THING...
SHE LEFT A CLEAR BLOOD TRAIL.
I HOPE ARCHIE APPRECIATES WHAT I'M DOIN' FOR HIM...

#2

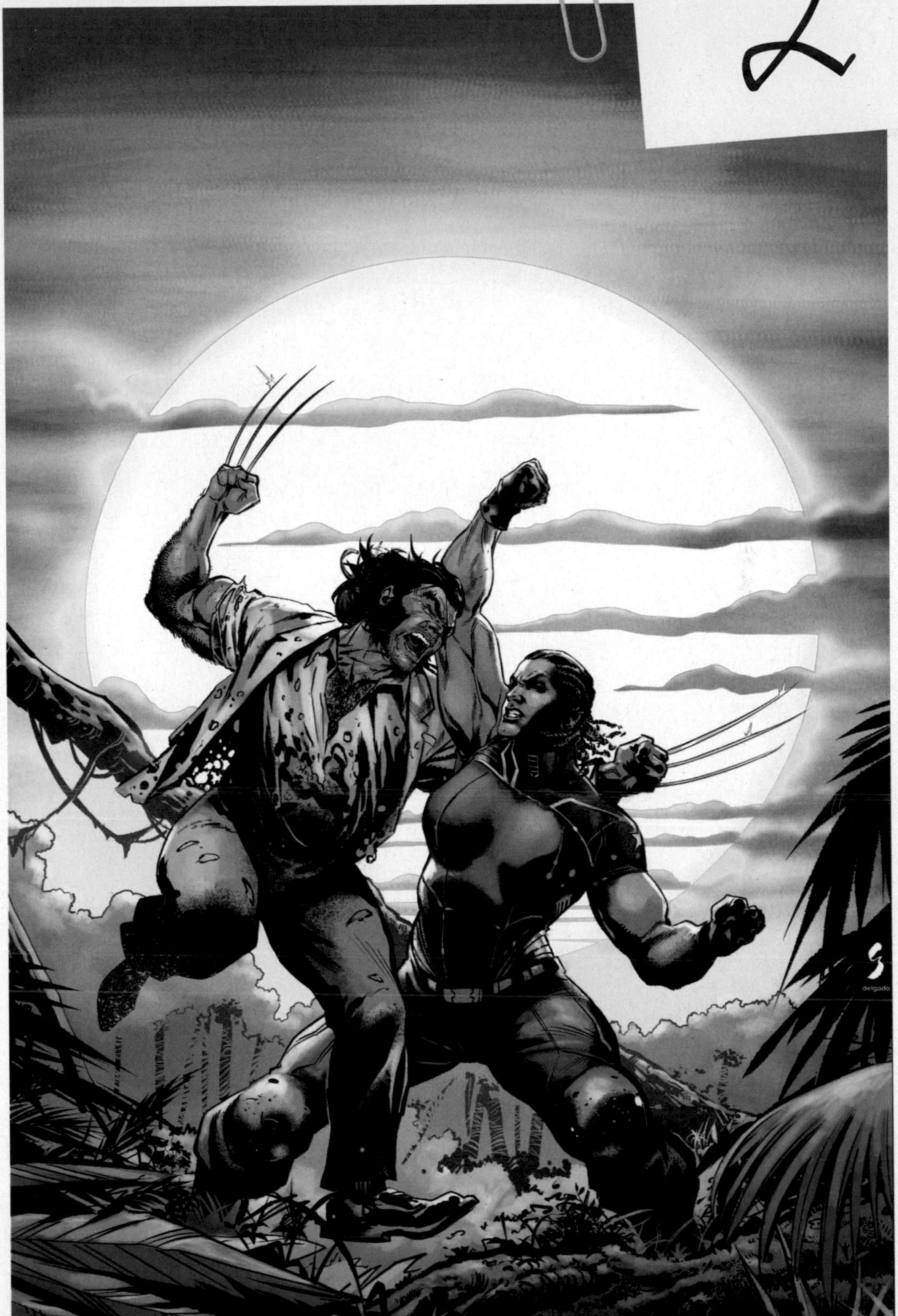

INTERNAL REVIEW ONLY

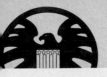

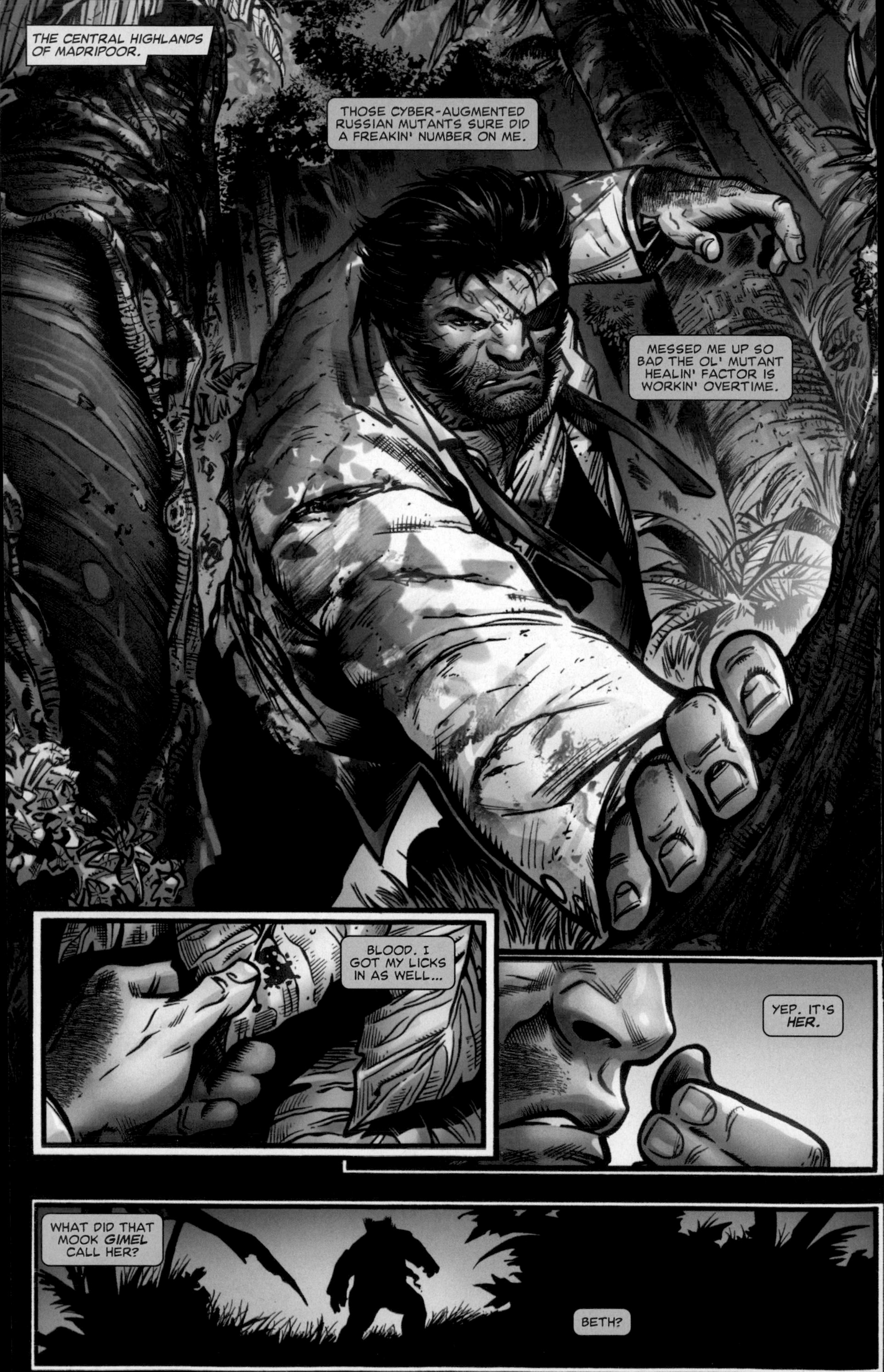
THE CENTRAL HIGHLANDS OF MADRIPOOR.
THOSE CYBER-AUGMENTED RUSSIAN MUTANTS SURE DID A FREAKIN' NUMBER ON ME.
MESSED ME UP SO BAD THE OL' MUTANT HEALIN' FACTOR IS WORKIN' OVERTIME.
BLOOD. I GOT MY LICKS IN AS WELL...
YEP. IT'S HER.
WHAT DID THAT MOOK GIMEL CALL HER?
BETH?

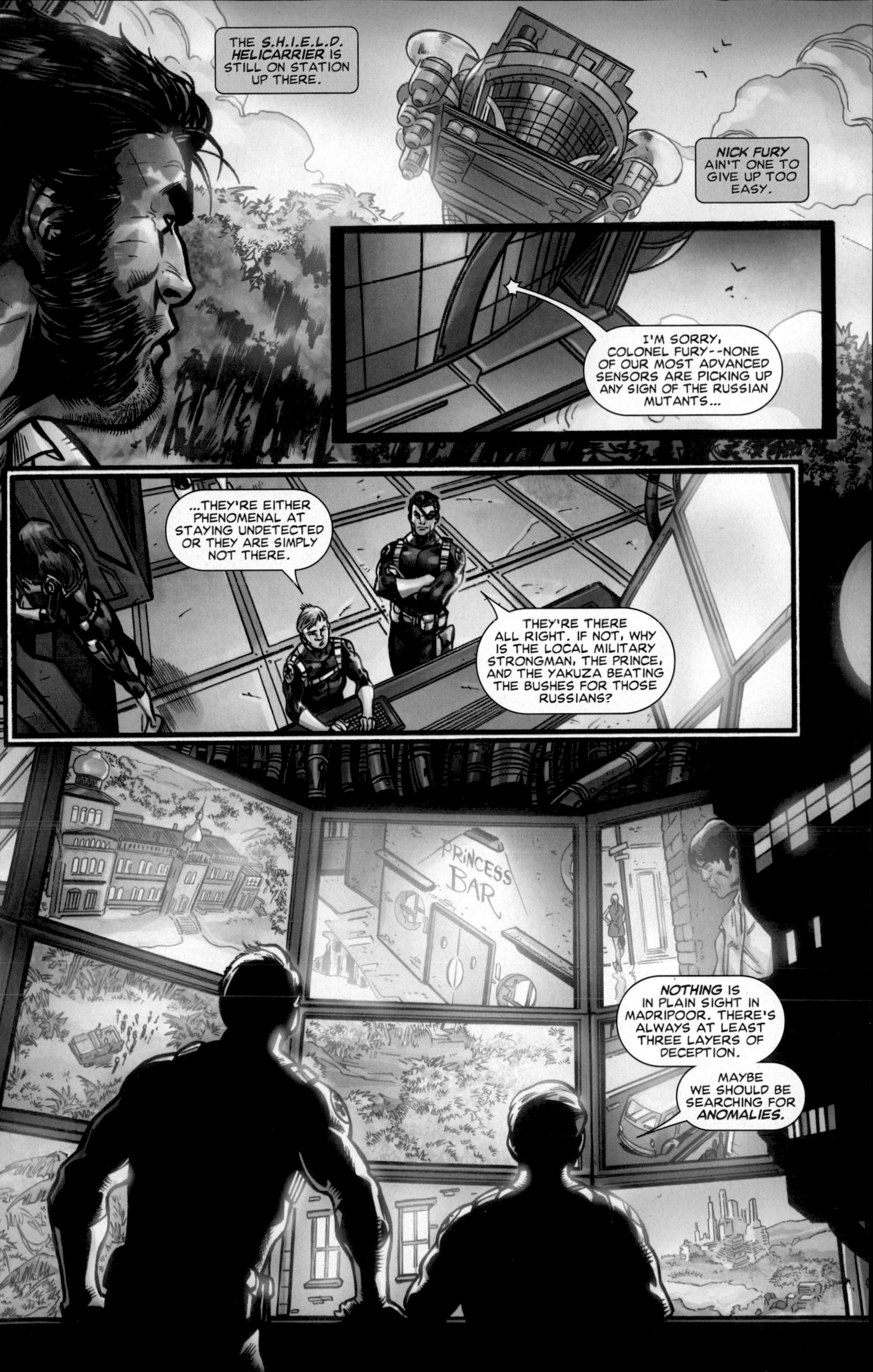
THE S.H.I.E.L.D. HELICARRIER IS STILL ON STATION UP THERE.
NICK FURY AIN'T ONE TO GIVE UP TOO EASY.
I'M SORRY, COLONEL FURY--NONE OF OUR MOST ADVANCED SENSORS ARE PICKING UP ANY SIGN OF THE RUSSIAN MUTANTS...
...THEY'RE EITHER PHENOMENAL AT STAYING UNDETECTED OR THEY ARE SIMPLY NOT THERE.
THEY'RE THERE ALL RIGHT. IF NOT, WHY IS THE LOCAL MILITARY STRONGMAN, THE PRINCE, AND THE YAKUZA BEATING THE BUSHES FOR THOSE RUSSIANS?
PRINCESS BAR
NOTHING IS IN PLAIN SIGHT IN MADRIPOOR. THERE'S ALWAYS AT LEAST THREE LAYERS OF DECEPTION.
MAYBE WE SHOULD BE SEARCHING FOR ANOMALIES.

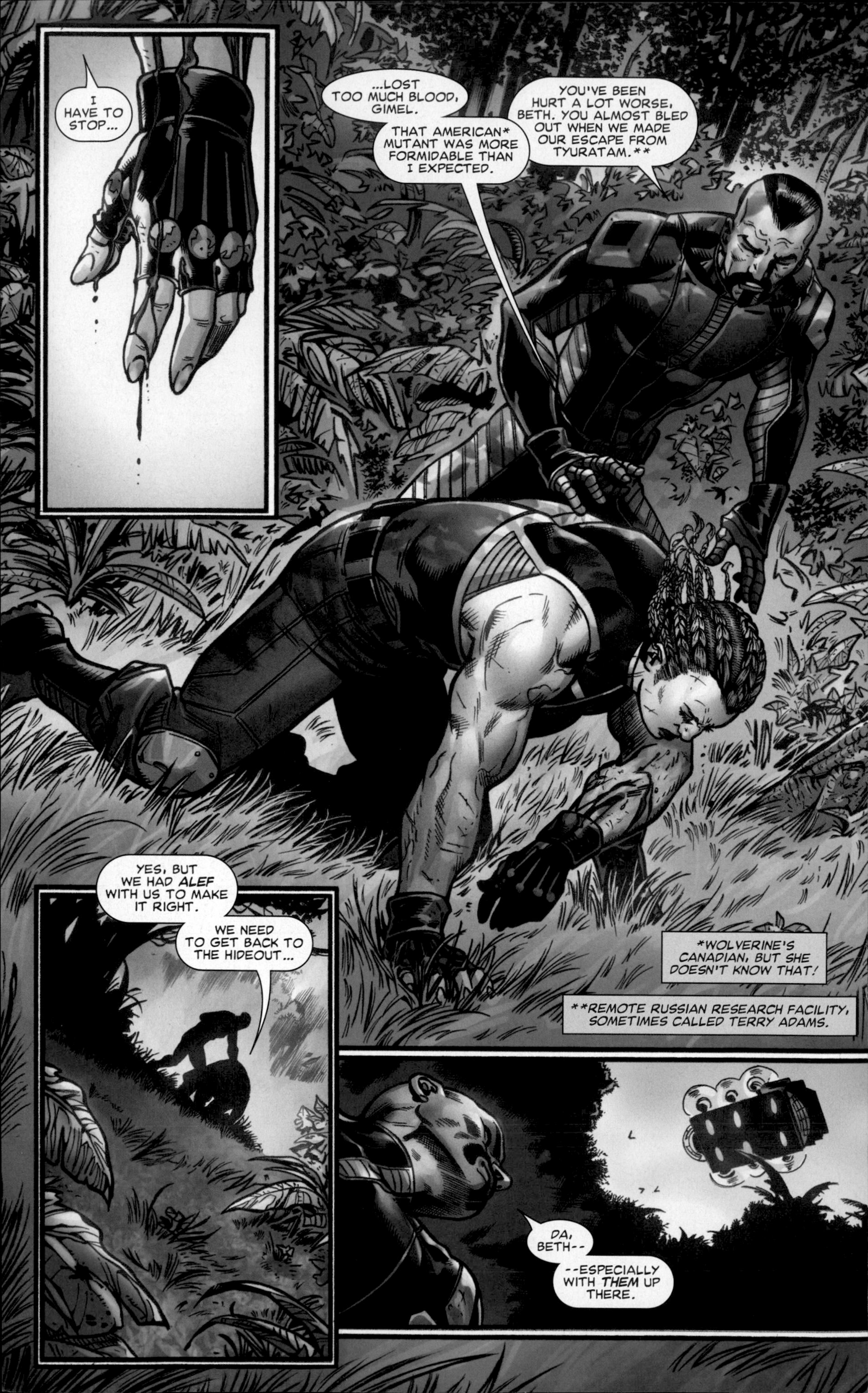
I HAVE TO STOP...
...LOST TOO MUCH BLOOD, GIMEL.
THAT AMERICAN* MUTANT WAS MORE FORMIDABLE THAN I EXPECTED.
YOU'VE BEEN HURT A LOT WORSE, BETH. YOU ALMOST BLED OUT WHEN WE MADE OUR ESCAPE FROM TYURATAM.**
*WOLVERINE'S CANADIAN, BUT SHE DOESN'T KNOW THAT!
**REMOTE RUSSIAN RESEARCH FACILITY, SOMETIMES CALLED TERRY ADAMS.
YES, BUT WE HAD ALEF WITH US TO MAKE IT RIGHT.
WE NEED TO GET BACK TO THE HIDEOUT...
DA, BETH--
--ESPECIALLY WITH THEM UP THERE.

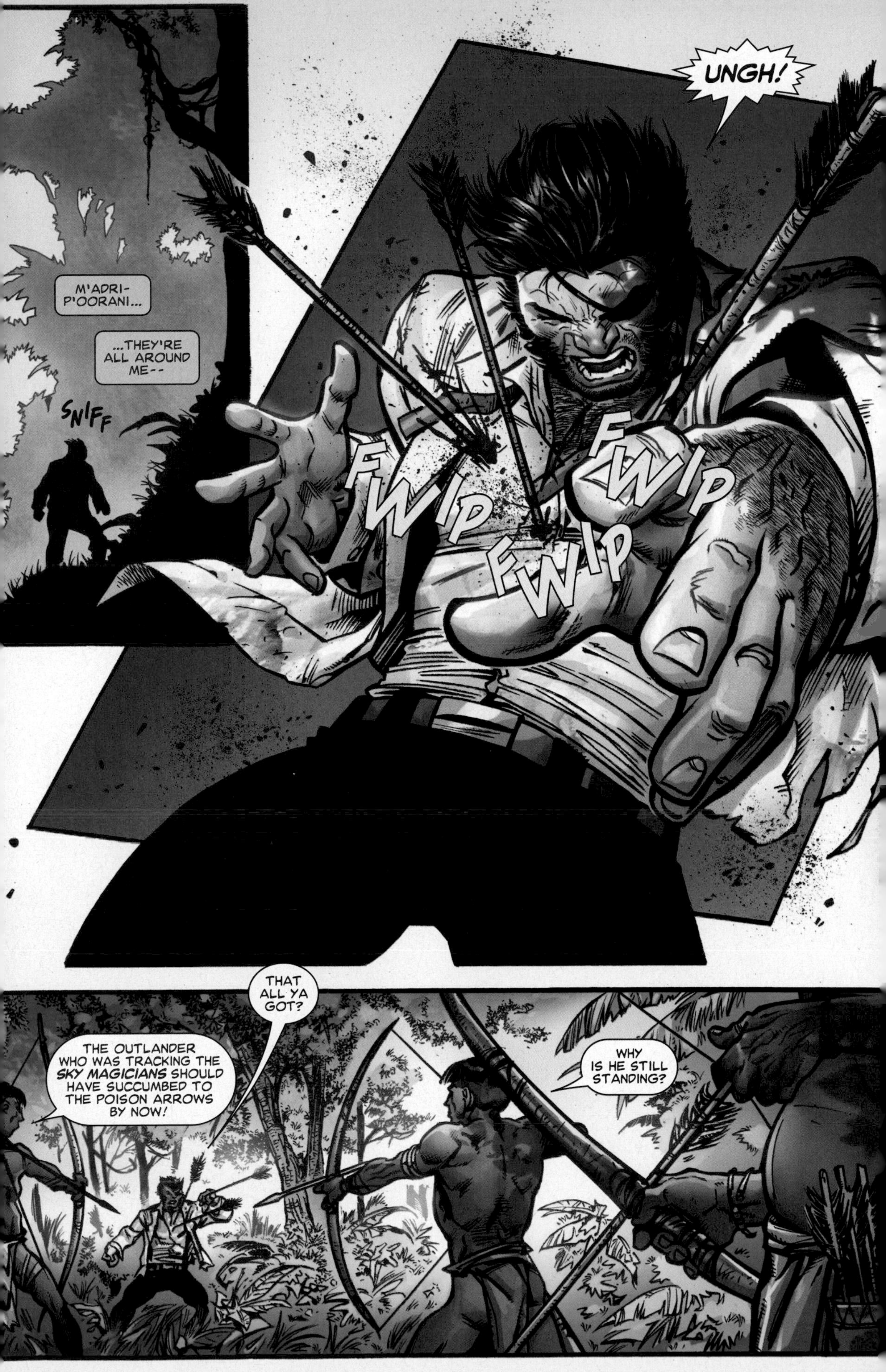

M'ADRI-P'OORANI...
...THEY'RE ALL AROUND ME--
SNIFF
UNGH!
FWIP
FWIP
FWIP
THE OUTLANDER WHO WAS TRACKING THE SKY MAGICIANS SHOULD HAVE SUCCUMBED TO THE POISON ARROWS BY NOW!
THAT ALL YA GOT?
WHY IS HE STILL STANDING?

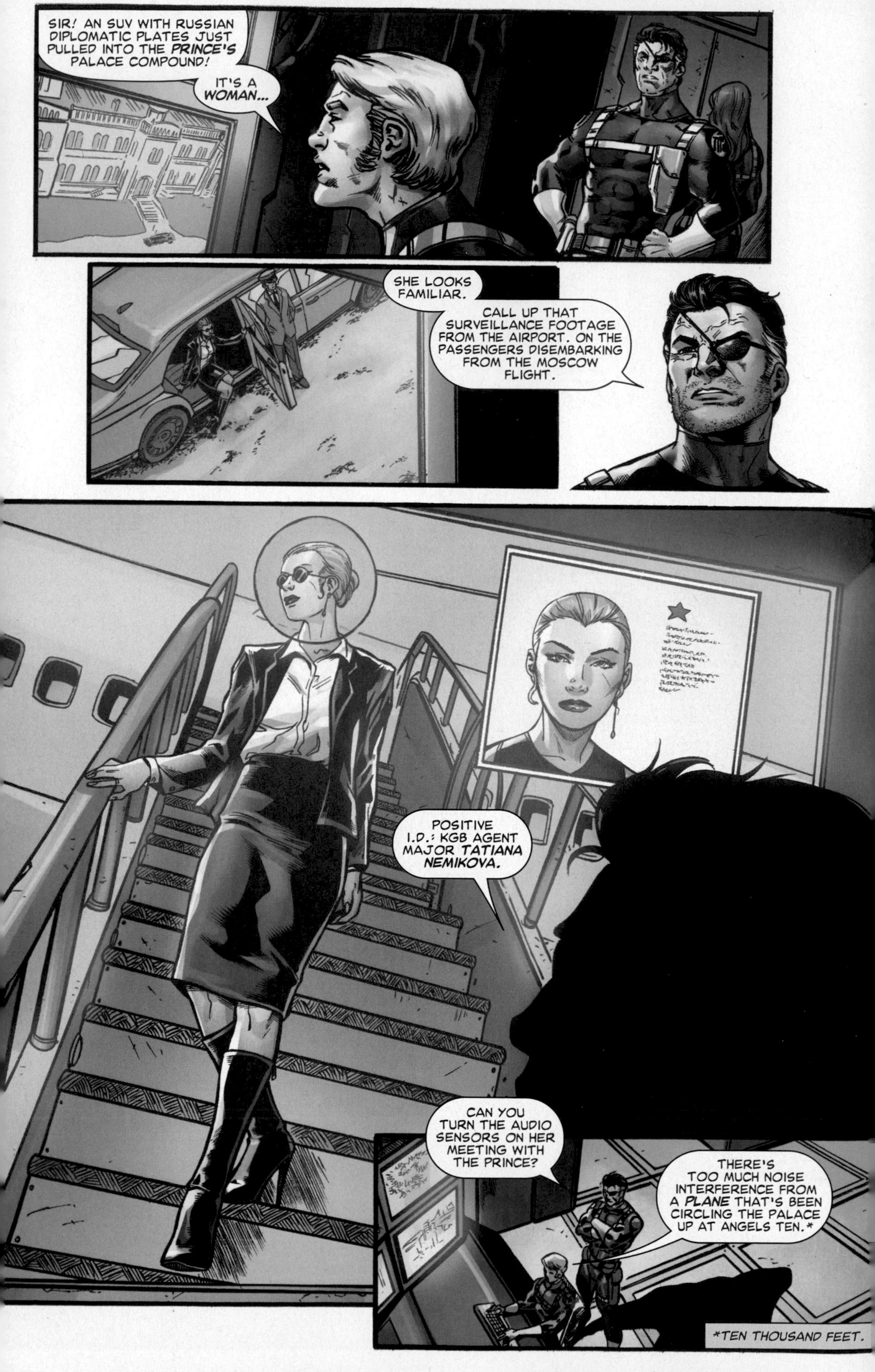
SIR! AN SUV WITH RUSSIAN DIPLOMATIC PLATES JUST PULLED INTO THE PRINCE'S PALACE COMPOUND!
IT'S A WOMAN...
SHE LOOKS FAMILIAR.
CALL UP THAT SURVEILLANCE FOOTAGE FROM THE AIRPORT. ON THE PASSENGERS DISEMBARKING FROM THE MOSCOW FLIGHT.
POSITIVE I.D.: KGB AGENT MAJOR TATIANA NEMIKOVA.
CAN YOU TURN THE AUDIO SENSORS ON HER MEETING WITH THE PRINCE?
THERE'S TOO MUCH NOISE INTERFERENCE FROM A PLANE THAT'S BEEN CIRCLING THE PALACE UP AT ANGELS TEN.*
*TEN THOUSAND FEET.

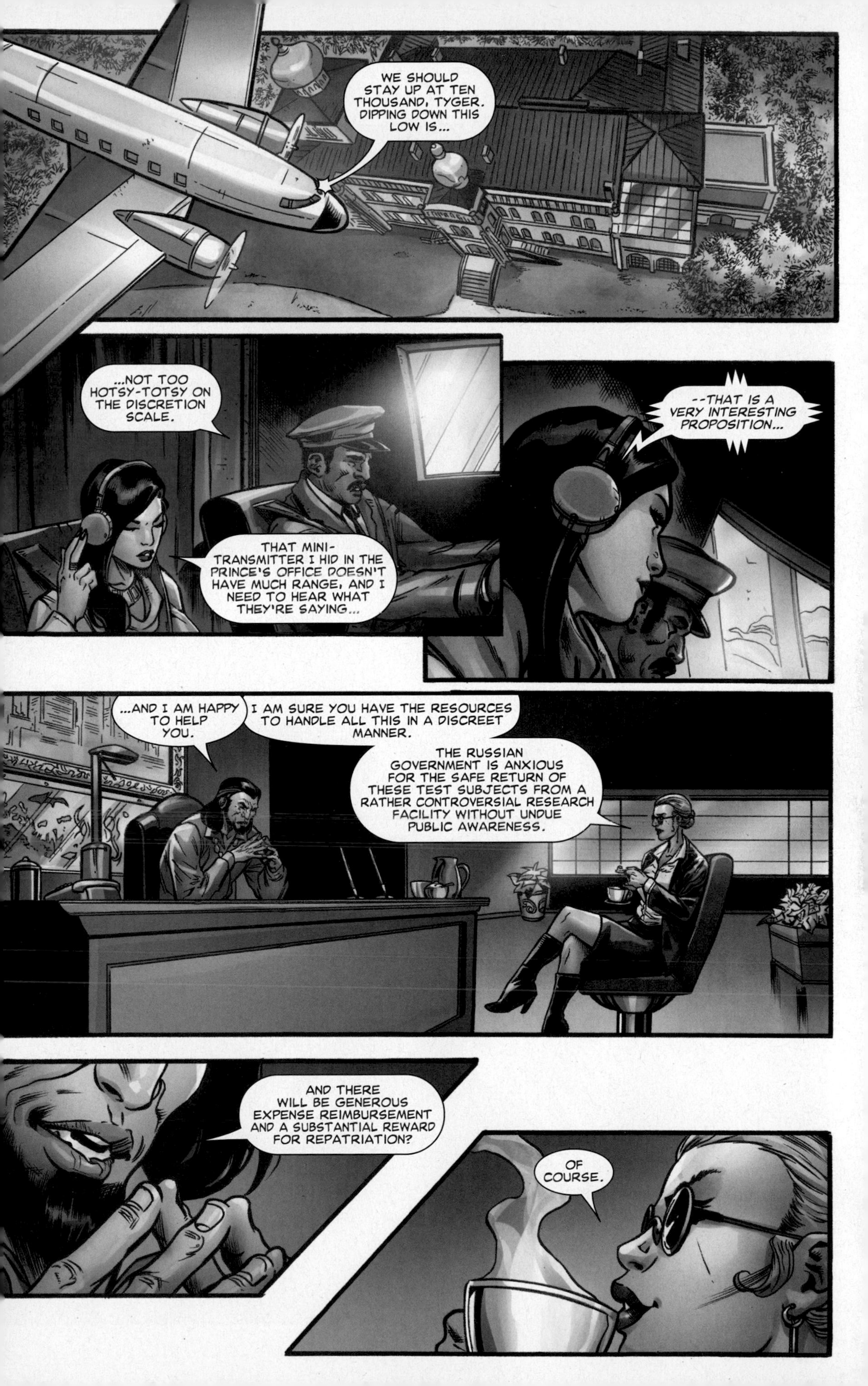
WE SHOULD STAY UP AT TEN THOUSAND, TYGER. DIPPING DOWN THIS LOW IS...
...NOT TOO HOTSY-TOTSY ON THE DISCRETION SCALE.
THAT MINI-TRANSMITTER I HID IN THE PRINCE'S OFFICE DOESN'T HAVE MUCH RANGE, AND I NEED TO HEAR WHAT THEY'RE SAYING...
--THAT IS A VERY INTERESTING PROPOSITION...
...AND I AM HAPPY TO HELP YOU.
I AM SURE YOU HAVE THE RESOURCES TO HANDLE ALL THIS IN A DISCREET MANNER.
THE RUSSIAN GOVERNMENT IS ANXIOUS FOR THE SAFE RETURN OF THESE TEST SUBJECTS FROM A RATHER CONTROVERSIAL RESEARCH FACILITY WITHOUT UNDUE PUBLIC AWARENESS.
AND THERE WILL BE GENEROUS EXPENSE REIMBURSEMENT AND A SUBSTANTIAL REWARD FOR REPATRIATION?
OF COURSE.

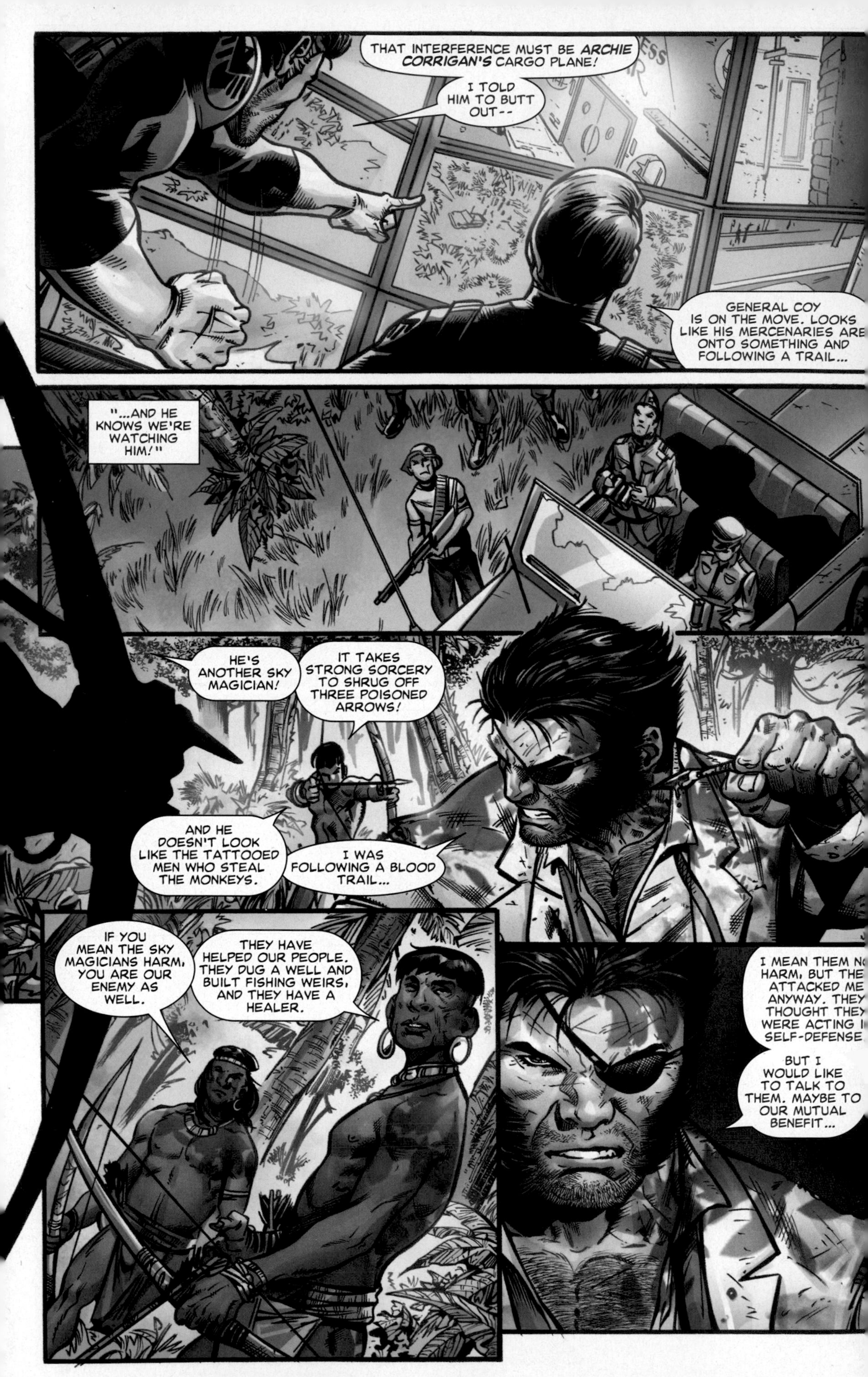

THAT INTERFERENCE MUST BE ARCHIE CORRIGAN'S CARGO PLANE!
I TOLD HIM TO BUTT OUT--
GENERAL COY IS ON THE MOVE. LOOKS LIKE HIS MERCENARIES ARE ONTO SOMETHING AND FOLLOWING A TRAIL...
"...AND HE KNOWS WE'RE WATCHING HIM!"
HE'S ANOTHER SKY MAGICIAN!
IT TAKES STRONG SORCERY TO SHRUG OFF THREE POISONED ARROWS!
AND HE DOESN'T LOOK LIKE THE TATTOOED MEN WHO STEAL THE MONKEYS.
I WAS FOLLOWING A BLOOD TRAIL...
IF YOU MEAN THE SKY MAGICIANS HARM, YOU ARE OUR ENEMY AS WELL.
THEY HAVE HELPED OUR PEOPLE. THEY DUG A WELL AND BUILT FISHING WEIRS, AND THEY HAVE A HEALER.
I MEAN THEM N HARM, BUT THE ATTACKED ME ANYWAY. THEY THOUGHT THEY WERE ACTING I SELF-DEFENSE
BUT I WOULD LIKE TO TALK TO THEM. MAYBE TO OUR MUTUAL BENEFIT...

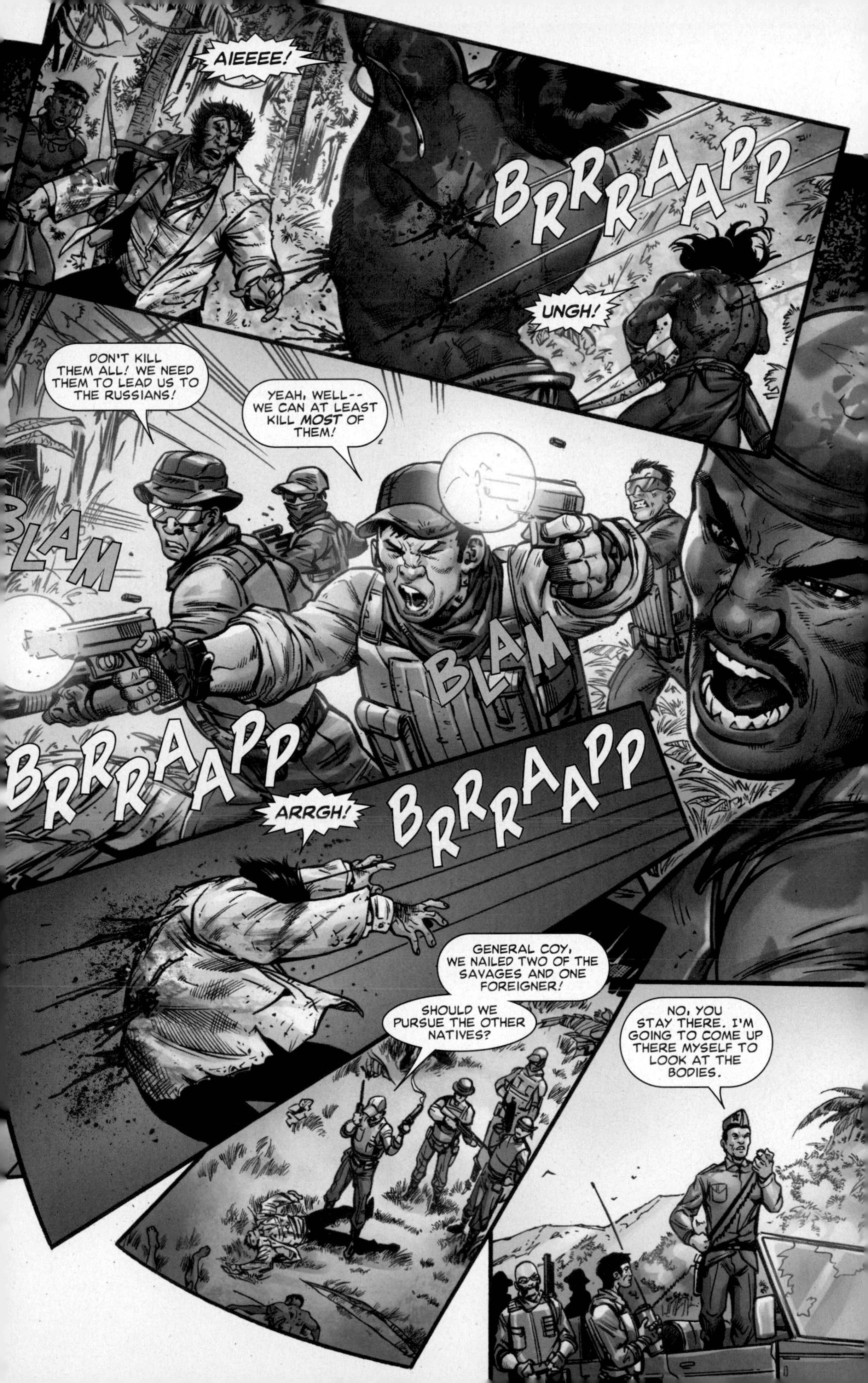
AIEEEE!
BRRRAAPP
UNGH!
DON'T KILL THEM ALL! WE NEED THEM TO LEAD US TO THE RUSSIANS!
YEAH, WELL-- WE CAN AT LEAST KILL *MOST* OF THEM!
BLAM
BLAM
BRRRAAPP
ARRGH!
BRRRAAPP
GENERAL COY, WE NAILED TWO OF THE SAVAGES AND ONE FOREIGNER!
SHOULD WE PURSUE THE OTHER NATIVES?
NO, YOU STAY THERE. I'M GOING TO COME UP THERE MYSELF TO LOOK AT THE BODIES.

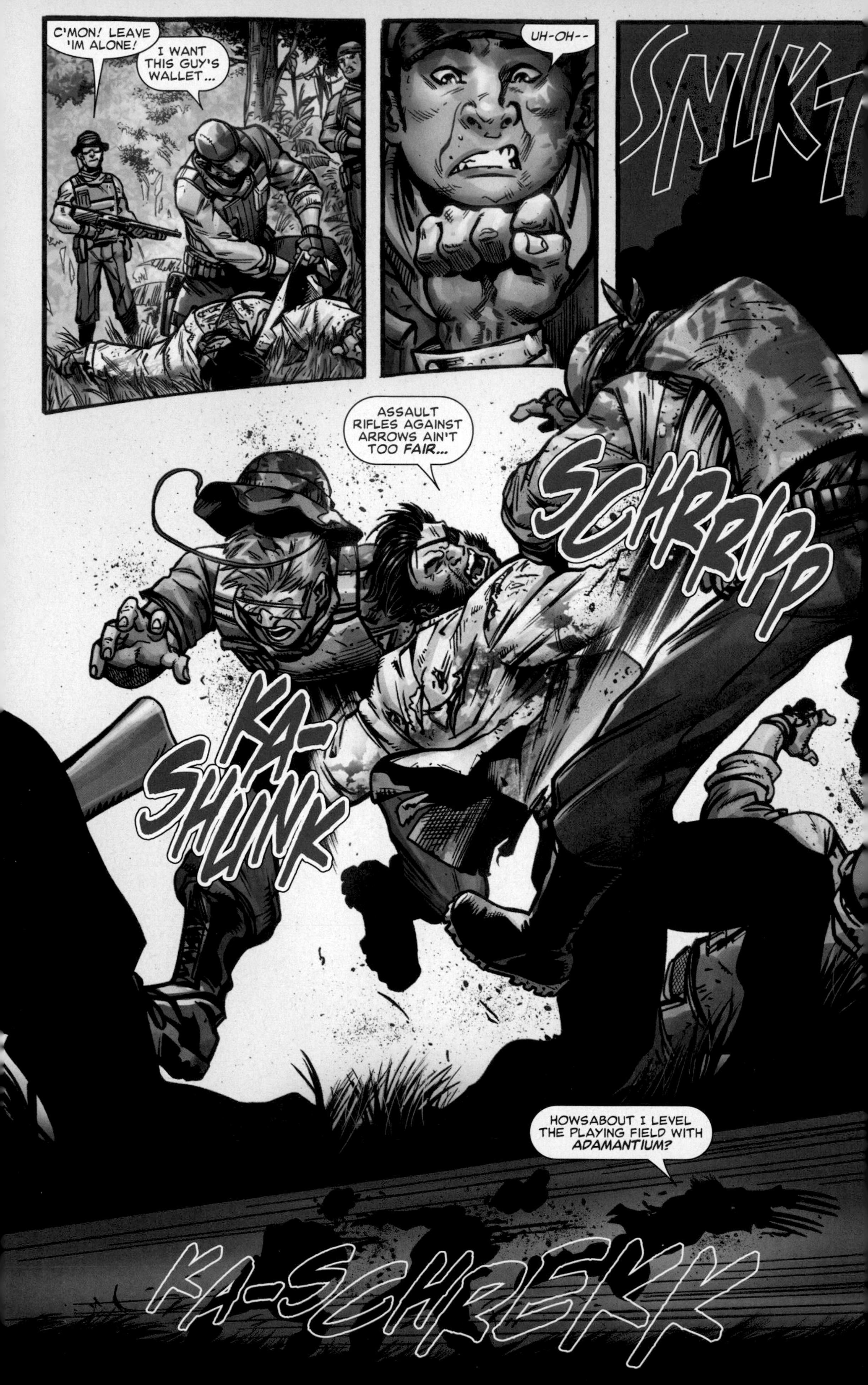
C'MON! LEAVE 'IM ALONE!
I WANT THIS GUY'S WALLET...
UH-OH--
SNIKT
ASSAULT RIFLES AGAINST ARROWS AIN'T TOO FAIR...
SCHRIPP
KA-SHUNK
HOWSABOUT I LEVEL THE PLAYING FIELD WITH ADAMANTIUM?
KA-SCHREKK

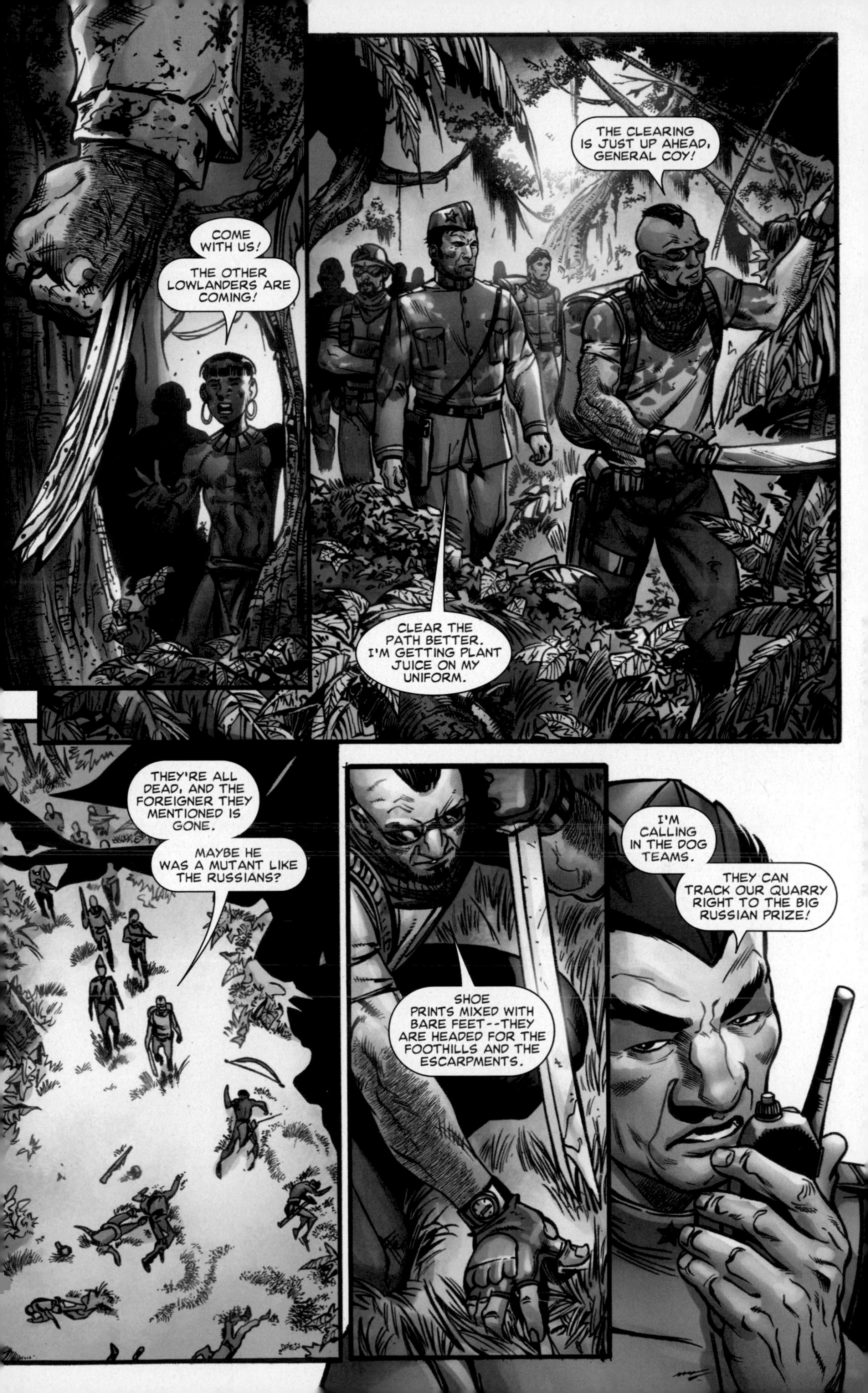
COME WITH US!
THE OTHER LOWLANDERS ARE COMING!
THE CLEARING IS JUST UP AHEAD, GENERAL COY!
CLEAR THE PATH BETTER. I'M GETTING PLANT JUICE ON MY UNIFORM.
THEY'RE ALL DEAD, AND THE FOREIGNER THEY MENTIONED IS GONE.
MAYBE HE WAS A MUTANT LIKE THE RUSSIANS?
SHOE PRINTS MIXED WITH BARE FEET--THEY ARE HEADED FOR THE FOOTHILLS AND THE ESCARPMENTS.
I'M CALLING IN THE DOG TEAMS.
THEY CAN TRACK OUR QUARRY RIGHT TO THE BIG RUSSIAN PRIZE!

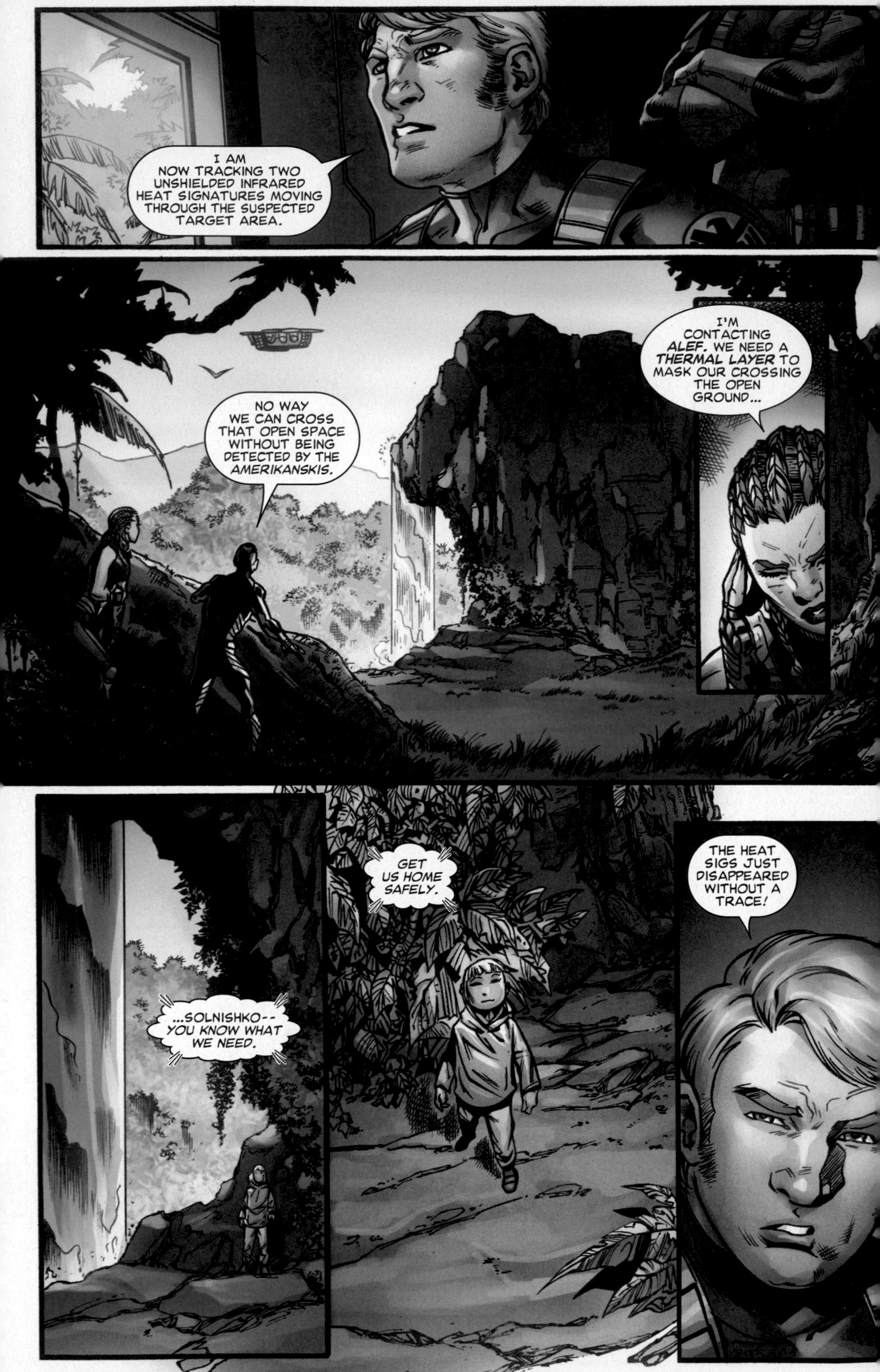
I AM NOW TRACKING TWO UNSHIELDED INFRARED HEAT SIGNATURES MOVING THROUGH THE SUSPECTED TARGET AREA.
NO WAY WE CAN CROSS THAT OPEN SPACE WITHOUT BEING DETECTED BY THE AMERIKANSKIS.
I'M CONTACTING ALEF. WE NEED A THERMAL LAYER TO MASK OUR CROSSING THE OPEN GROUND...
...SOLNISHKO-- YOU KNOW WHAT WE NEED.
GET US HOME SAFELY.
THE HEAT SIGS JUST DISAPPEARED WITHOUT A TRACE!

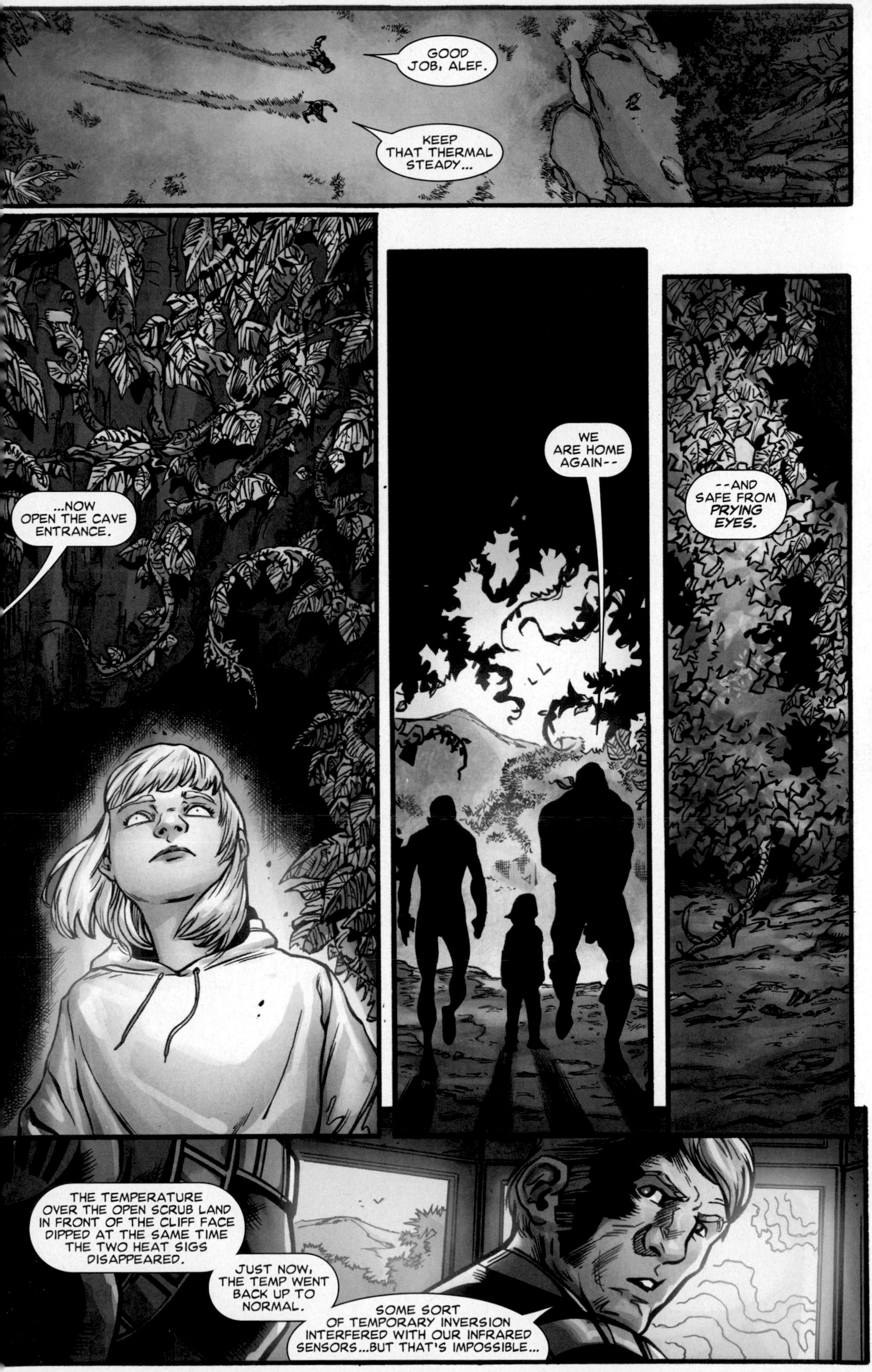
GOOD JOB, ALEF.
KEEP THAT THERMAL STEADY...
...NOW OPEN THE CAVE ENTRANCE.
WE ARE HOME AGAIN--
--AND SAFE FROM PRYING EYES.
THE TEMPERATURE OVER THE OPEN SCRUB LAND IN FRONT OF THE CLIFF FACE DIPPED AT THE SAME TIME THE TWO HEAT SIGS DISAPPEARED.
JUST NOW, THE TEMP WENT BACK UP TO NORMAL.
SOME SORT OF TEMPORARY INVERSION INTERFERED WITH OUR INFRARED SENSORS...BUT THAT'S IMPOSSIBLE...

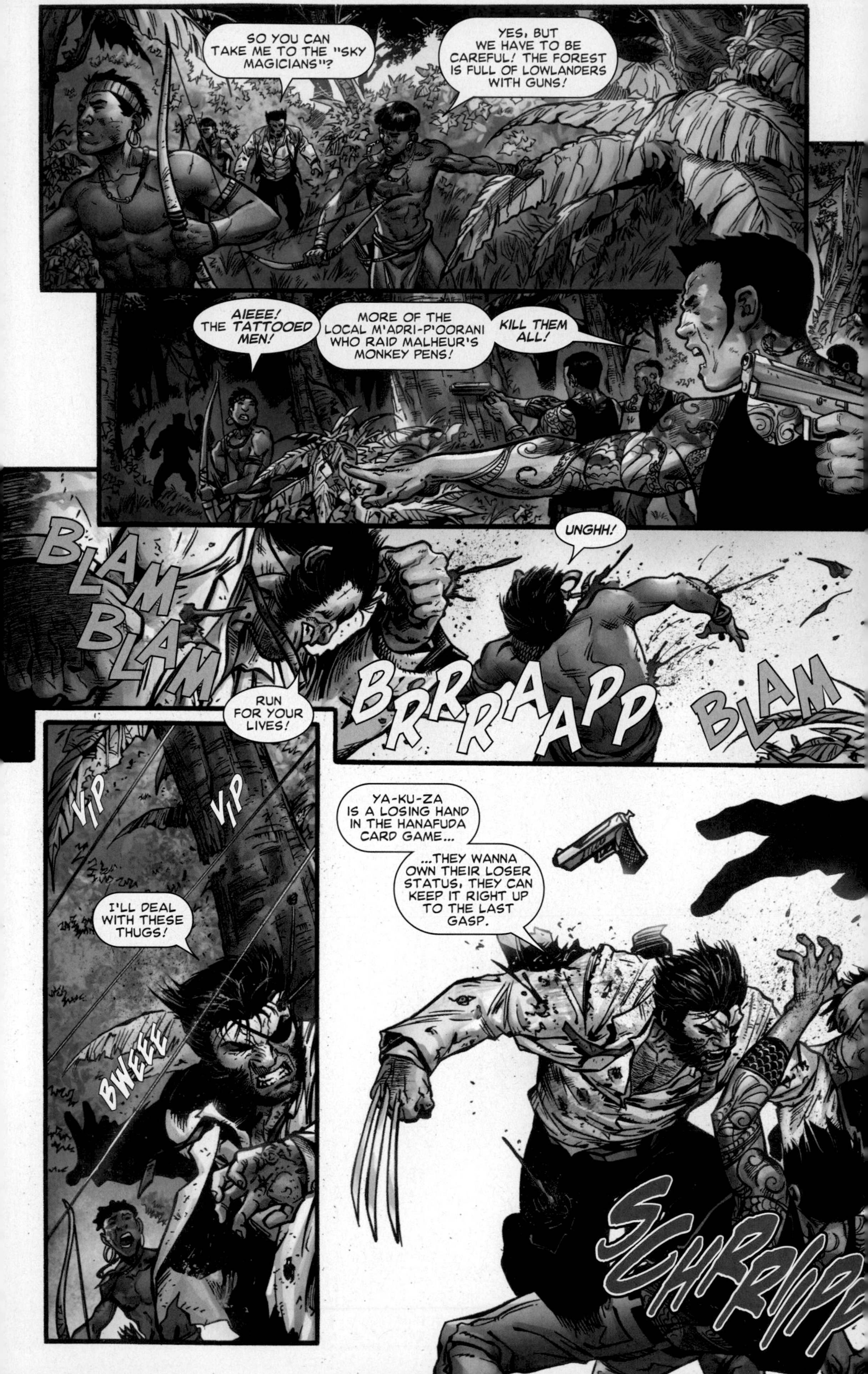
SO YOU CAN TAKE ME TO THE "SKY MAGICIANS"?
YES, BUT WE HAVE TO BE CAREFUL! THE FOREST IS FULL OF LOWLANDERS WITH GUNS!
AIEEE! THE TATTOOED MEN!
MORE OF THE LOCAL M'ADRI-P'OORANI WHO RAID MALHEUR'S MONKEY PENS!
KILL THEM ALL!
BLAM BLAM
UNGHH!
RUN FOR YOUR LIVES!
BRRRAAPP
BLAM
VIP
VIP
I'LL DEAL WITH THESE THUGS!
BWEEE
YA-KU-ZA IS A LOSING HAND IN THE HANAFUDA CARD GAME...
...THEY WANNA OWN THEIR LOSER STATUS, THEY CAN KEEP IT RIGHT UP TO THE LAST GASP.
SCHRIPP

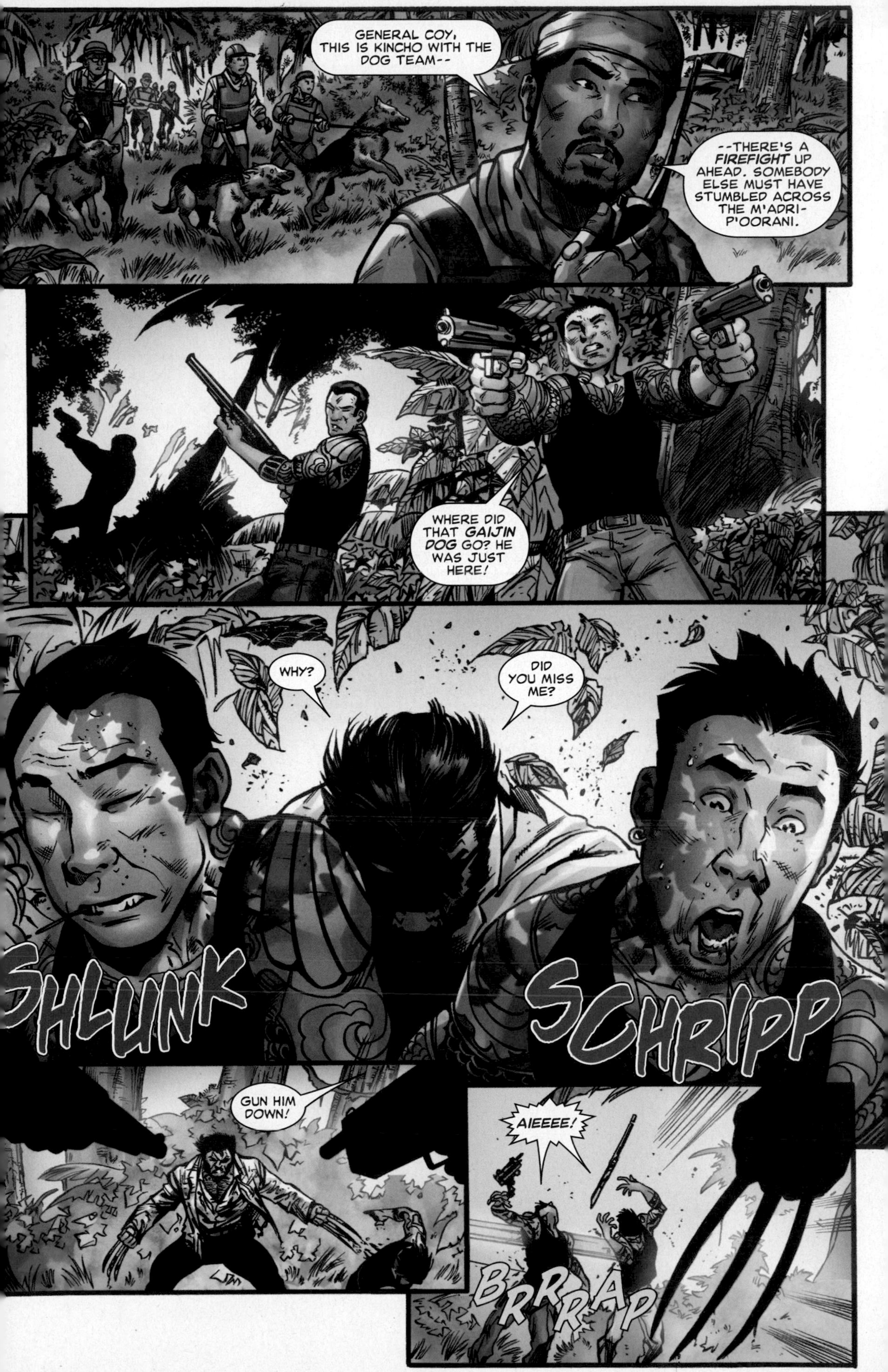
GENERAL COY, THIS IS KINCHO WITH THE DOG TEAM--
--THERE'S A FIREFIGHT UP AHEAD. SOMEBODY ELSE MUST HAVE STUMBLED ACROSS THE M'ADRI-P'OORANI.
WHERE DID THAT GAIJIN DOG GO? HE WAS JUST HERE!
WHY?
DID YOU MISS ME?
SHLUNK
SCHRIPP
GUN HIM DOWN!
AIEEEE!
BRRRAP

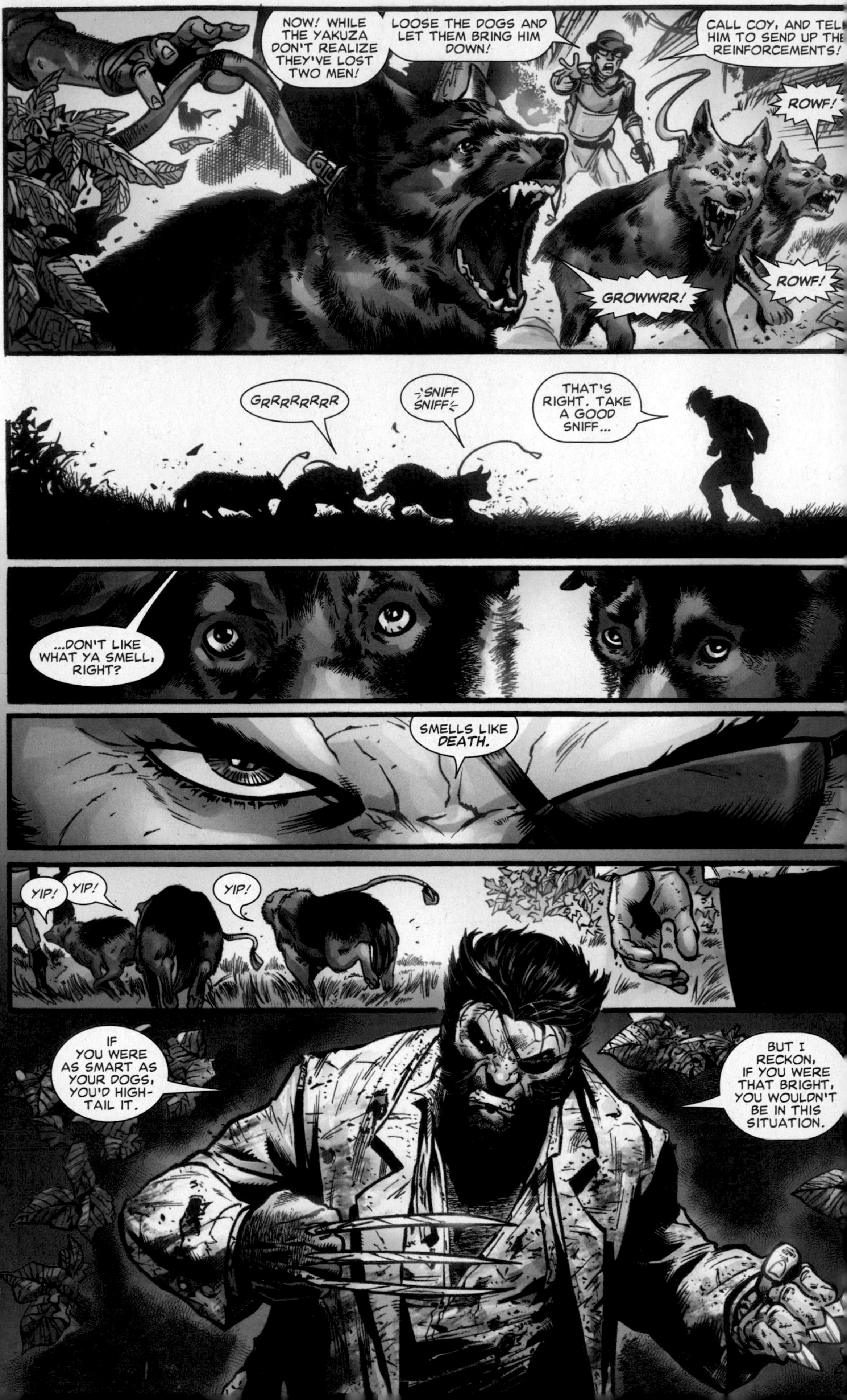
NOW! WHILE THE YAKUZA DON'T REALIZE THEY'VE LOST TWO MEN!
LOOSE THE DOGS AND LET THEM BRING HIM DOWN!
CALL COY, AND TELL HIM TO SEND UP THE REINFORCEMENTS!
ROWF!
GROWWRR!
ROWF!
GRRRRRRRR
SNIFF SNIFF
THAT'S RIGHT. TAKE A GOOD SNIFF...
...DON'T LIKE WHAT YA SMELL, RIGHT?
SMELLS LIKE DEATH.
YIP!
YIP!
YIP!
IF YOU WERE AS SMART AS YOUR DOGS, YOU'D HIGH-TAIL IT.
BUT I RECKON, IF YOU WERE THAT BRIGHT, YOU WOULDN'T BE IN THIS SITUATION.

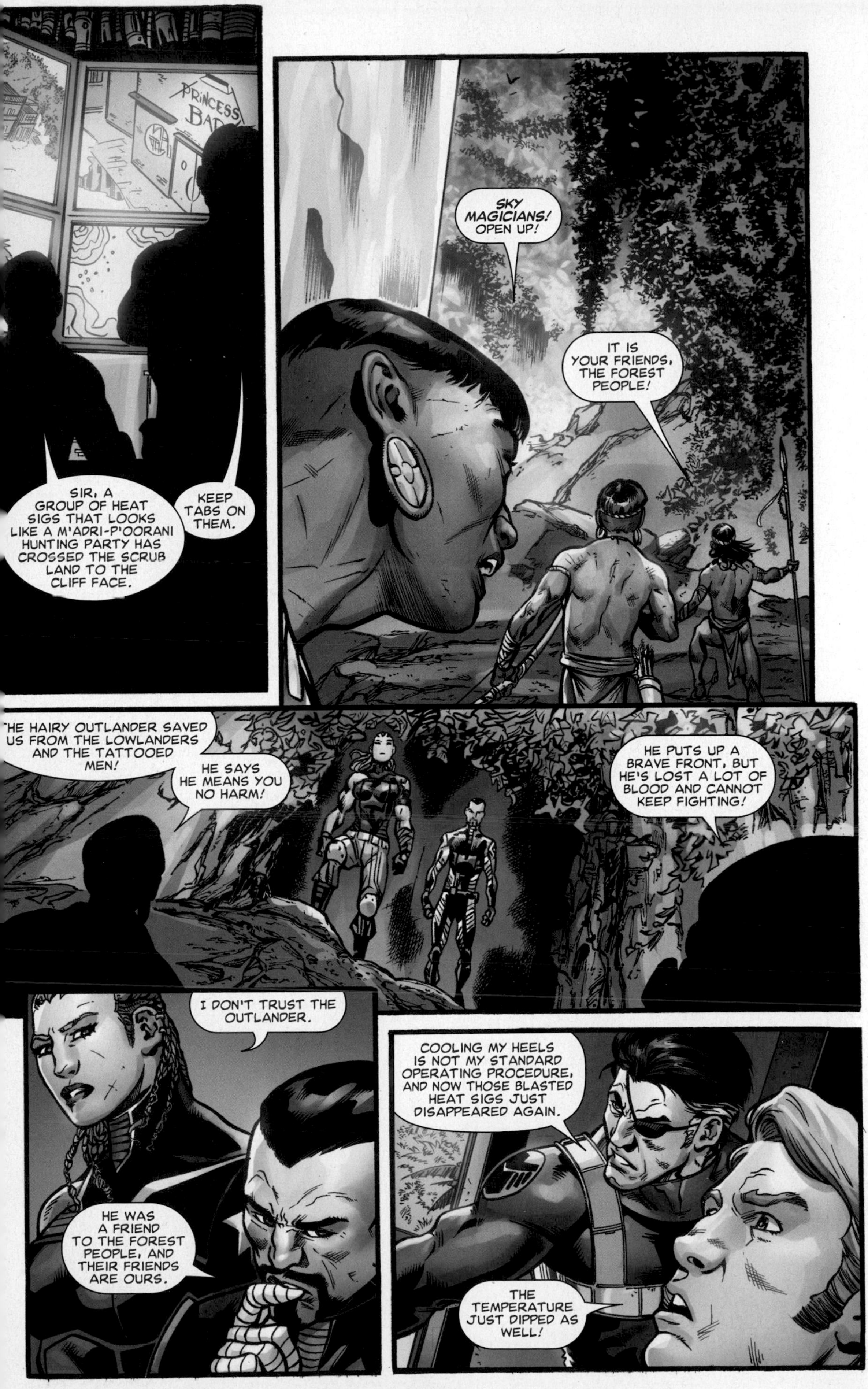
PRINCESS BAR
SIR, A GROUP OF HEAT SIGS THAT LOOKS LIKE A M'ADRI-P'OORANI HUNTING PARTY HAS CROSSED THE SCRUB LAND TO THE CLIFF FACE.
KEEP TABS ON THEM.
SKY MAGICIANS! OPEN UP!
IT IS YOUR FRIENDS, THE FOREST PEOPLE!
THE HAIRY OUTLANDER SAVED US FROM THE LOWLANDERS AND THE TATTOOED MEN!
HE SAYS HE MEANS YOU NO HARM!
HE PUTS UP A BRAVE FRONT, BUT HE'S LOST A LOT OF BLOOD AND CANNOT KEEP FIGHTING!
I DON'T TRUST THE OUTLANDER.
HE WAS A FRIEND TO THE FOREST PEOPLE, AND THEIR FRIENDS ARE OURS.
COOLING MY HEELS IS NOT MY STANDARD OPERATING PROCEDURE, AND NOW THOSE BLASTED HEAT SIGS JUST DISAPPEARED AGAIN.
THE TEMPERATURE JUST DIPPED AS WELL!

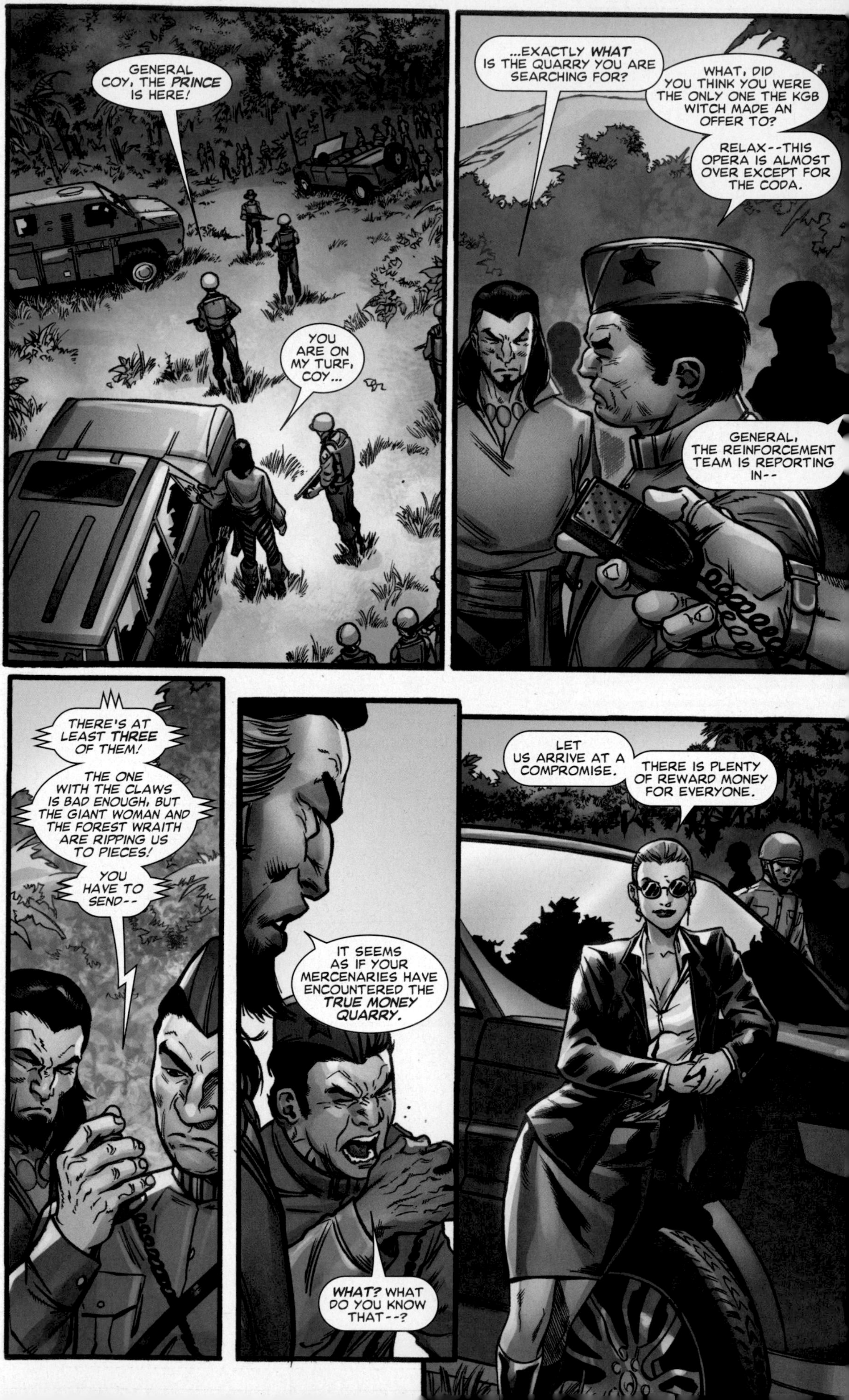
GENERAL COY, THE *PRINCE* IS HERE!
YOU ARE ON MY TURF, COY...
...EXACTLY *WHAT* IS THE QUARRY YOU ARE SEARCHING FOR?
WHAT, DID YOU THINK YOU WERE THE ONLY ONE THE KGB WITCH MADE AN OFFER TO?
RELAX--THIS OPERA IS ALMOST OVER EXCEPT FOR THE CODA.
GENERAL, THE REINFORCEMENT TEAM IS REPORTING IN--
THERE'S AT LEAST *THREE* OF THEM!
THE ONE WITH THE CLAWS IS BAD ENOUGH, BUT THE GIANT WOMAN AND THE FOREST WRAITH ARE RIPPING US TO PIECES!
YOU HAVE TO SEND--
IT SEEMS AS IF YOUR MERCENARIES HAVE ENCOUNTERED THE *TRUE MONEY QUARRY.*
WHAT? WHAT DO YOU KNOW THAT--?
LET US ARRIVE AT A COMPROMISE.
THERE IS PLENTY OF REWARD MONEY FOR EVERYONE.

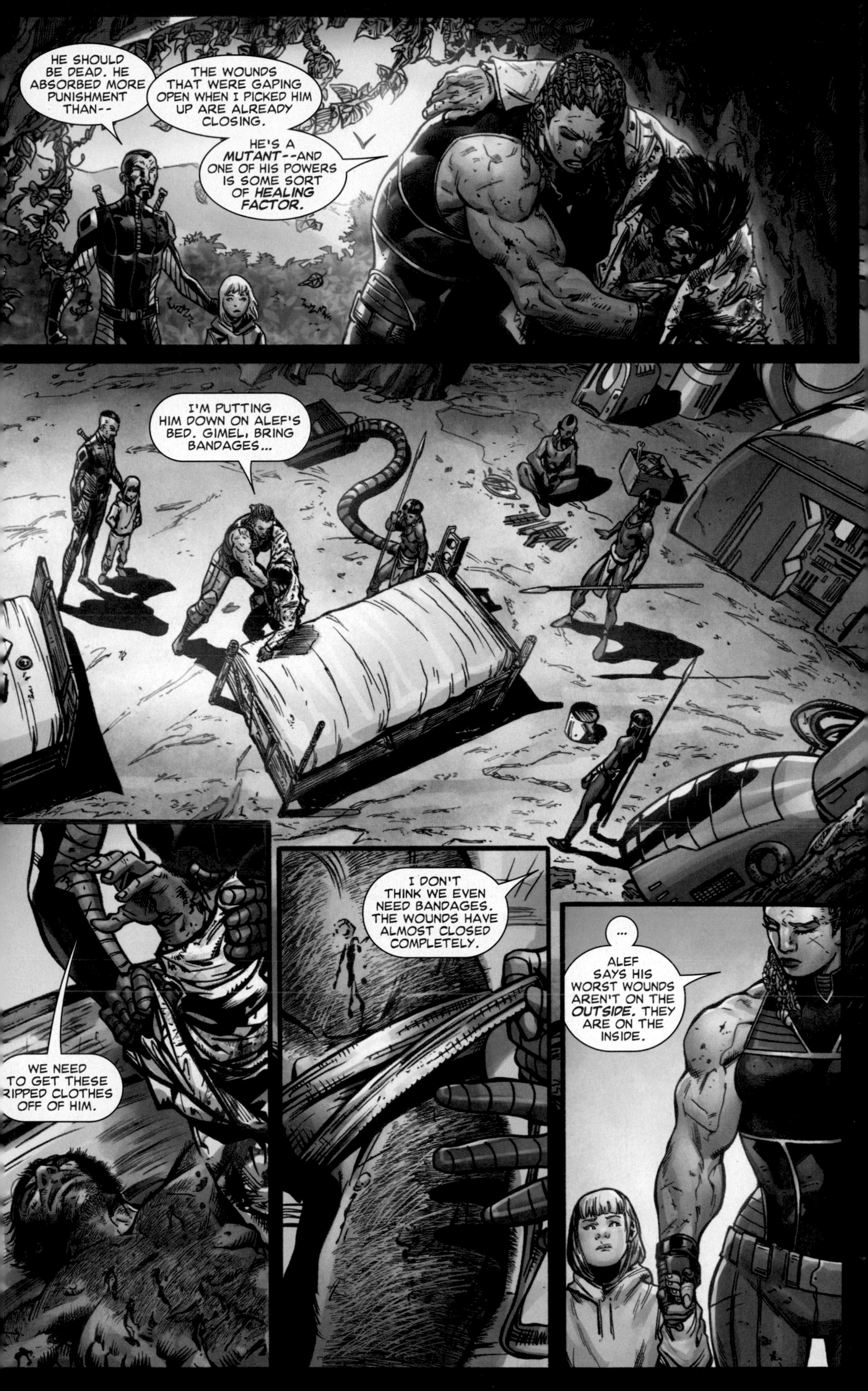
HE SHOULD BE DEAD. HE ABSORBED MORE PUNISHMENT THAN--
THE WOUNDS THAT WERE GAPING OPEN WHEN I PICKED HIM UP ARE ALREADY CLOSING.
HE'S A MUTANT--AND ONE OF HIS POWERS IS SOME SORT OF HEALING FACTOR.
I'M PUTTING HIM DOWN ON ALEF'S BED. GIMEL, BRING BANDAGES...
WE NEED TO GET THESE RIPPED CLOTHES OFF OF HIM.
I DON'T THINK WE EVEN NEED BANDAGES. THE WOUNDS HAVE ALMOST CLOSED COMPLETELY.
...
ALEF SAYS HIS WORST WOUNDS AREN'T ON THE OUTSIDE. THEY ARE ON THE INSIDE.

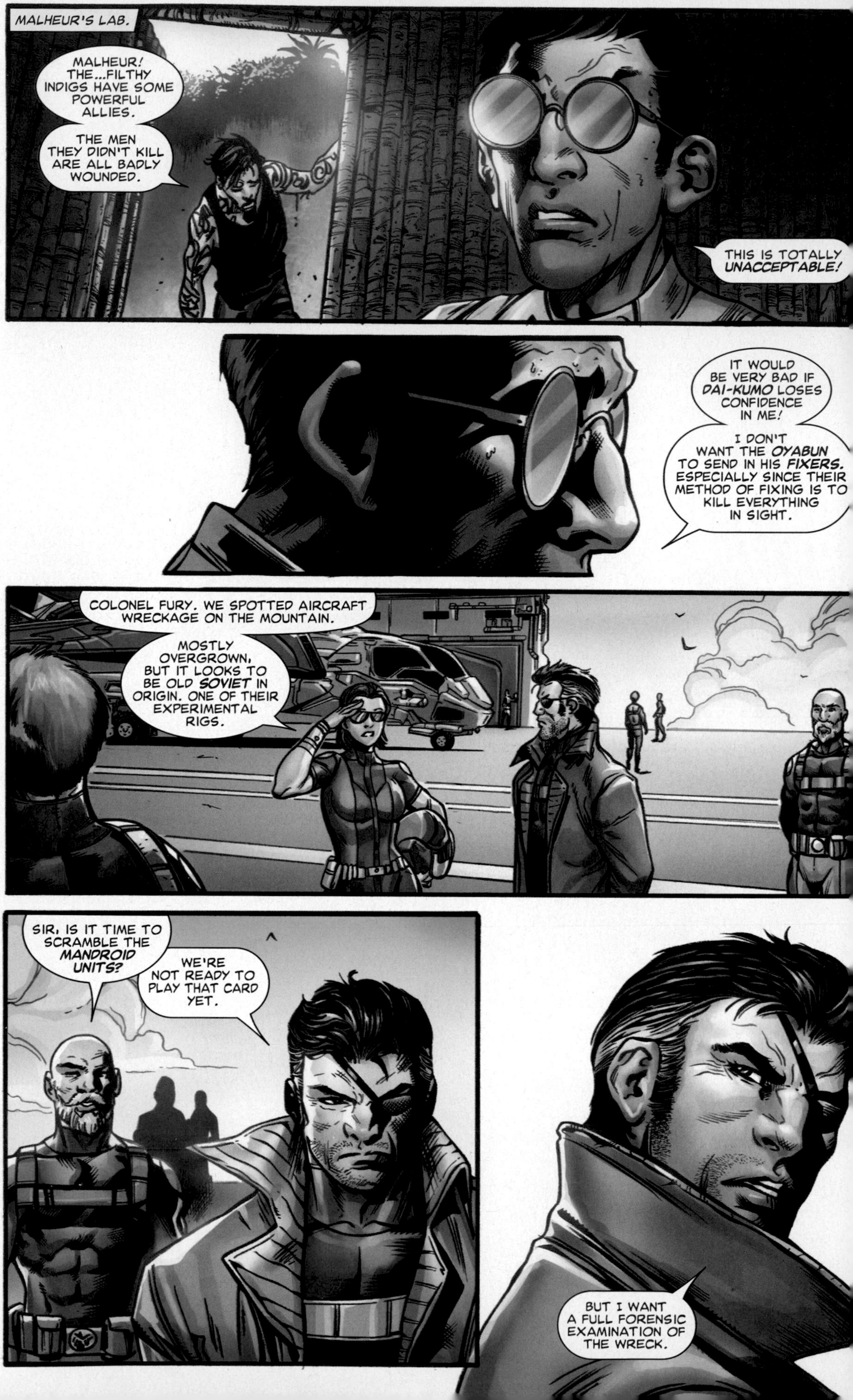
MALHEUR'S LAB.
MALHEUR! THE...FILTHY INDIGS HAVE SOME POWERFUL ALLIES.
THE MEN THEY DIDN'T KILL ARE ALL BADLY WOUNDED.
THIS IS TOTALLY UNACCEPTABLE!
IT WOULD BE VERY BAD IF DAI-KUMO LOSES CONFIDENCE IN ME!
I DON'T WANT THE OYABUN TO SEND IN HIS FIXERS. ESPECIALLY SINCE THEIR METHOD OF FIXING IS TO KILL EVERYTHING IN SIGHT.
COLONEL FURY. WE SPOTTED AIRCRAFT WRECKAGE ON THE MOUNTAIN.
MOSTLY OVERGROWN, BUT IT LOOKS TO BE OLD SOVIET IN ORIGIN. ONE OF THEIR EXPERIMENTAL RIGS.
SIR, IS IT TIME TO SCRAMBLE THE MANDROID UNITS?
WE'RE NOT READY TO PLAY THAT CARD YET.
BUT I WANT A FULL FORENSIC EXAMINATION OF THE WRECK.

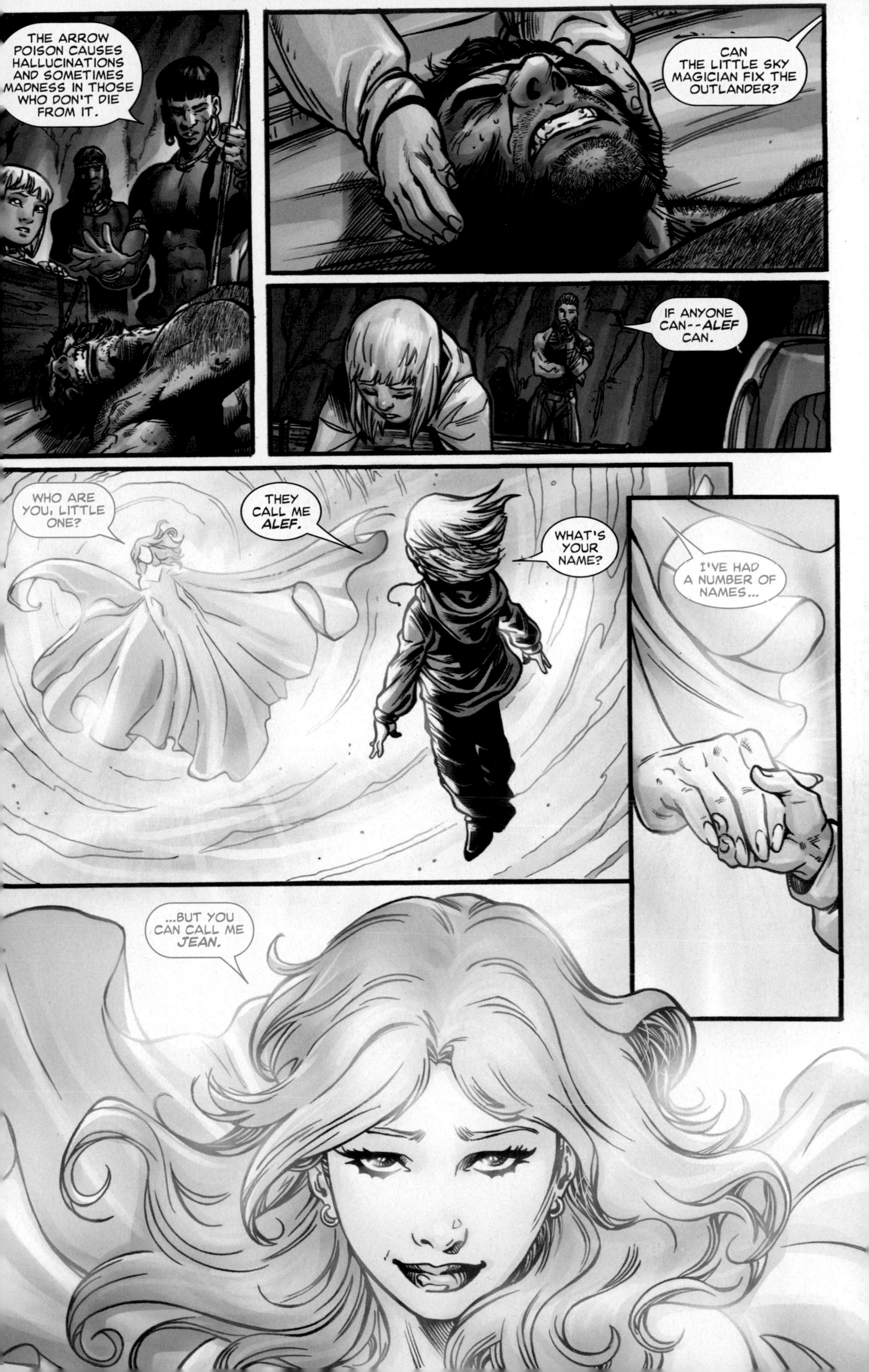
THE ARROW POISON CAUSES HALLUCINATIONS AND SOMETIMES MADNESS IN THOSE WHO DON'T DIE FROM IT.
CAN THE LITTLE SKY MAGICIAN FIX THE OUTLANDER?
IF ANYONE CAN--ALEF CAN.
WHO ARE YOU, LITTLE ONE?
THEY CALL ME ALEF.
WHAT'S YOUR NAME?
I'VE HAD A NUMBER OF NAMES...
...BUT YOU CAN CALL ME JEAN.

#3

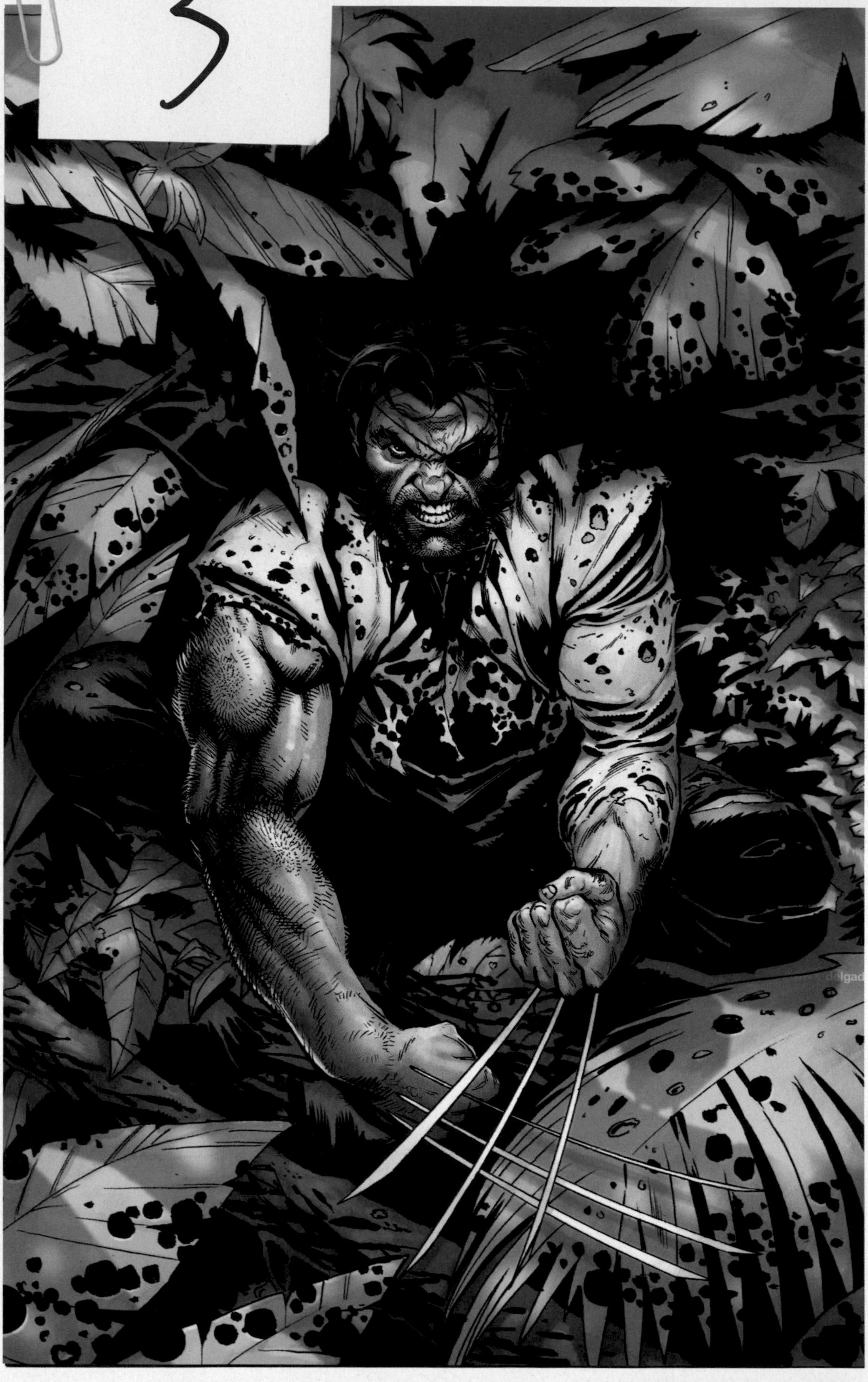

INTERNAL REVIEW ONLY

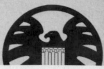

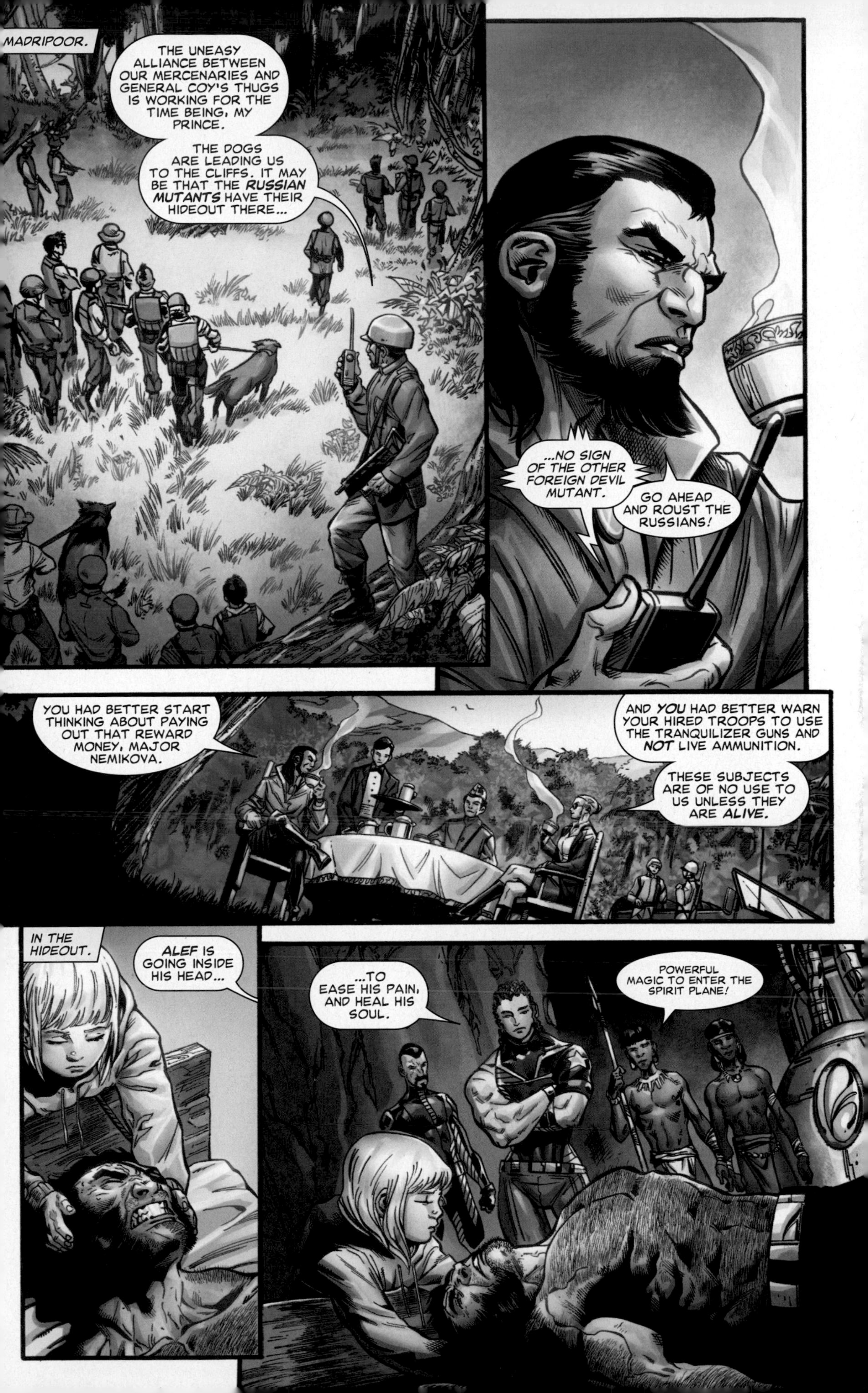
MADRIPOOR.
THE UNEASY ALLIANCE BETWEEN OUR MERCENARIES AND GENERAL COY'S THUGS IS WORKING FOR THE TIME BEING, MY PRINCE.
THE DOGS ARE LEADING US TO THE CLIFFS. IT MAY BE THAT THE RUSSIAN MUTANTS HAVE THEIR HIDEOUT THERE...
...NO SIGN OF THE OTHER FOREIGN DEVIL MUTANT.
GO AHEAD AND ROUST THE RUSSIANS!
YOU HAD BETTER START THINKING ABOUT PAYING OUT THAT REWARD MONEY, MAJOR NEMIKOVA.
AND YOU HAD BETTER WARN YOUR HIRED TROOPS TO USE THE TRANQUILIZER GUNS AND NOT LIVE AMMUNITION.
THESE SUBJECTS ARE OF NO USE TO US UNLESS THEY ARE ALIVE.
IN THE HIDEOUT.
ALEF IS GOING INSIDE HIS HEAD...
...TO EASE HIS PAIN, AND HEAL HIS SOUL.
POWERFUL MAGIC TO ENTER THE SPIRIT PLANE!

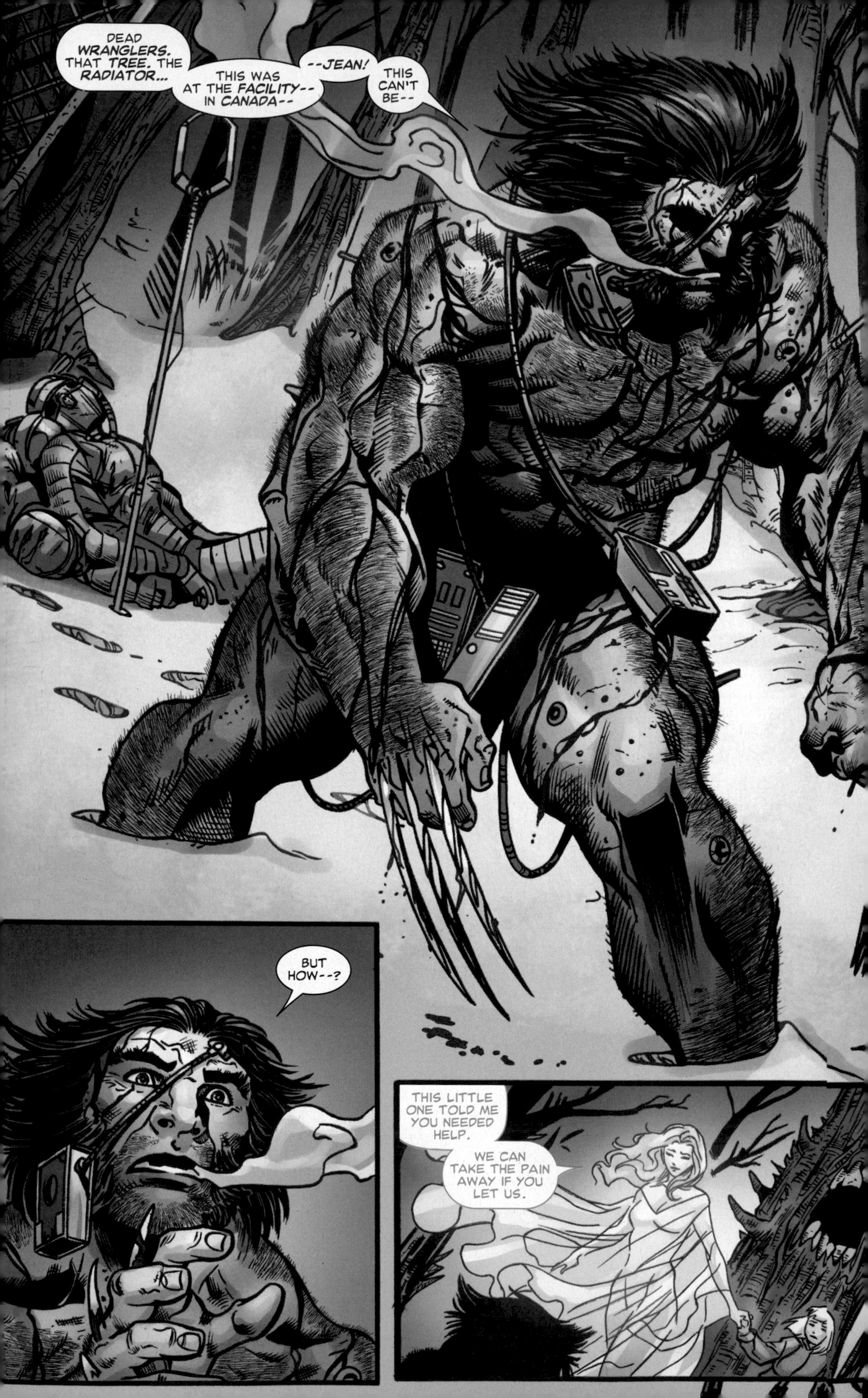
DEAD WRANGLERS. THAT TREE. THE RADIATOR...
THIS WAS AT THE FACILITY-- IN CANADA--
--JEAN!
THIS CAN'T BE--
BUT HOW--?
THIS LITTLE ONE TOLD ME YOU NEEDED HELP.
WE CAN TAKE THE PAIN AWAY IF YOU LET US.

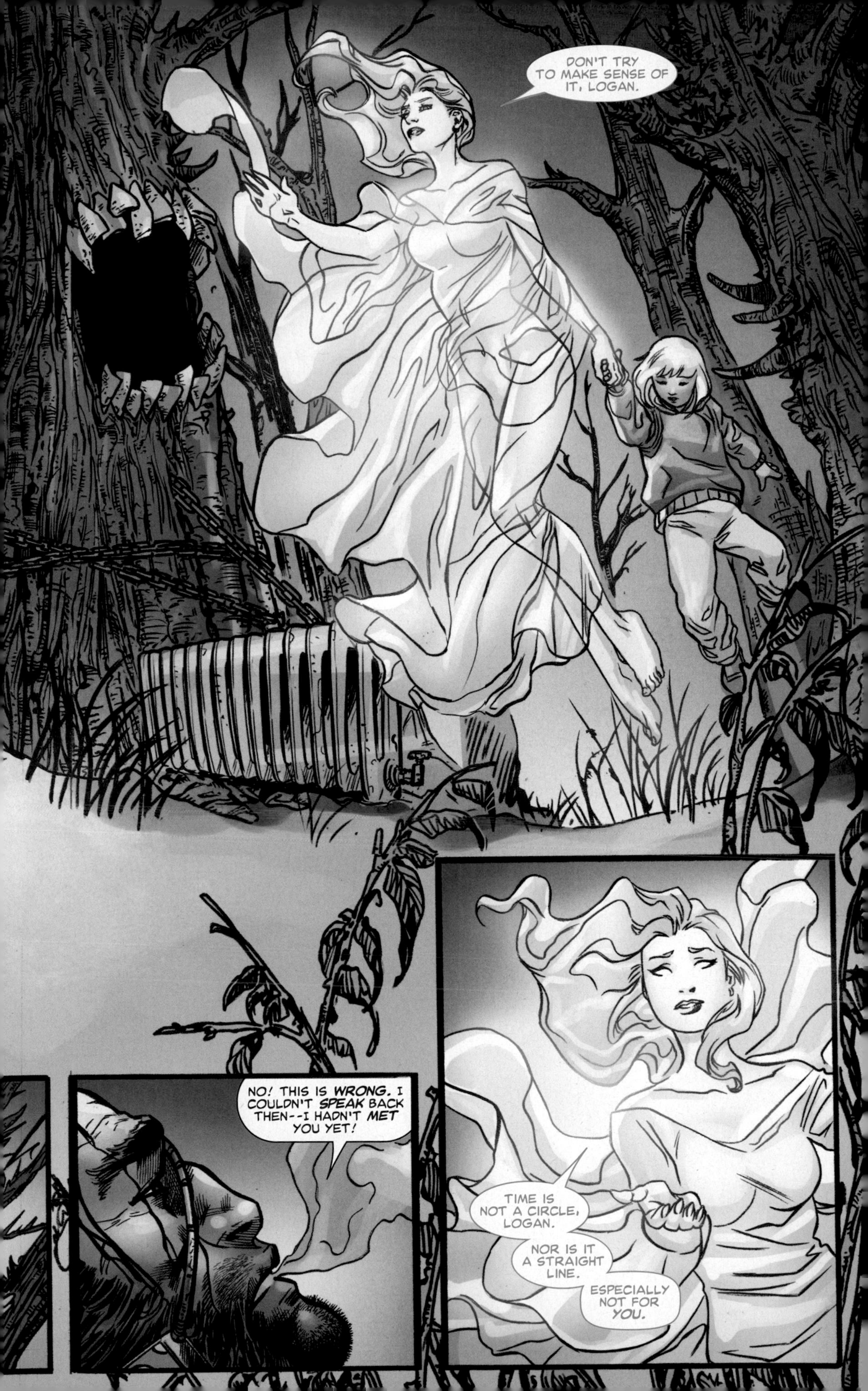
DON'T TRY TO MAKE SENSE OF IT, LOGAN.
NO! THIS IS WRONG. I COULDN'T SPEAK BACK THEN--I HADN'T MET YOU YET!
TIME IS NOT A CIRCLE, LOGAN.
NOR IS IT A STRAIGHT LINE.
ESPECIALLY NOT FOR YOU.

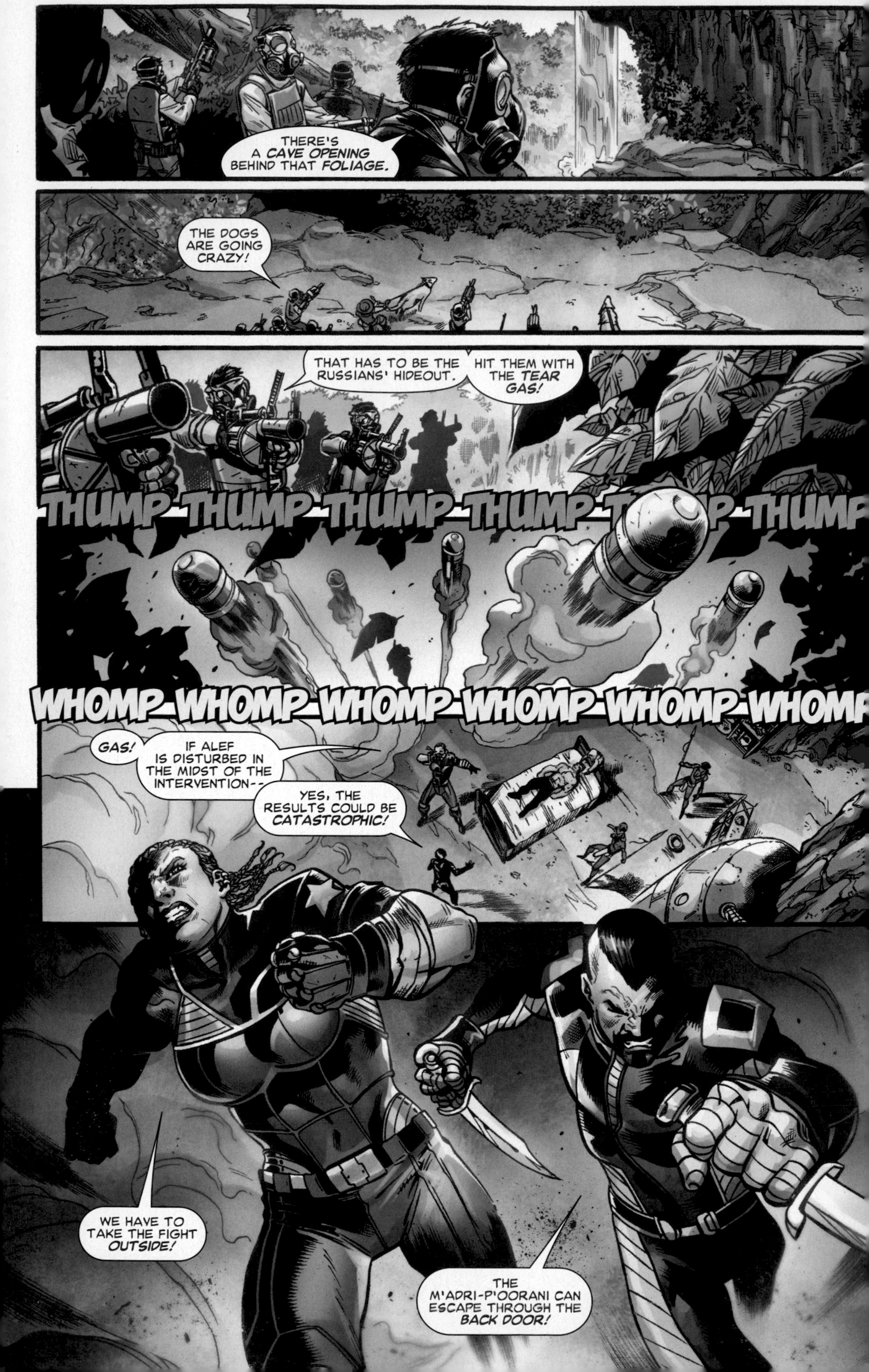
THERE'S A CAVE OPENING BEHIND THAT FOLIAGE.
THE DOGS ARE GOING CRAZY!
THAT HAS TO BE THE RUSSIANS' HIDEOUT.
HIT THEM WITH THE TEAR GAS!
THUMP THUMP THUMP THUMP THUMP THUMP
WHOMP WHOMP WHOMP WHOMP WHOMP WHOMP
GAS!
IF ALEF IS DISTURBED IN THE MIDST OF THE INTERVENTION--
YES, THE RESULTS COULD BE CATASTROPHIC!
WE HAVE TO TAKE THE FIGHT OUTSIDE!
THE M'ADRI-P'OORANI CAN ESCAPE THROUGH THE BACK DOOR!

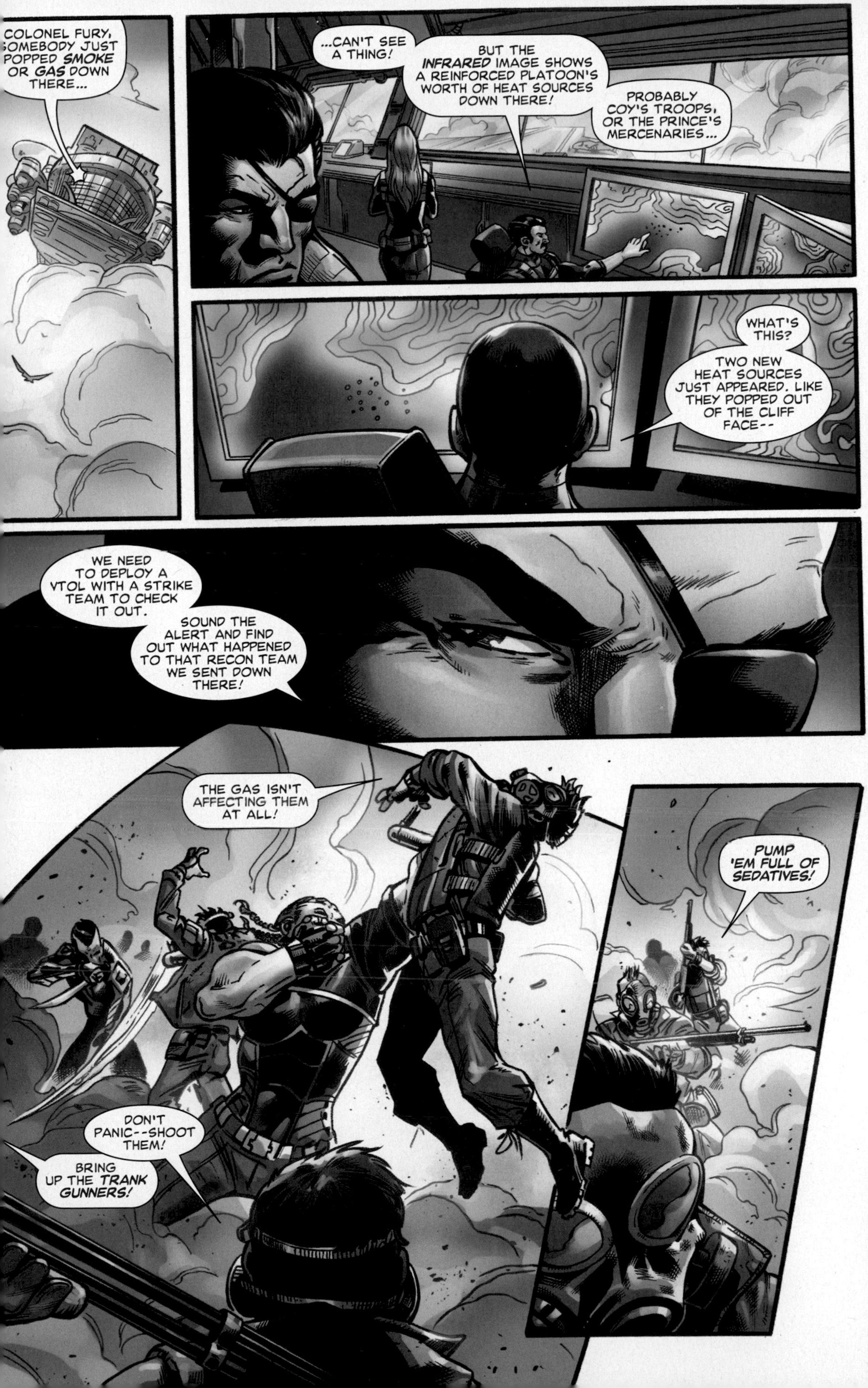
COLONEL FURY, SOMEBODY JUST POPPED **SMOKE** OR **GAS** DOWN THERE...
...CAN'T SEE A THING!
BUT THE ***INFRARED*** IMAGE SHOWS A REINFORCED PLATOON'S WORTH OF HEAT SOURCES DOWN THERE!
PROBABLY COY'S TROOPS, OR THE PRINCE'S MERCENARIES...
WHAT'S THIS?
TWO NEW HEAT SOURCES JUST APPEARED. LIKE THEY POPPED OUT OF THE CLIFF FACE--
WE NEED TO DEPLOY A VTOL WITH A STRIKE TEAM TO CHECK IT OUT.
SOUND THE ALERT AND FIND OUT WHAT HAPPENED TO THAT RECON TEAM WE SENT DOWN THERE!
THE GAS ISN'T AFFECTING THEM AT ALL!
DON'T PANIC--SHOOT THEM!
BRING UP THE ***TRANK GUNNERS!***
PUMP 'EM FULL OF SEDATIVES!

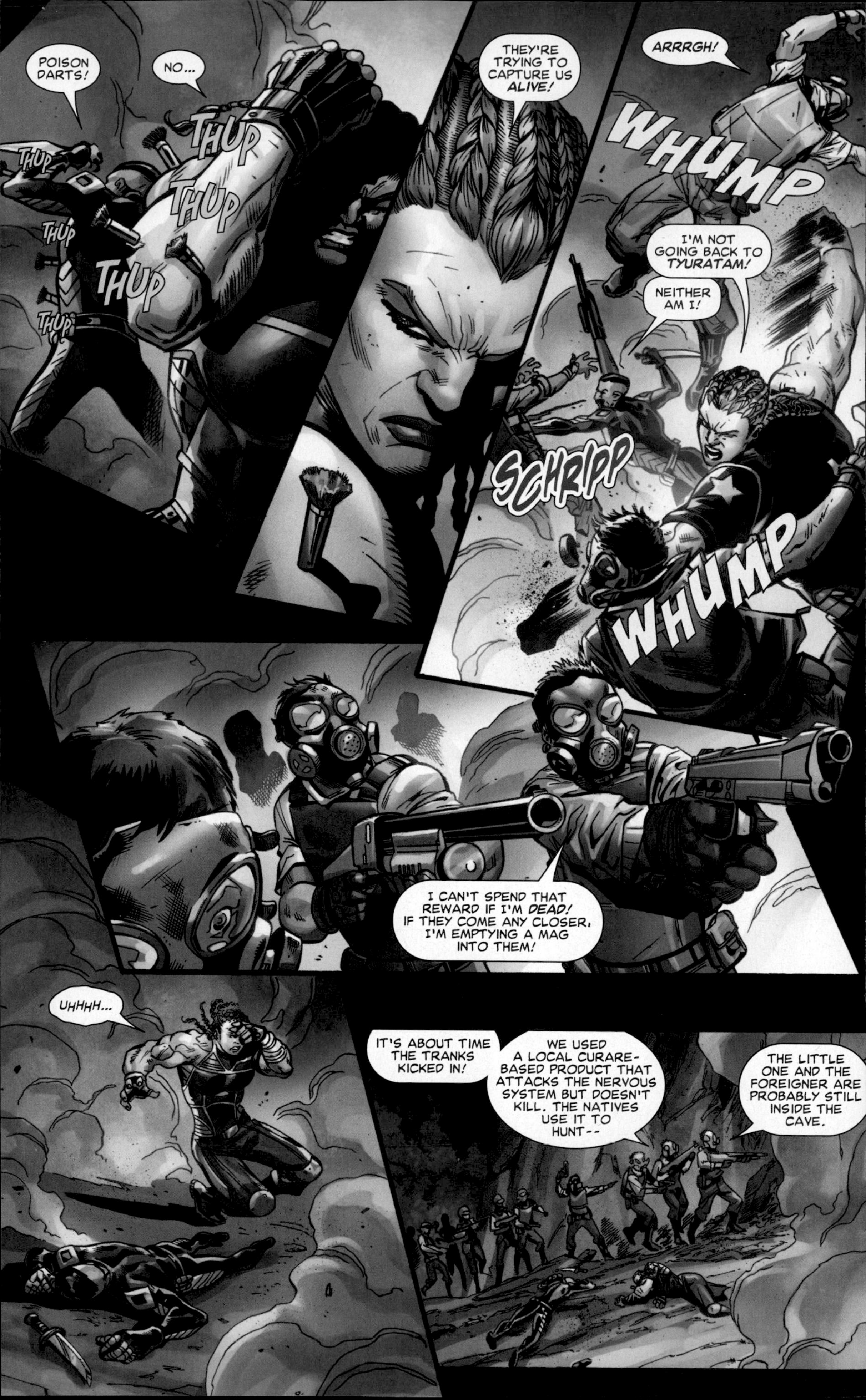
POISON DARTS!
NO...
THUP
THUP
THUP
THUP
THUP
THUP
THUP
THEY'RE TRYING TO CAPTURE US ALIVE!
ARRRGH!
WHUMP
I'M NOT GOING BACK TO TYURATAM!
NEITHER AM I!
SCHRIPP
WHUMP
I CAN'T SPEND THAT REWARD IF I'M DEAD! IF THEY COME ANY CLOSER, I'M EMPTYING A MAG INTO THEM!
UHHHH...
IT'S ABOUT TIME THE TRANKS KICKED IN!
WE USED A LOCAL CURARE-BASED PRODUCT THAT ATTACKS THE NERVOUS SYSTEM BUT DOESN'T KILL. THE NATIVES USE IT TO HUNT--
THE LITTLE ONE AND THE FOREIGNER ARE PROBABLY STILL INSIDE THE CAVE.

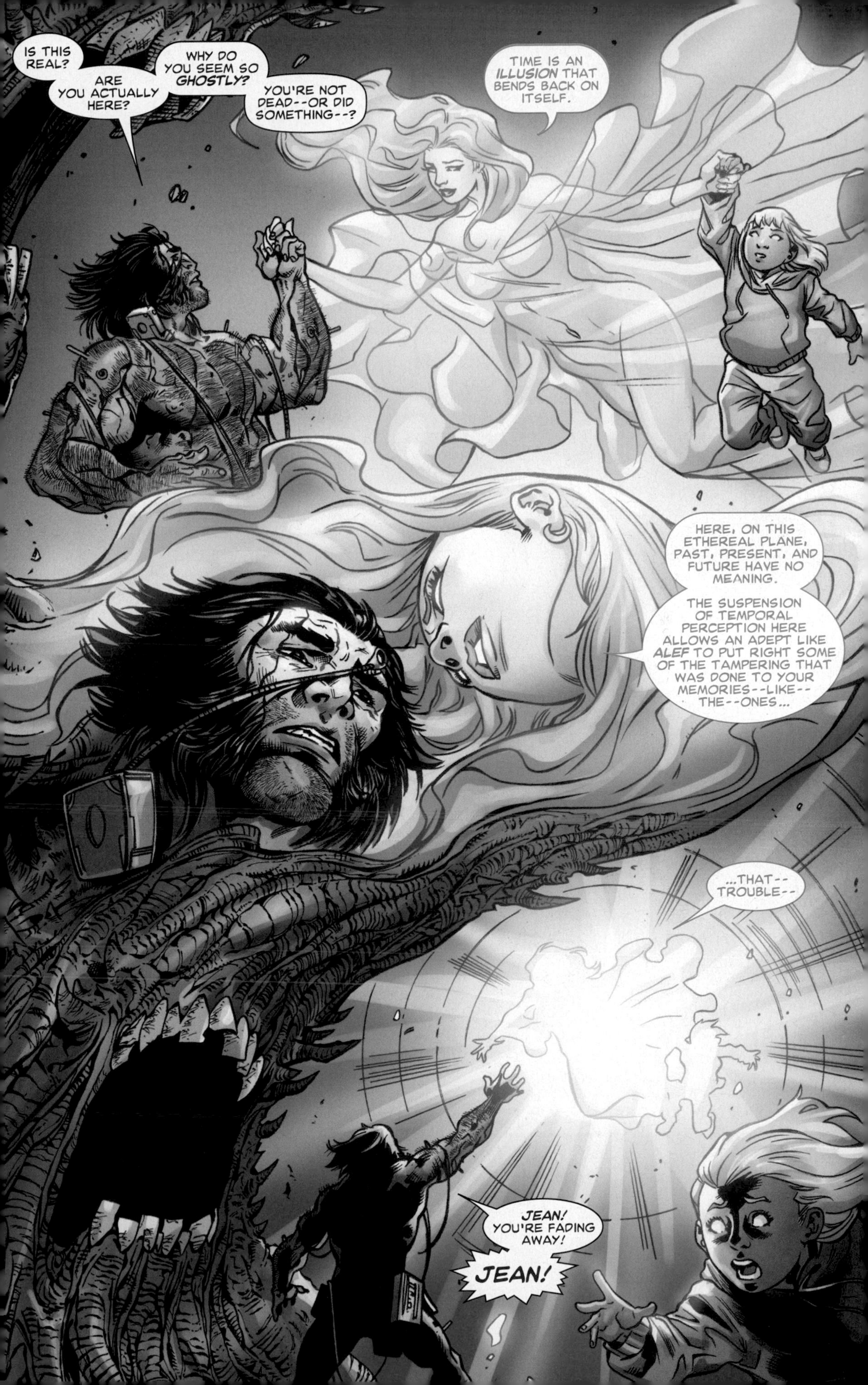
IS THIS REAL?
ARE YOU ACTUALLY HERE?
WHY DO YOU SEEM SO GHOSTLY?
YOU'RE NOT DEAD--OR DID SOMETHING--?
TIME IS AN ILLUSION THAT BENDS BACK ON ITSELF.
HERE, ON THIS ETHEREAL PLANE, PAST, PRESENT, AND FUTURE HAVE NO MEANING.
THE SUSPENSION OF TEMPORAL PERCEPTION HERE ALLOWS AN ADEPT LIKE ALEF TO PUT RIGHT SOME OF THE TAMPERING THAT WAS DONE TO YOUR MEMORIES--LIKE--THE--ONES...
...THAT--TROUBLE--
JEAN! YOU'RE FADING AWAY!
JEAN!

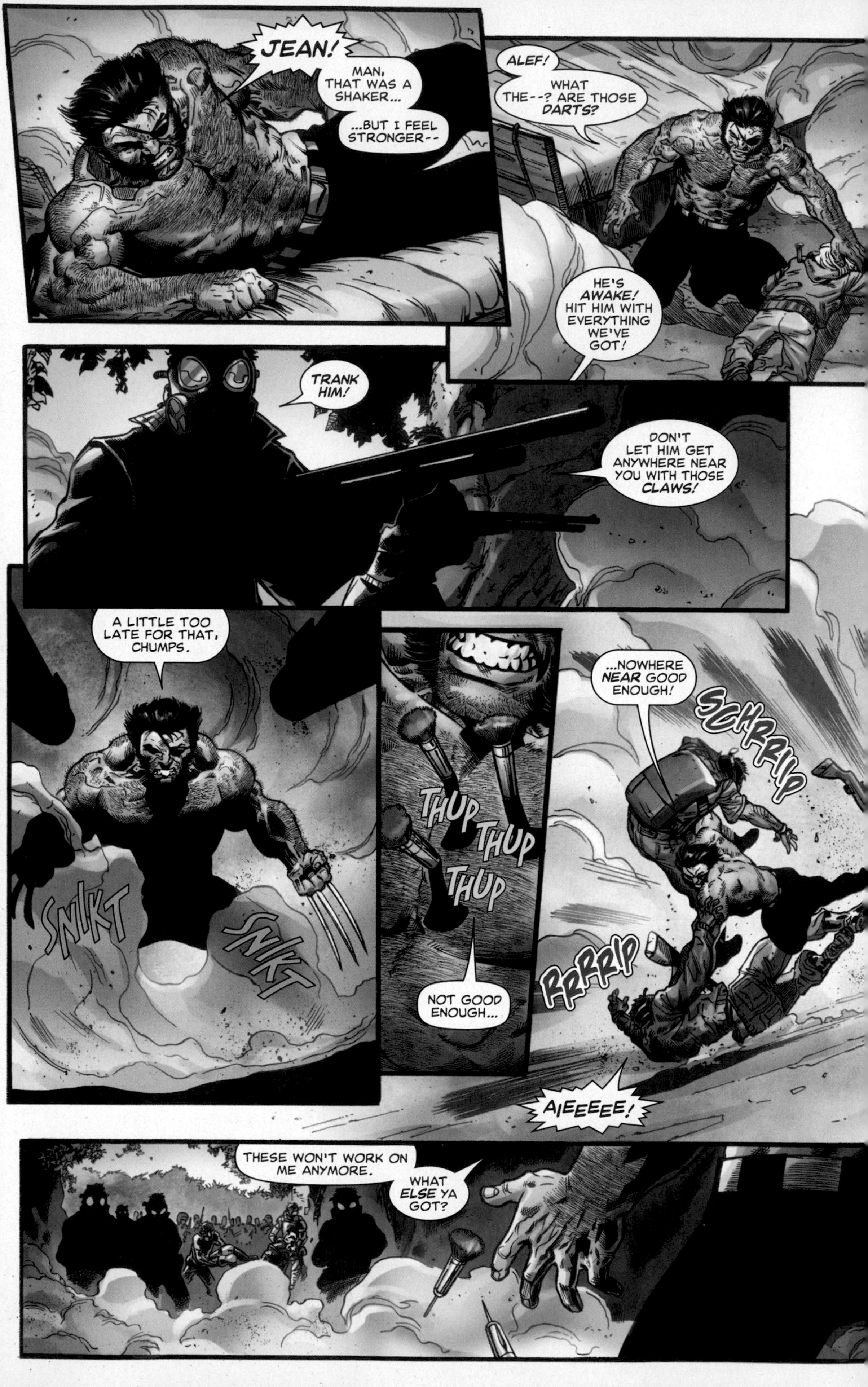
JEAN!
MAN, THAT WAS A SHAKER...
...BUT I FEEL STRONGER--
ALEF!
WHAT THE--? ARE THOSE DARTS?
HE'S AWAKE! HIT HIM WITH EVERYTHING WE'VE GOT!
TRANK HIM!
DON'T LET HIM GET ANYWHERE NEAR YOU WITH THOSE CLAWS!
A LITTLE TOO LATE FOR THAT, CHUMPS.
SNIKT
SNIKT
THUP
THUP
THUP
NOT GOOD ENOUGH...
...NOWHERE NEAR GOOD ENOUGH!
SCHRRIP
RRRRIP
AIEEEEE!
THESE WON'T WORK ON ME ANYMORE.
WHAT ELSE YA GOT?

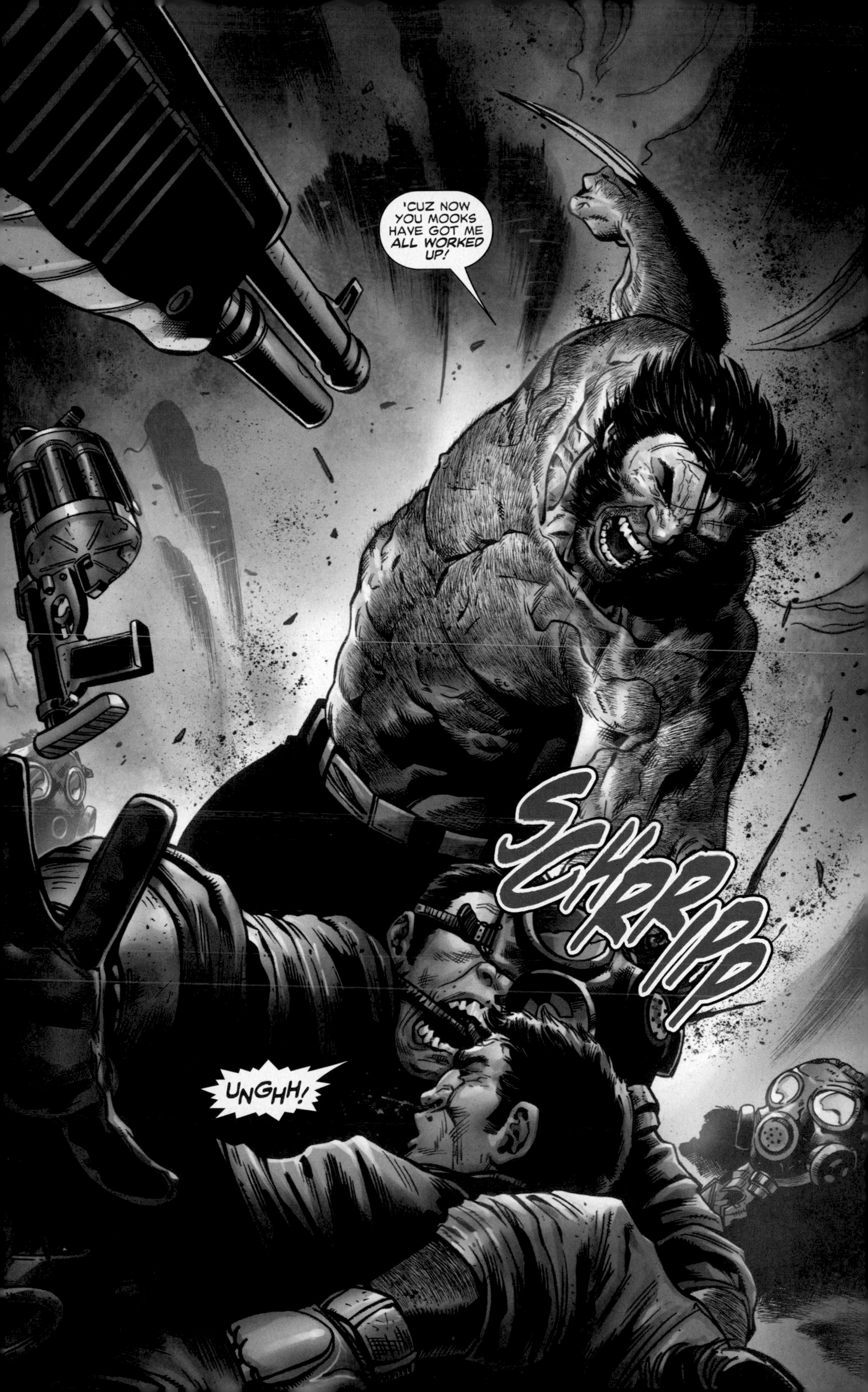
'CUZ NOW YOU MOOKS HAVE GOT ME ALL WORKED UP!
SCHRIPP
UNGHH!

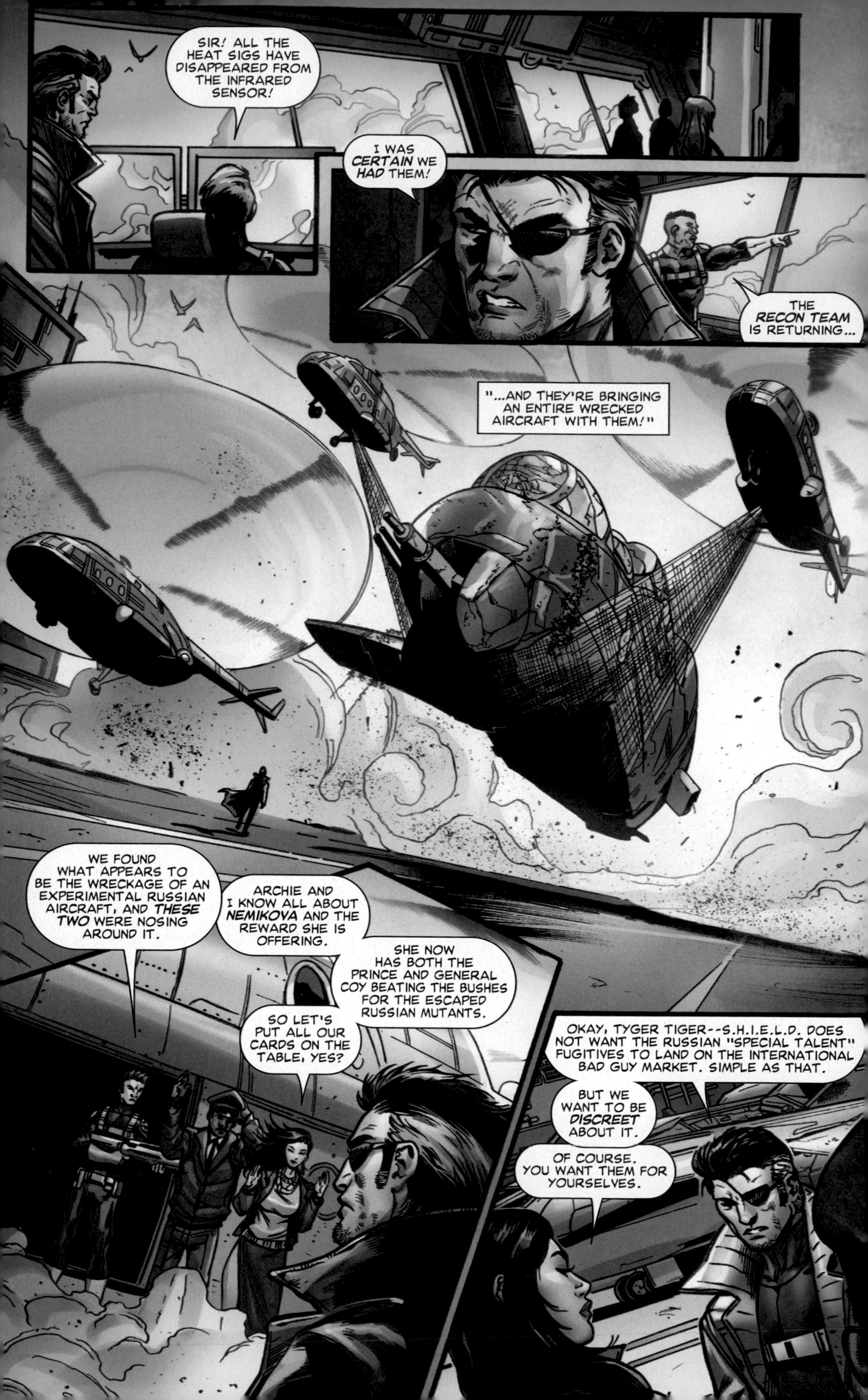
SIR! ALL THE HEAT SIGS HAVE DISAPPEARED FROM THE INFRARED SENSOR!
I WAS CERTAIN WE HAD THEM!
THE RECON TEAM IS RETURNING...
"...AND THEY'RE BRINGING AN ENTIRE WRECKED AIRCRAFT WITH THEM!"
WE FOUND WHAT APPEARS TO BE THE WRECKAGE OF AN EXPERIMENTAL RUSSIAN AIRCRAFT, AND THESE TWO WERE NOSING AROUND IT.
ARCHIE AND I KNOW ALL ABOUT NEMIKOVA AND THE REWARD SHE IS OFFERING.
SHE NOW HAS BOTH THE PRINCE AND GENERAL COY BEATING THE BUSHES FOR THE ESCAPED RUSSIAN MUTANTS.
SO LET'S PUT ALL OUR CARDS ON THE TABLE, YES?
OKAY, TYGER TIGER--S.H.I.E.L.D. DOES NOT WANT THE RUSSIAN "SPECIAL TALENT" FUGITIVES TO LAND ON THE INTERNATIONAL BAD GUY MARKET. SIMPLE AS THAT.
BUT WE WANT TO BE DISCREET ABOUT IT.
OF COURSE. YOU WANT THEM FOR YOURSELVES.

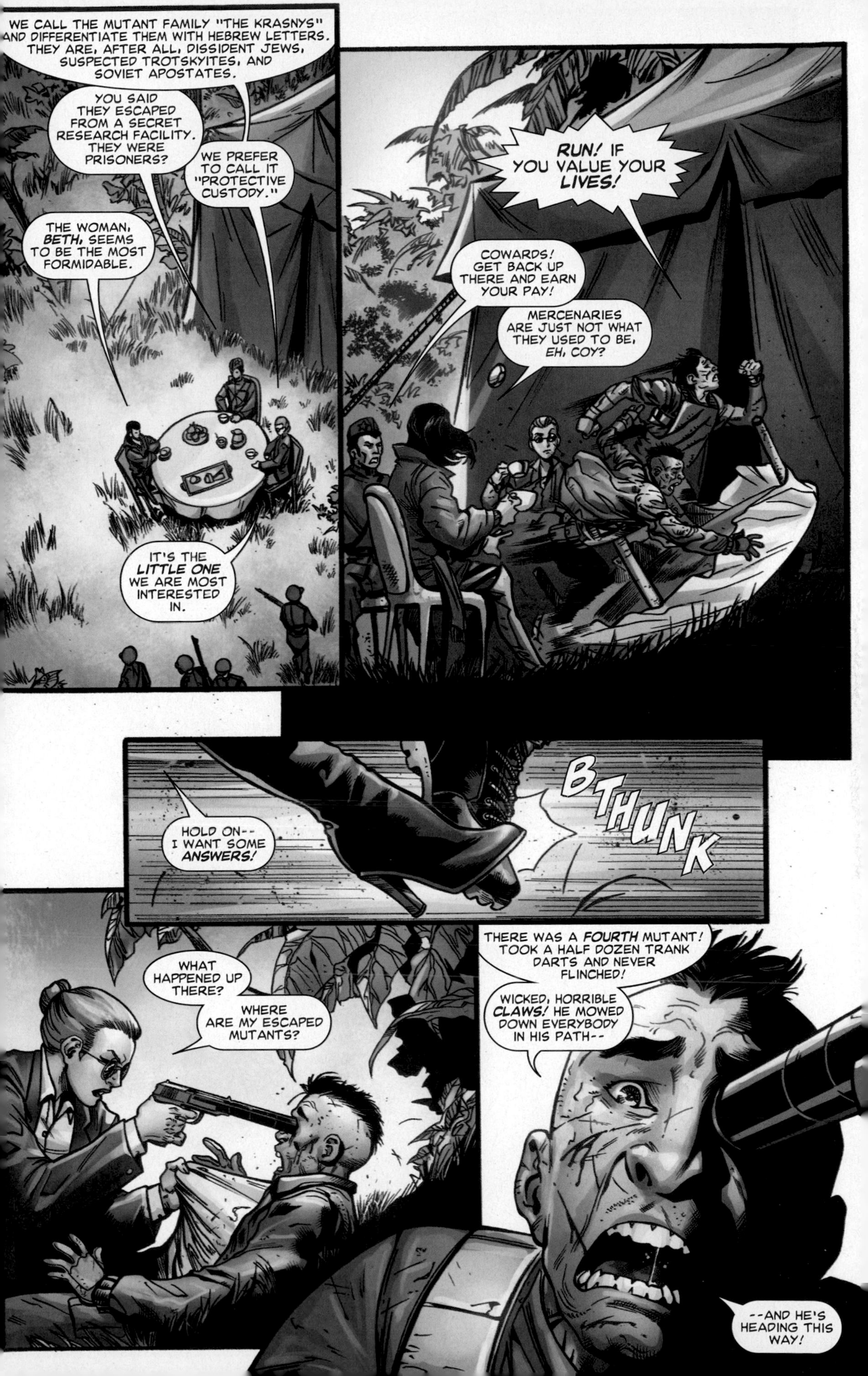
WE CALL THE MUTANT FAMILY "THE KRASNYS" AND DIFFERENTIATE THEM WITH HEBREW LETTERS. THEY ARE, AFTER ALL, DISSIDENT JEWS, SUSPECTED TROTSKYITES, AND SOVIET APOSTATES.
YOU SAID THEY ESCAPED FROM A SECRET RESEARCH FACILITY. THEY WERE PRISONERS?
WE PREFER TO CALL IT "PROTECTIVE CUSTODY."
THE WOMAN, BETH, SEEMS TO BE THE MOST FORMIDABLE.
IT'S THE LITTLE ONE WE ARE MOST INTERESTED IN.
RUN! IF YOU VALUE YOUR LIVES!
COWARDS! GET BACK UP THERE AND EARN YOUR PAY!
MERCENARIES ARE JUST NOT WHAT THEY USED TO BE, EH, COY?
HOLD ON-- I WANT SOME ANSWERS!
BTHUNK
WHAT HAPPENED UP THERE?
WHERE ARE MY ESCAPED MUTANTS?
THERE WAS A FOURTH MUTANT! TOOK A HALF DOZEN TRANK DARTS AND NEVER FLINCHED!
WICKED, HORRIBLE CLAWS! HE MOWED DOWN EVERYBODY IN HIS PATH--
--AND HE'S HEADING THIS WAY!

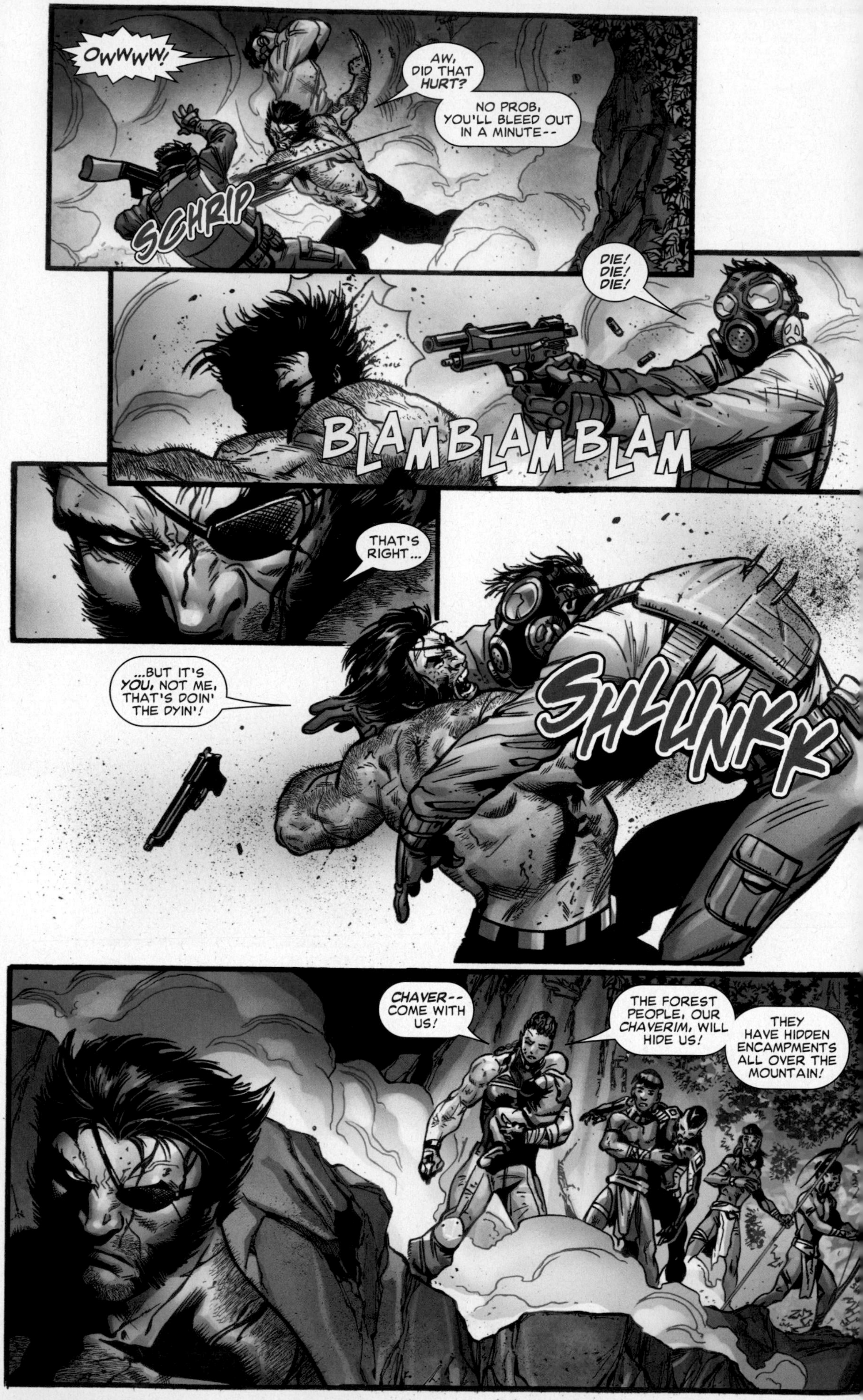
OWWWW!
AW, DID THAT HURT?
NO PROB, YOU'LL BLEED OUT IN A MINUTE--
SCHRIP
DIE! DIE! DIE!
BLAMBLAMBLAM
THAT'S RIGHT...
...BUT IT'S YOU, NOT ME, THAT'S DOIN' THE DYIN'!
SHLUNKK
CHAVER-- COME WITH US!
THE FOREST PEOPLE, OUR CHAVERIM, WILL HIDE US!
THEY HAVE HIDDEN ENCAMPMENTS ALL OVER THE MOUNTAIN!

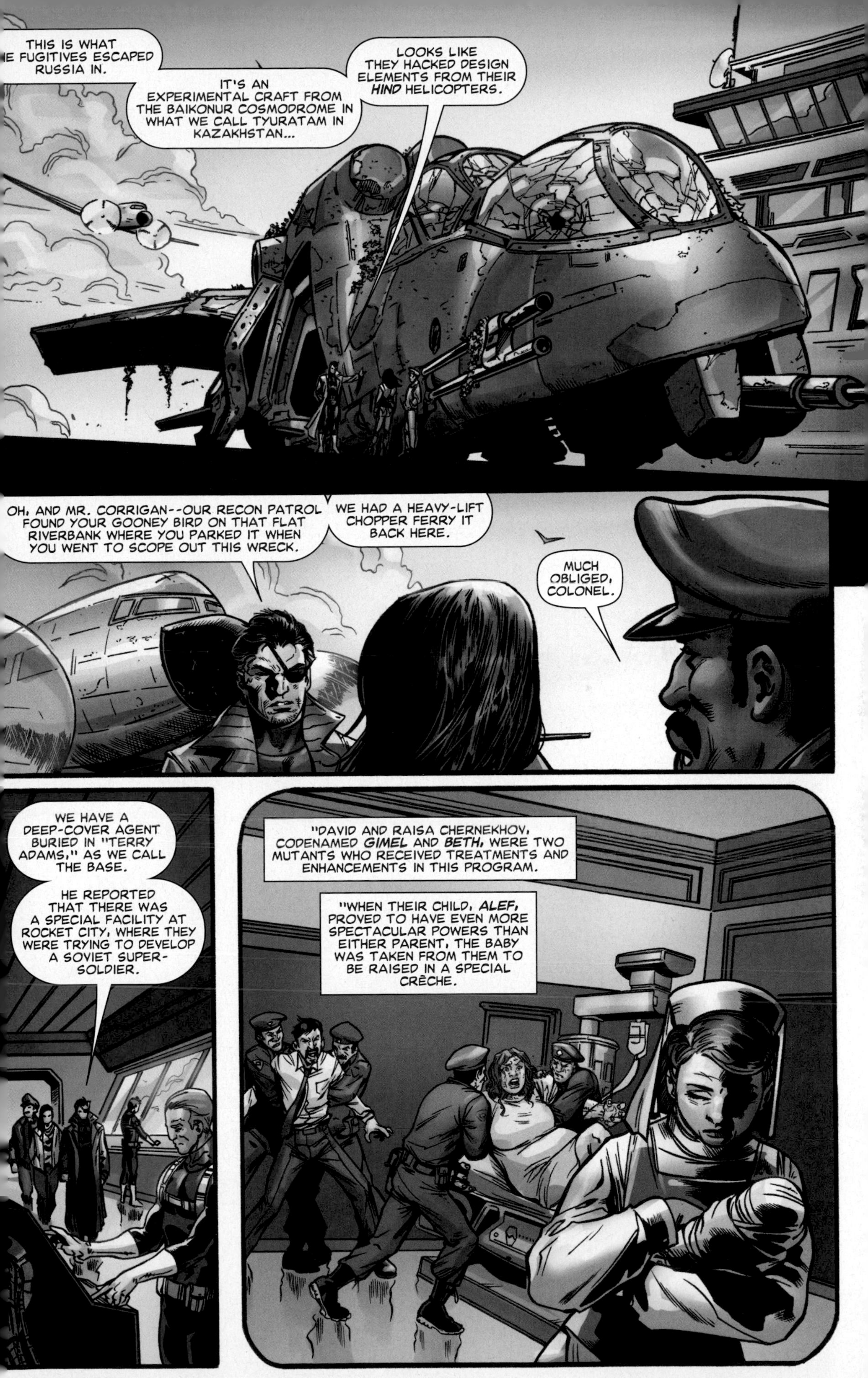
THIS IS WHAT E FUGITIVES ESCAPED RUSSIA IN.
IT'S AN EXPERIMENTAL CRAFT FROM THE BAIKONUR COSMODROME IN WHAT WE CALL TYURATAM IN KAZAKHSTAN...
LOOKS LIKE THEY HACKED DESIGN ELEMENTS FROM THEIR *HIND* HELICOPTERS.
OH, AND MR. CORRIGAN--OUR RECON PATROL FOUND YOUR GOONEY BIRD ON THAT FLAT RIVERBANK WHERE YOU PARKED IT WHEN YOU WENT TO SCOPE OUT THIS WRECK.
WE HAD A HEAVY-LIFT CHOPPER FERRY IT BACK HERE.
MUCH OBLIGED, COLONEL.
WE HAVE A DEEP-COVER AGENT BURIED IN "TERRY ADAMS," AS WE CALL THE BASE.
HE REPORTED THAT THERE WAS A SPECIAL FACILITY AT ROCKET CITY, WHERE THEY WERE TRYING TO DEVELOP A SOVIET SUPER-SOLDIER.
"DAVID AND RAISA CHERNEKHOV, CODENAMED *GIMEL* AND *BETH*, WERE TWO MUTANTS WHO RECEIVED TREATMENTS AND ENHANCEMENTS IN THIS PROGRAM.
"WHEN THEIR CHILD, *ALEF*, PROVED TO HAVE EVEN MORE SPECTACULAR POWERS THAN EITHER PARENT, THE BABY WAS TAKEN FROM THEM TO BE RAISED IN A SPECIAL CRÈCHE.

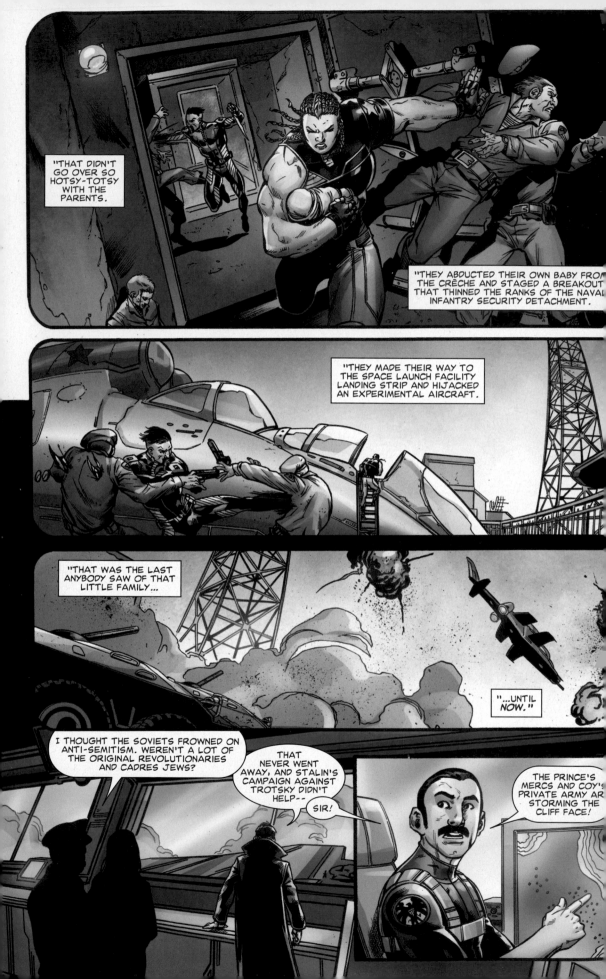

"THAT DIDN'T GO OVER SO HOTSY-TOTSY WITH THE PARENTS.

"THEY ABDUCTED THEIR OWN BABY FROM THE CRÈCHE AND STAGED A BREAKOUT THAT THINNED THE RANKS OF THE NAVAL INFANTRY SECURITY DETACHMENT.

"THEY MADE THEIR WAY TO THE SPACE LAUNCH FACILITY LANDING STRIP AND HIJACKED AN EXPERIMENTAL AIRCRAFT.

"THAT WAS THE LAST ANYBODY SAW OF THAT LITTLE FAMILY...

"...UNTIL NOW."

I THOUGHT THE SOVIETS FROWNED ON ANTI-SEMITISM. WEREN'T A LOT OF THE ORIGINAL REVOLUTIONARIES AND CADRES JEWS?

THAT NEVER WENT AWAY, AND STALIN'S CAMPAIGN AGAINST TROTSKY DIDN'T HELP--

SIR!

THE PRINCE'S MERCS AND COY'S PRIVATE ARMY ARE STORMING THE CLIFF FACE!

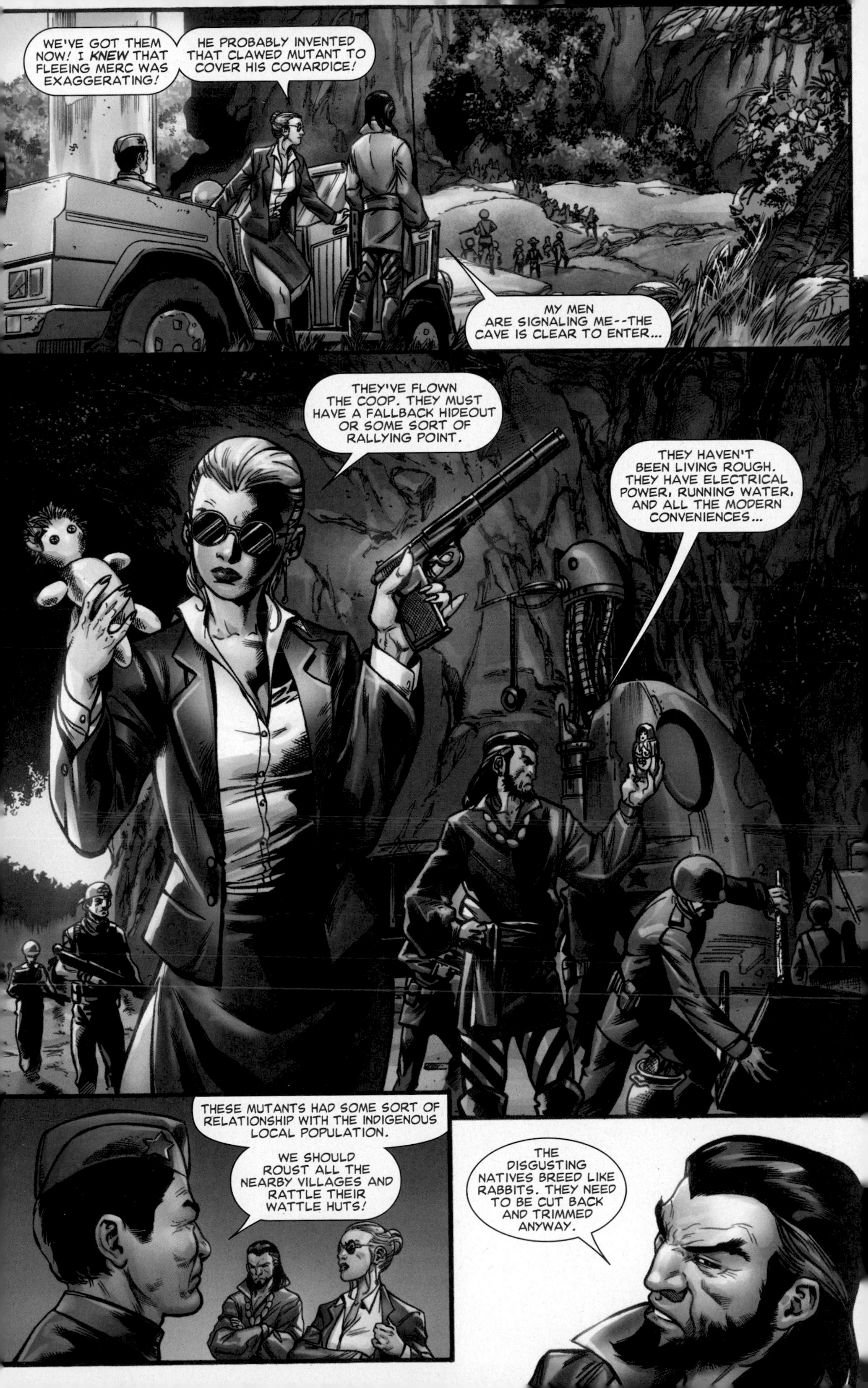
WE'VE GOT THEM NOW! I KNEW THAT FLEEING MERC WAS EXAGGERATING!
HE PROBABLY INVENTED THAT CLAWED MUTANT TO COVER HIS COWARDICE!
MY MEN ARE SIGNALING ME--THE CAVE IS CLEAR TO ENTER...
THEY'VE FLOWN THE COOP. THEY MUST HAVE A FALLBACK HIDEOUT OR SOME SORT OF RALLYING POINT.
THEY HAVEN'T BEEN LIVING ROUGH. THEY HAVE ELECTRICAL POWER, RUNNING WATER, AND ALL THE MODERN CONVENIENCES...
THESE MUTANTS HAD SOME SORT OF RELATIONSHIP WITH THE INDIGENOUS LOCAL POPULATION.
WE SHOULD ROUST ALL THE NEARBY VILLAGES AND RATTLE THEIR WATTLE HUTS!
THE DISGUSTING NATIVES BREED LIKE RABBITS. THEY NEED TO BE CUT BACK AND TRIMMED ANYWAY.

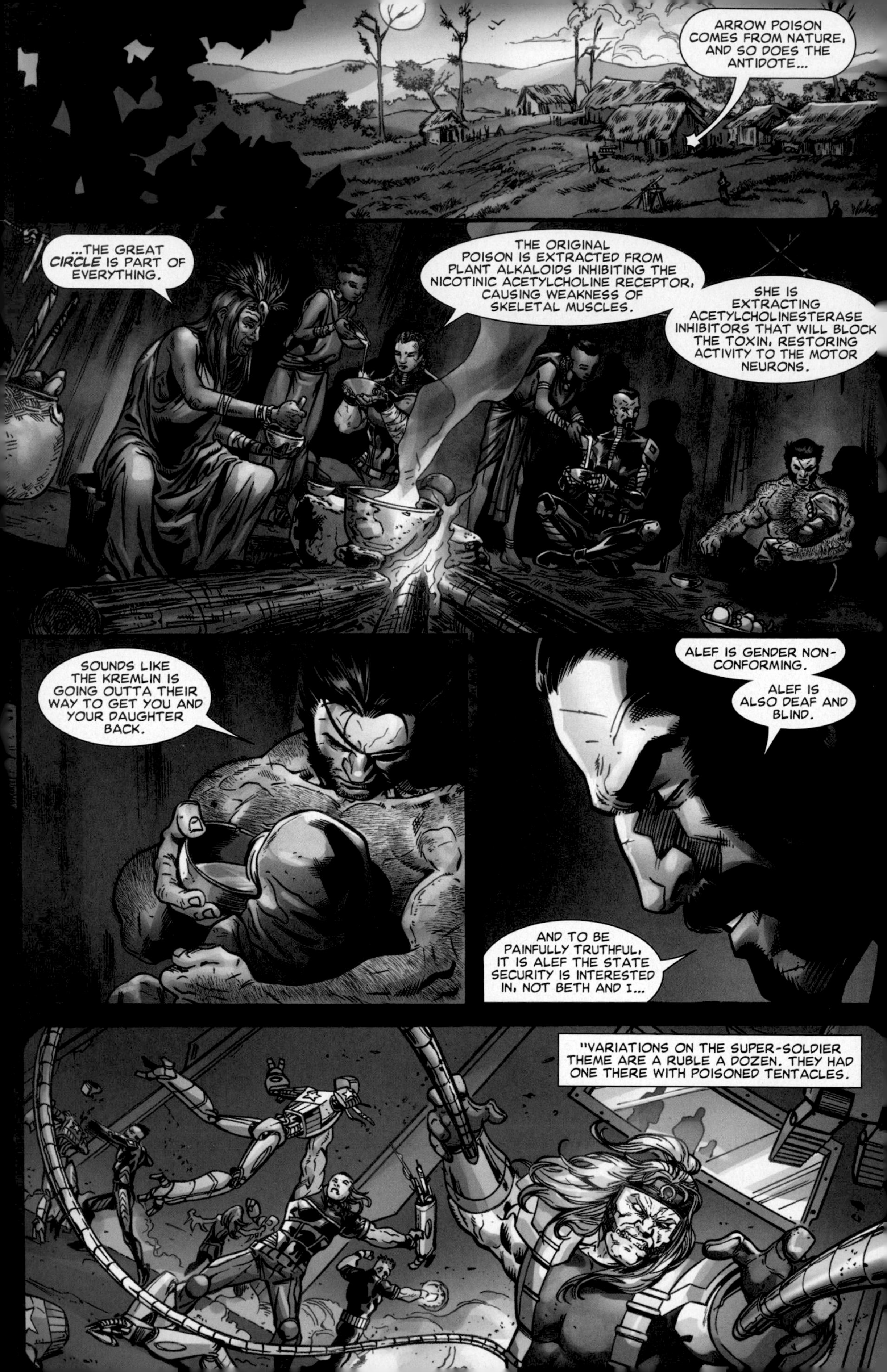
ARROW POISON COMES FROM NATURE, AND SO DOES THE ANTIDOTE...
...THE GREAT CIRCLE IS PART OF EVERYTHING.
THE ORIGINAL POISON IS EXTRACTED FROM PLANT ALKALOIDS INHIBITING THE NICOTINIC ACETYLCHOLINE RECEPTOR, CAUSING WEAKNESS OF SKELETAL MUSCLES.
SHE IS EXTRACTING ACETYLCHOLINESTERASE INHIBITORS THAT WILL BLOCK THE TOXIN, RESTORING ACTIVITY TO THE MOTOR NEURONS.
SOUNDS LIKE THE KREMLIN IS GOING OUTTA THEIR WAY TO GET YOU AND YOUR DAUGHTER BACK.
ALEF IS GENDER NON-CONFORMING.
ALEF IS ALSO DEAF AND BLIND.
AND TO BE PAINFULLY TRUTHFUL, IT IS ALEF THE STATE SECURITY IS INTERESTED IN, NOT BETH AND I...
"VARIATIONS ON THE SUPER-SOLDIER THEME ARE A RUBLE A DOZEN. THEY HAD ONE THERE WITH POISONED TENTACLES.

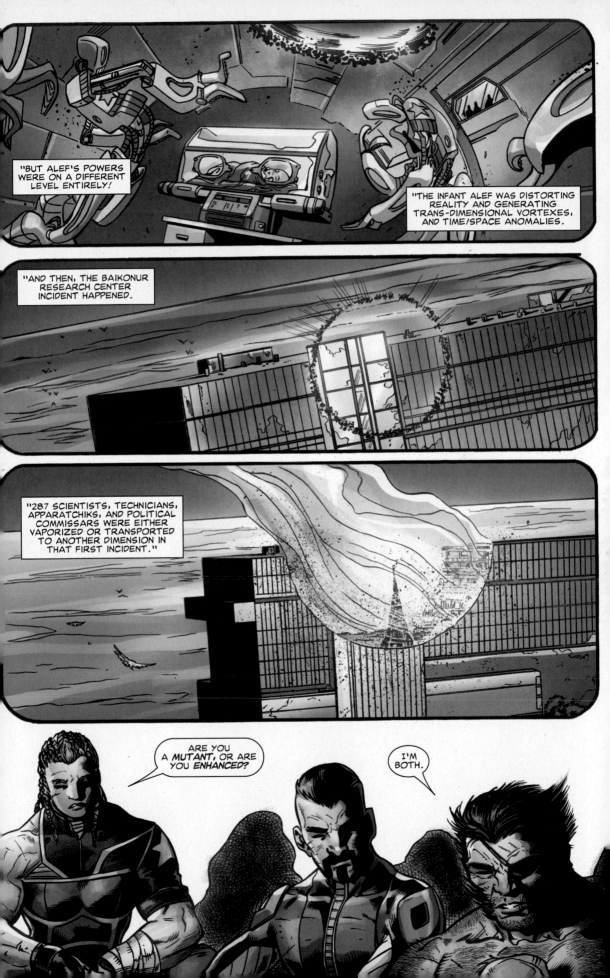

"BUT ALEF'S POWERS WERE ON A DIFFERENT LEVEL ENTIRELY!

"THE INFANT ALEF WAS DISTORTING REALITY AND GENERATING TRANS-DIMENSIONAL VORTEXES, AND TIME/SPACE ANOMALIES.

"AND THEN, THE BAIKONUR RESEARCH CENTER INCIDENT HAPPENED.

"287 SCIENTISTS, TECHNICIANS, APPARATCHIKS, AND POLITICAL COMMISSARS WERE EITHER VAPORIZED OR TRANSPORTED TO ANOTHER DIMENSION IN THAT FIRST INCIDENT."

ARE YOU A *MUTANT*, OR ARE YOU *ENHANCED*?

I'M *BOTH*.

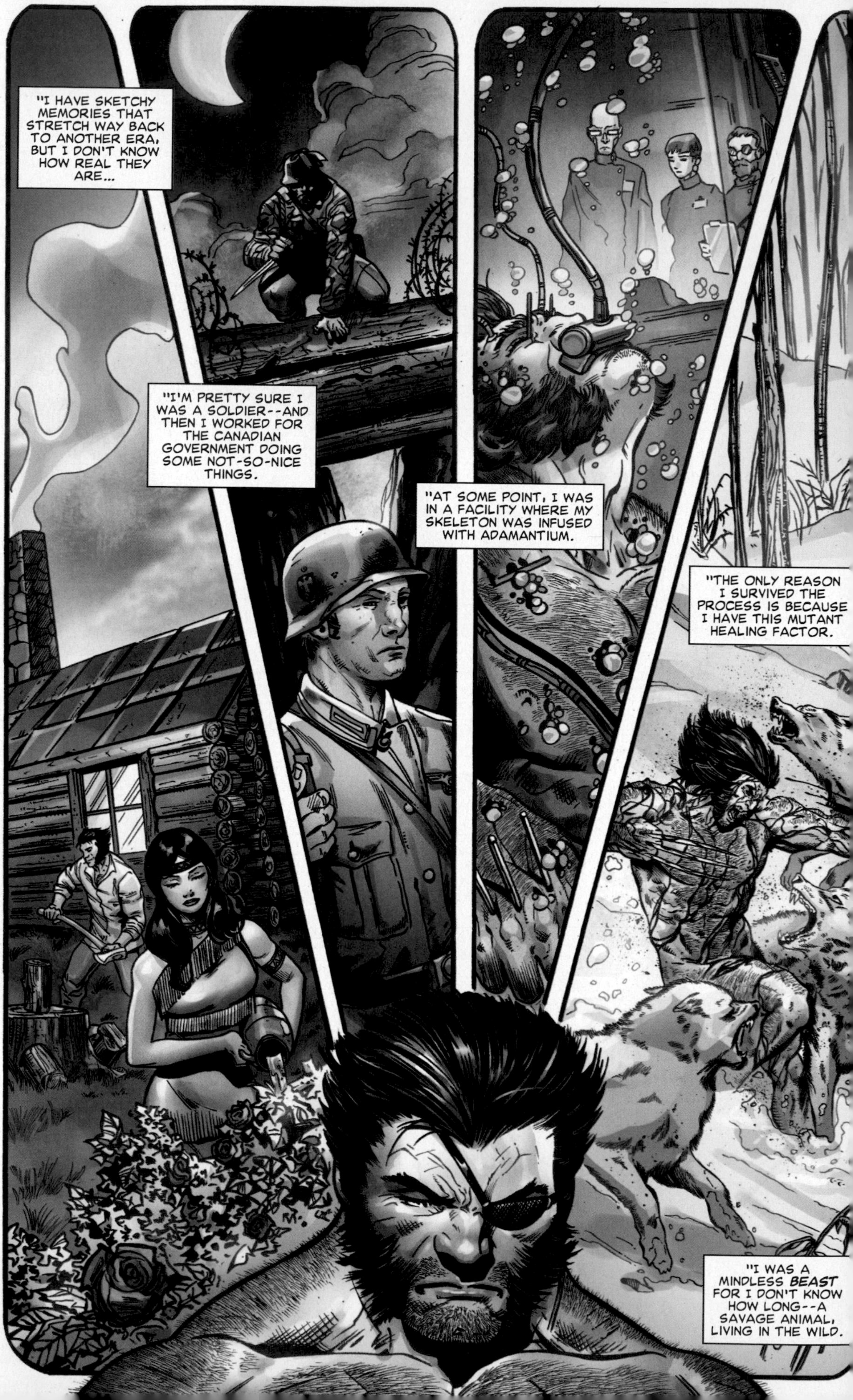
"I HAVE SKETCHY MEMORIES THAT STRETCH WAY BACK TO ANOTHER ERA, BUT I DON'T KNOW HOW REAL THEY ARE...
"I'M PRETTY SURE I WAS A SOLDIER--AND THEN I WORKED FOR THE CANADIAN GOVERNMENT DOING SOME NOT-SO-NICE THINGS.
"AT SOME POINT, I WAS IN A FACILITY WHERE MY SKELETON WAS INFUSED WITH ADAMANTIUM.
"THE ONLY REASON I SURVIVED THE PROCESS IS BECAUSE I HAVE THIS MUTANT HEALING FACTOR.
"I WAS A MINDLESS BEAST FOR I DON'T KNOW HOW LONG--A SAVAGE ANIMAL, LIVING IN THE WILD.

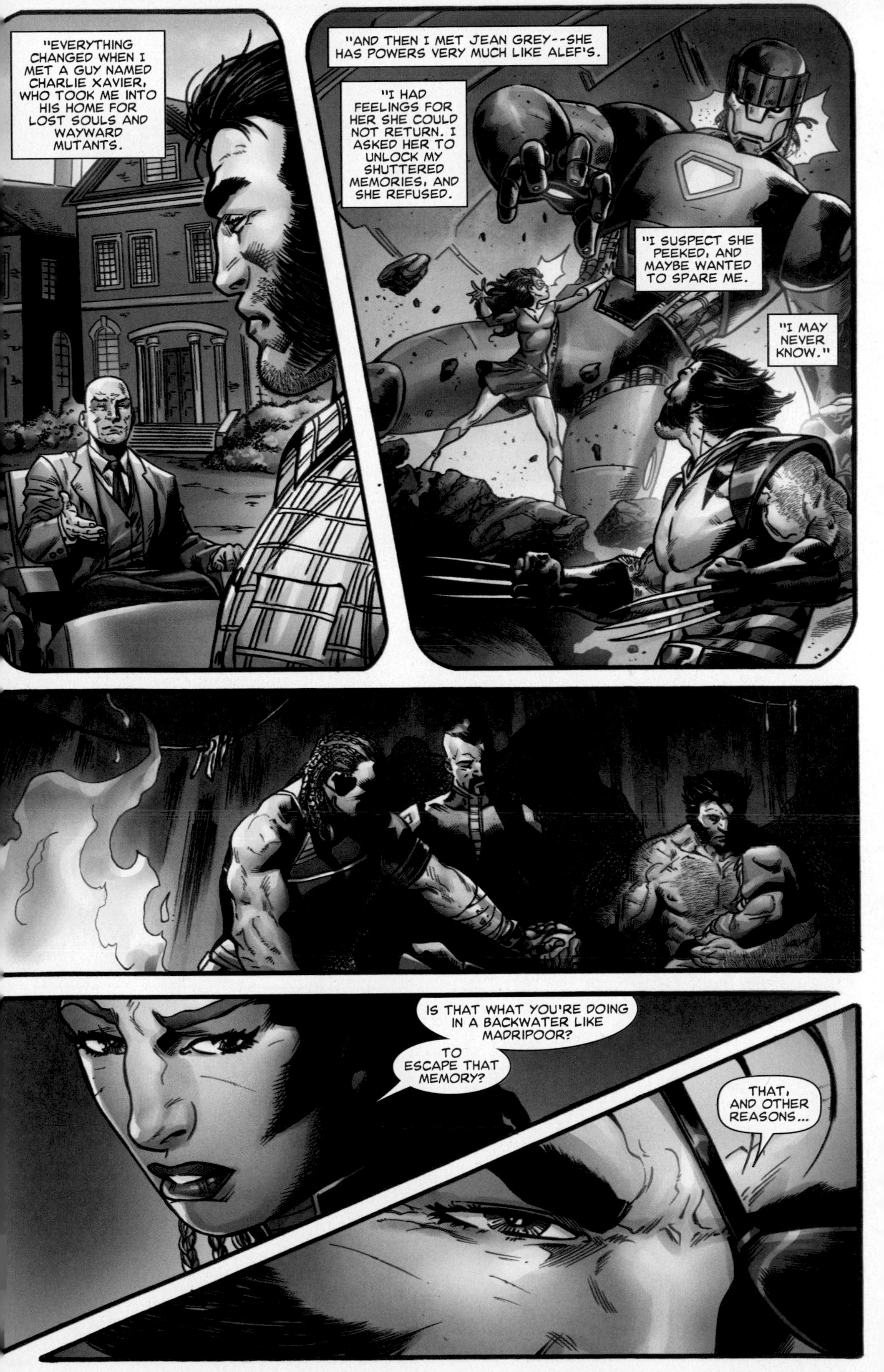
"EVERYTHING CHANGED WHEN I MET A GUY NAMED CHARLIE XAVIER, WHO TOOK ME INTO HIS HOME FOR LOST SOULS AND WAYWARD MUTANTS.
"AND THEN I MET JEAN GREY--SHE HAS POWERS VERY MUCH LIKE ALEF'S.
"I HAD FEELINGS FOR HER SHE COULD NOT RETURN. I ASKED HER TO UNLOCK MY SHUTTERED MEMORIES, AND SHE REFUSED.
"I SUSPECT SHE PEEKED, AND MAYBE WANTED TO SPARE ME.
"I MAY NEVER KNOW."
IS THAT WHAT YOU'RE DOING IN A BACKWATER LIKE MADRIPOOR?
TO ESCAPE THAT MEMORY?
THAT, AND OTHER REASONS...

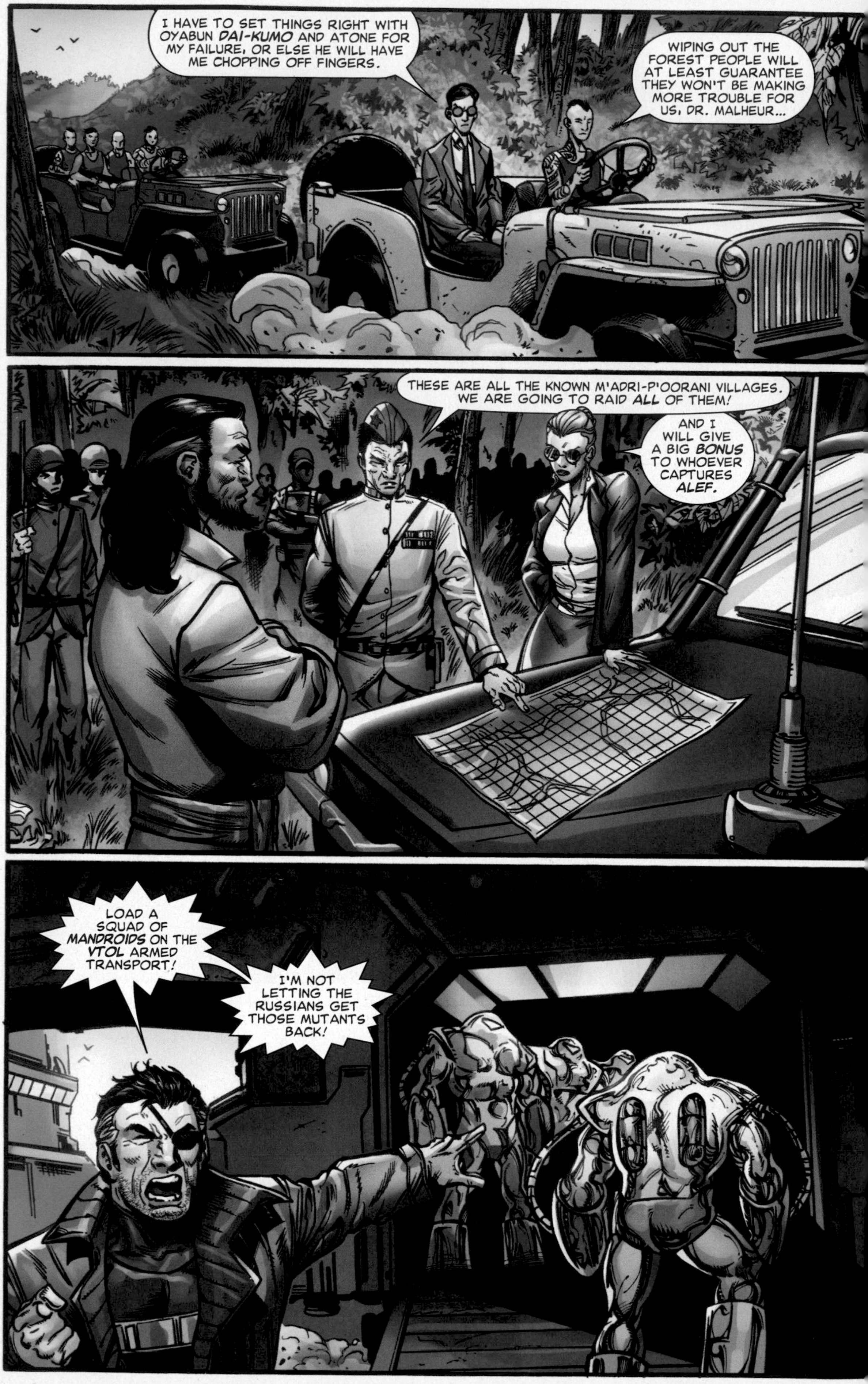
I HAVE TO SET THINGS RIGHT WITH OYABUN DAI-KUMO AND ATONE FOR MY FAILURE, OR ELSE HE WILL HAVE ME CHOPPING OFF FINGERS.
WIPING OUT THE FOREST PEOPLE WILL AT LEAST GUARANTEE THEY WON'T BE MAKING MORE TROUBLE FOR US, DR. MALHEUR...
THESE ARE ALL THE KNOWN M'ADRI-P'OORANI VILLAGES. WE ARE GOING TO RAID ALL OF THEM!
AND I WILL GIVE A BIG BONUS TO WHOEVER CAPTURES ALEF.
LOAD A SQUAD OF MANDROIDS ON THE VTOL ARMED TRANSPORT!
I'M NOT LETTING THE RUSSIANS GET THOSE MUTANTS BACK!

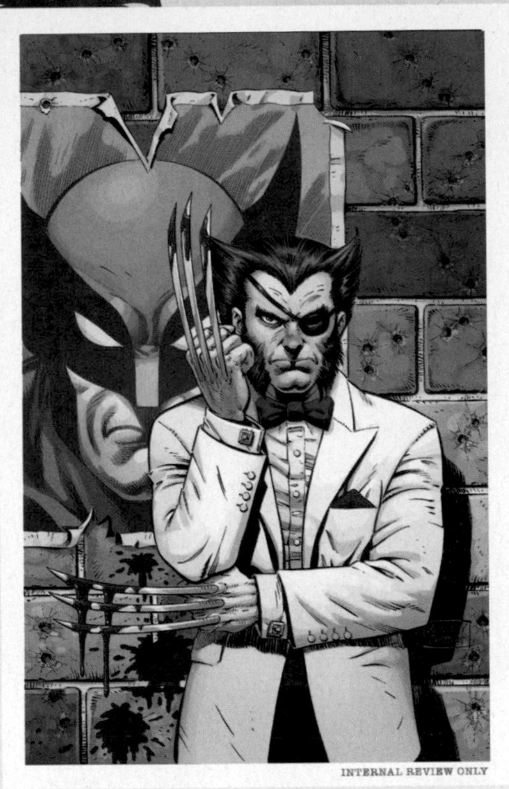

#1 VARIANT BY DAN JURGENS, BRETT BREEDING & JAVA TARTAGLIA

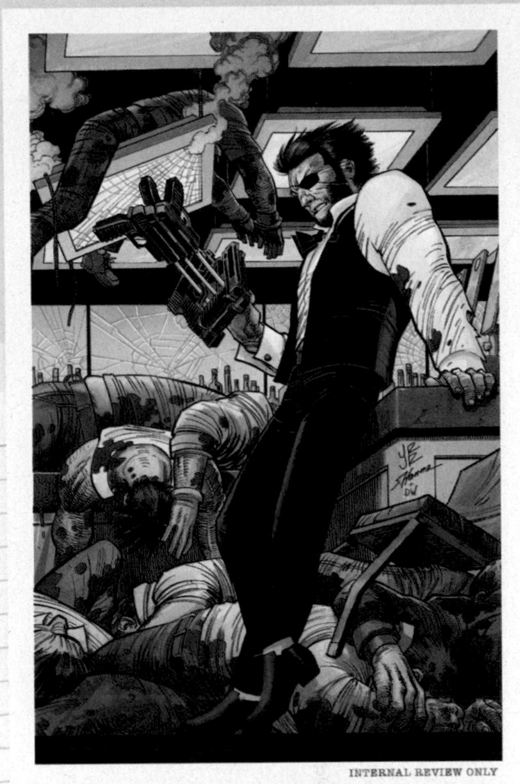

#1 VARIANT BY JOHN ROMITA JR., SCOTT HANNA & DEAN WHITE

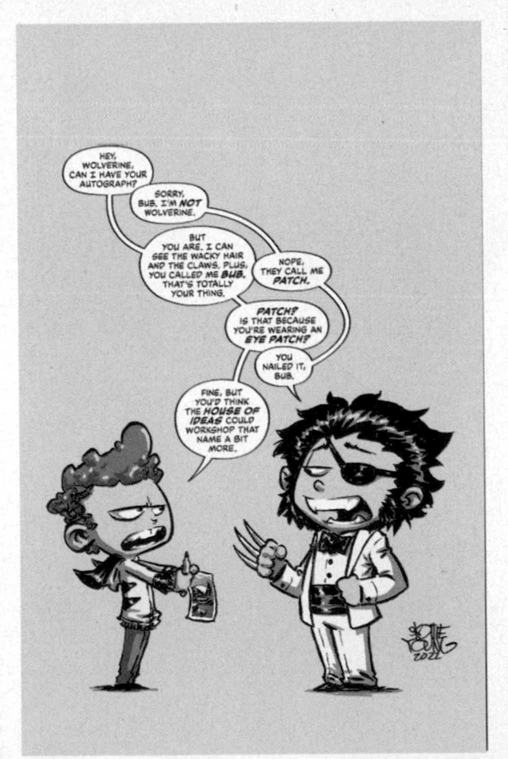
HEY, WOLVERINE, CAN I HAVE YOUR AUTOGRAPH?
SORRY, BUB, I'M NOT WOLVERINE.
BUT YOU ARE. I CAN SEE THE WACKY HAIR AND THE CLAWS. PLUS, YOU CALLED ME BUB. THAT'S TOTALLY YOUR THING.
NOPE, THEY CALL ME PATCH.
PATCH? IS THAT BECAUSE YOU'RE WEARING AN EYE PATCH?
YOU NAILED IT, BUB.
FINE, BUT YOU'D THINK THE HOUSE OF IDEAS COULD WORKSHOP THAT NAME A BIT MORE.
INTERNAL REVIEW ONLY

#1 VARIANT BY SKOTTIE YOUNG

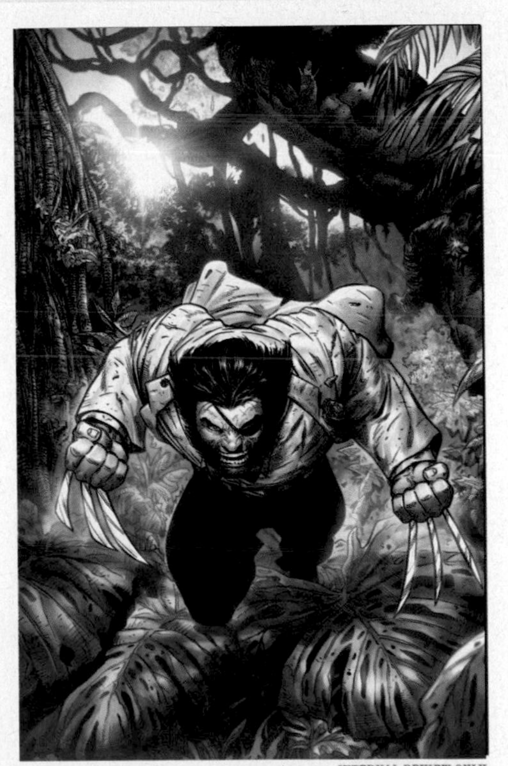

#1 VARIANT BY ANDREA DI VITO, LE BEAU UNDERWOOD & SEBASTIAN CHENG

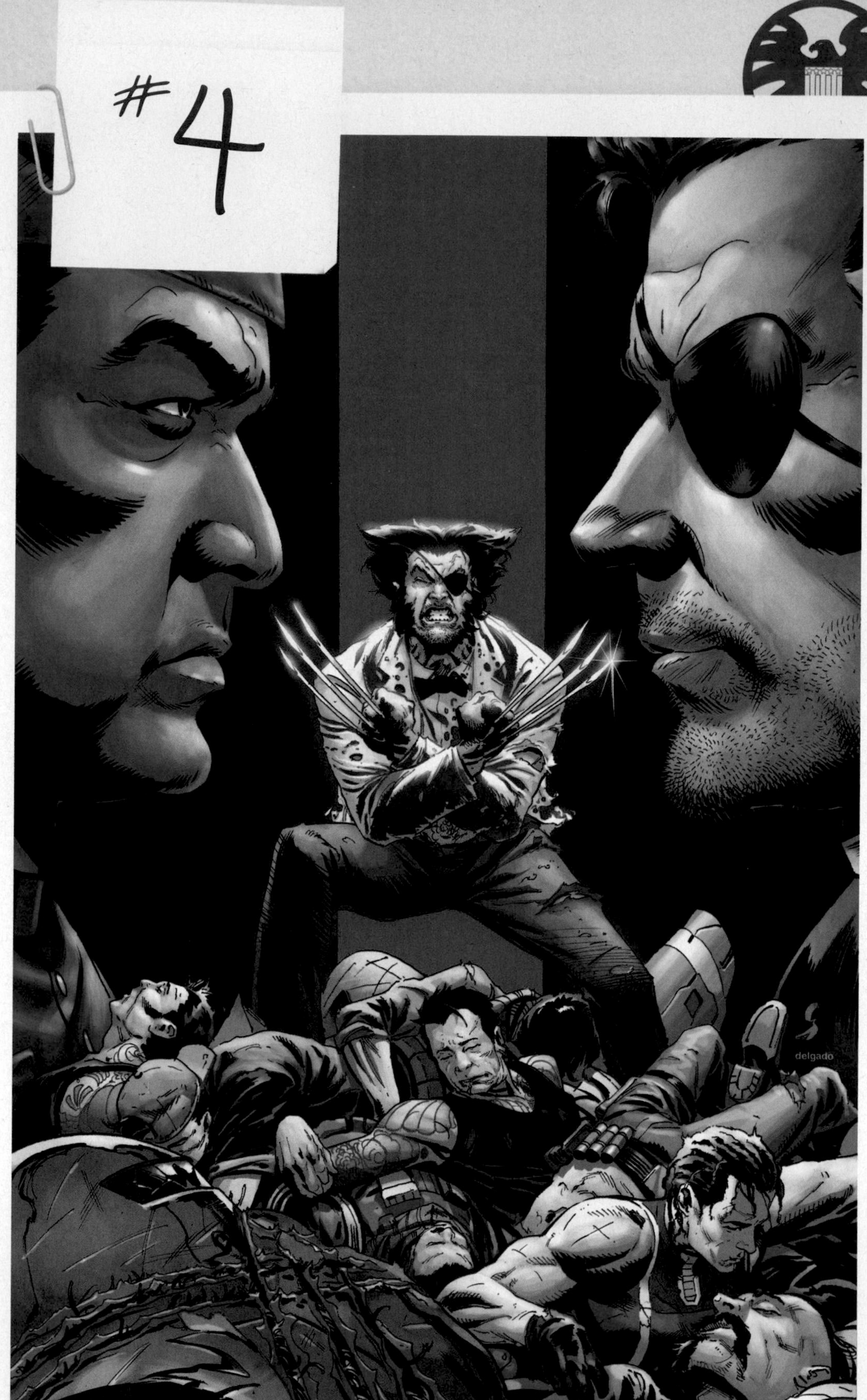
#4
delgado

INTERNAL REVIEW ONLY

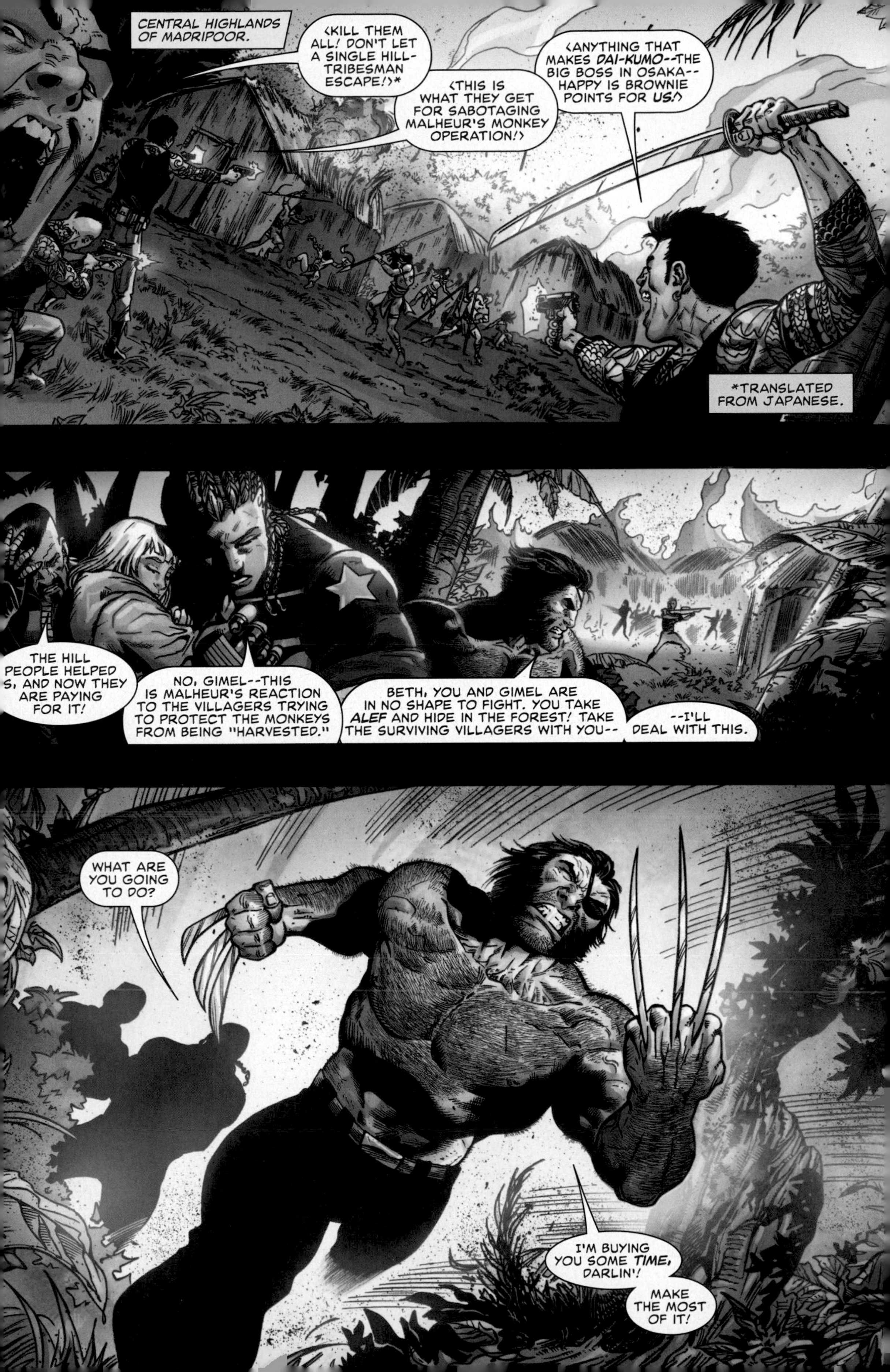
CENTRAL HIGHLANDS OF MADRIPOOR.
<KILL THEM ALL! DON'T LET A SINGLE HILL-TRIBESMAN ESCAPE!>*
<THIS IS WHAT THEY GET FOR SABOTAGING MALHEUR'S MONKEY OPERATION!>
<ANYTHING THAT MAKES DAI-KUMO--THE BIG BOSS IN OSAKA--HAPPY IS BROWNIE POINTS FOR US!>
*TRANSLATED FROM JAPANESE.
THE HILL PEOPLE HELPED S, AND NOW THEY ARE PAYING FOR IT!
NO, GIMEL--THIS IS MALHEUR'S REACTION TO THE VILLAGERS TRYING TO PROTECT THE MONKEYS FROM BEING "HARVESTED."
BETH, YOU AND GIMEL ARE IN NO SHAPE TO FIGHT. YOU TAKE ALEF AND HIDE IN THE FOREST! TAKE THE SURVIVING VILLAGERS WITH YOU--
--I'LL DEAL WITH THIS.
WHAT ARE YOU GOING TO DO?
I'M BUYING YOU SOME TIME, DARLIN'!
MAKE THE MOST OF IT!

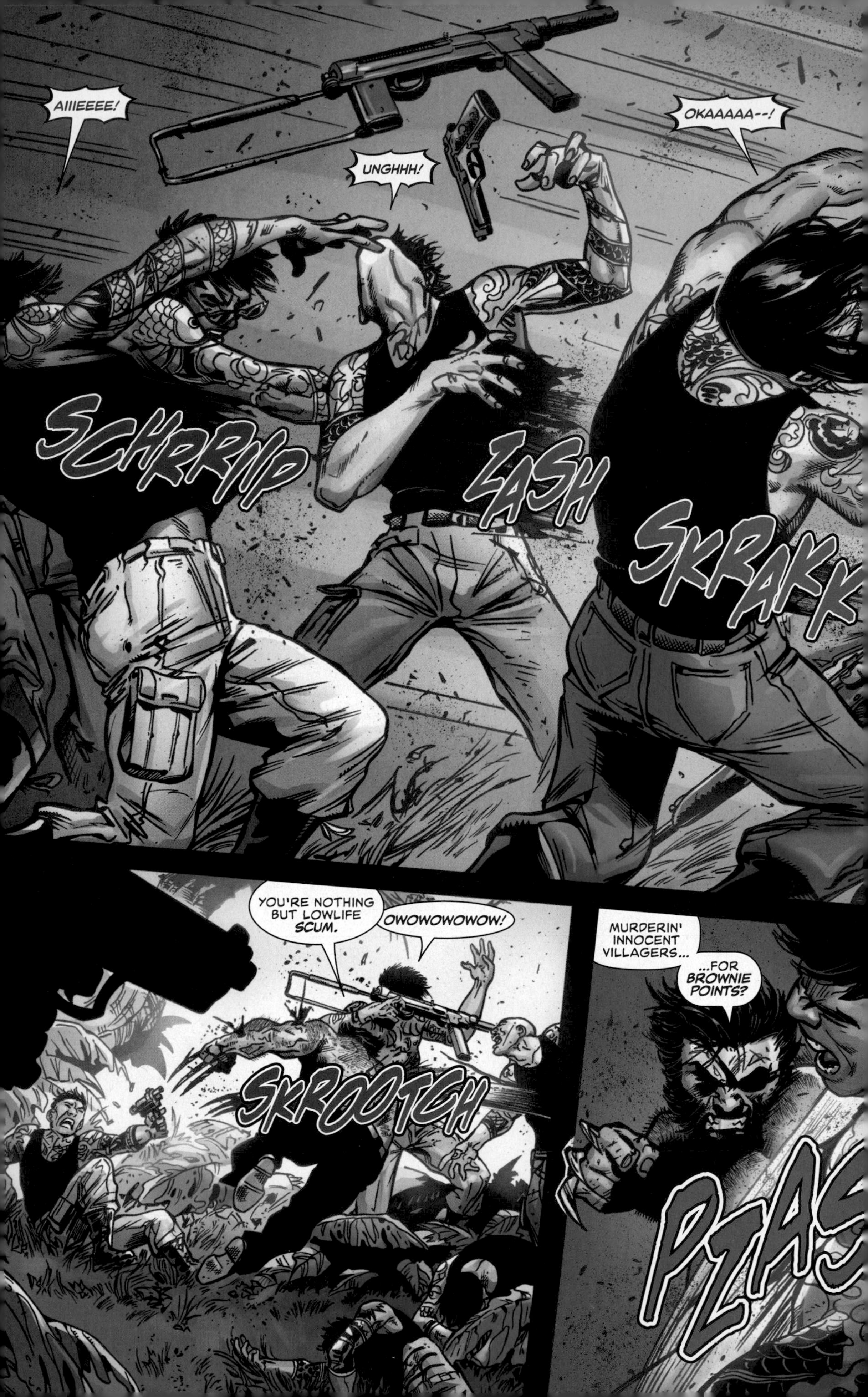
AIIIEEEE!
UNGHHH!
OKAAAAA--!
SCHRRIIP
ZASH
SKRAKK
YOU'RE NOTHING BUT LOWLIFE SCUM.
OWOWOWOWOW!
SKROOTCH
MURDERIN' INNOCENT VILLAGERS...
...FOR BROWNIE POINTS?
PZAS

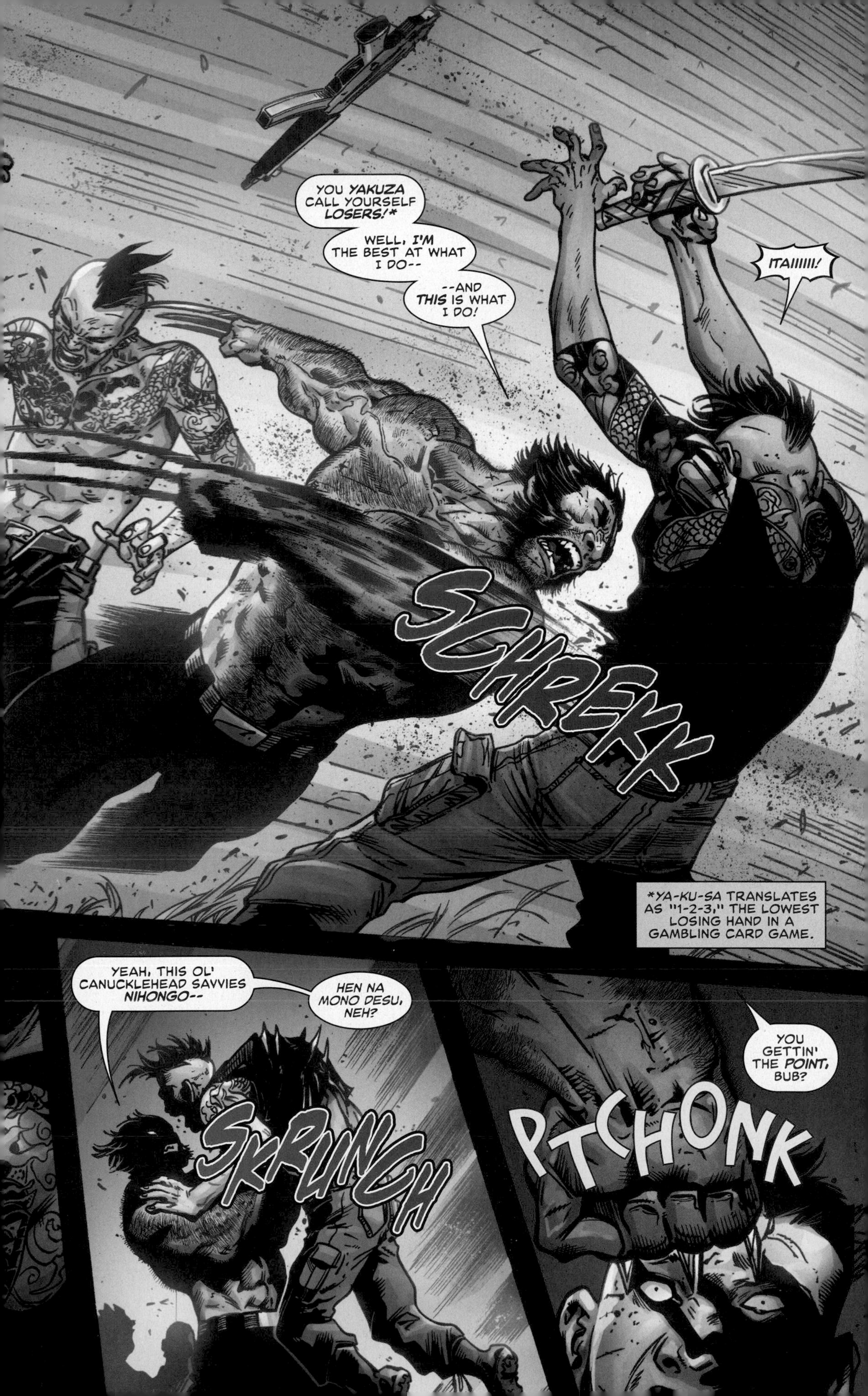
YOU YAKUZA CALL YOURSELF LOSERS!*
WELL, I'M THE BEST AT WHAT I DO--
--AND THIS IS WHAT I DO!
ITAIIIIII!
SCHREKK
*YA-KU-SA TRANSLATES AS "1-2-3," THE LOWEST LOSING HAND IN A GAMBLING CARD GAME.
YEAH, THIS OL' CANUCKLEHEAD SAVVIES NIHONGO--
HEN NA MONO DESU, NEH?
SKRUNCH
YOU GETTIN' THE POINT, BUB?
PTCHONK

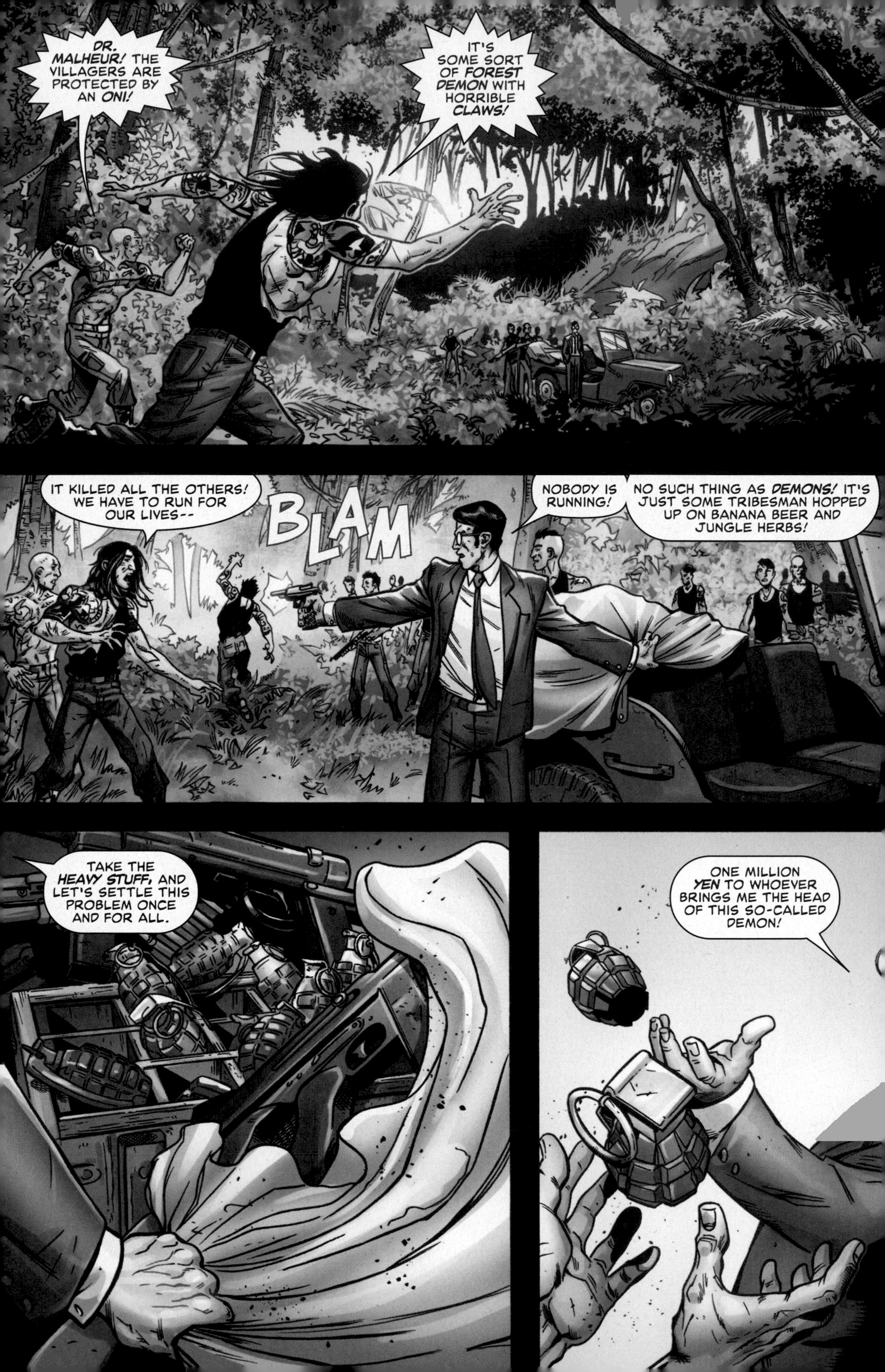
DR. MALHEUR! THE VILLAGERS ARE PROTECTED BY AN ONI!
IT'S SOME SORT OF FOREST DEMON WITH HORRIBLE CLAWS!
IT KILLED ALL THE OTHERS! WE HAVE TO RUN FOR OUR LIVES--
BLAM
NOBODY IS RUNNING!
NO SUCH THING AS DEMONS! IT'S JUST SOME TRIBESMAN HOPPED UP ON BANANA BEER AND JUNGLE HERBS!
TAKE THE HEAVY STUFF, AND LET'S SETTLE THIS PROBLEM ONCE AND FOR ALL.
ONE MILLION YEN TO WHOEVER BRINGS ME THE HEAD OF THIS SO-CALLED DEMON!

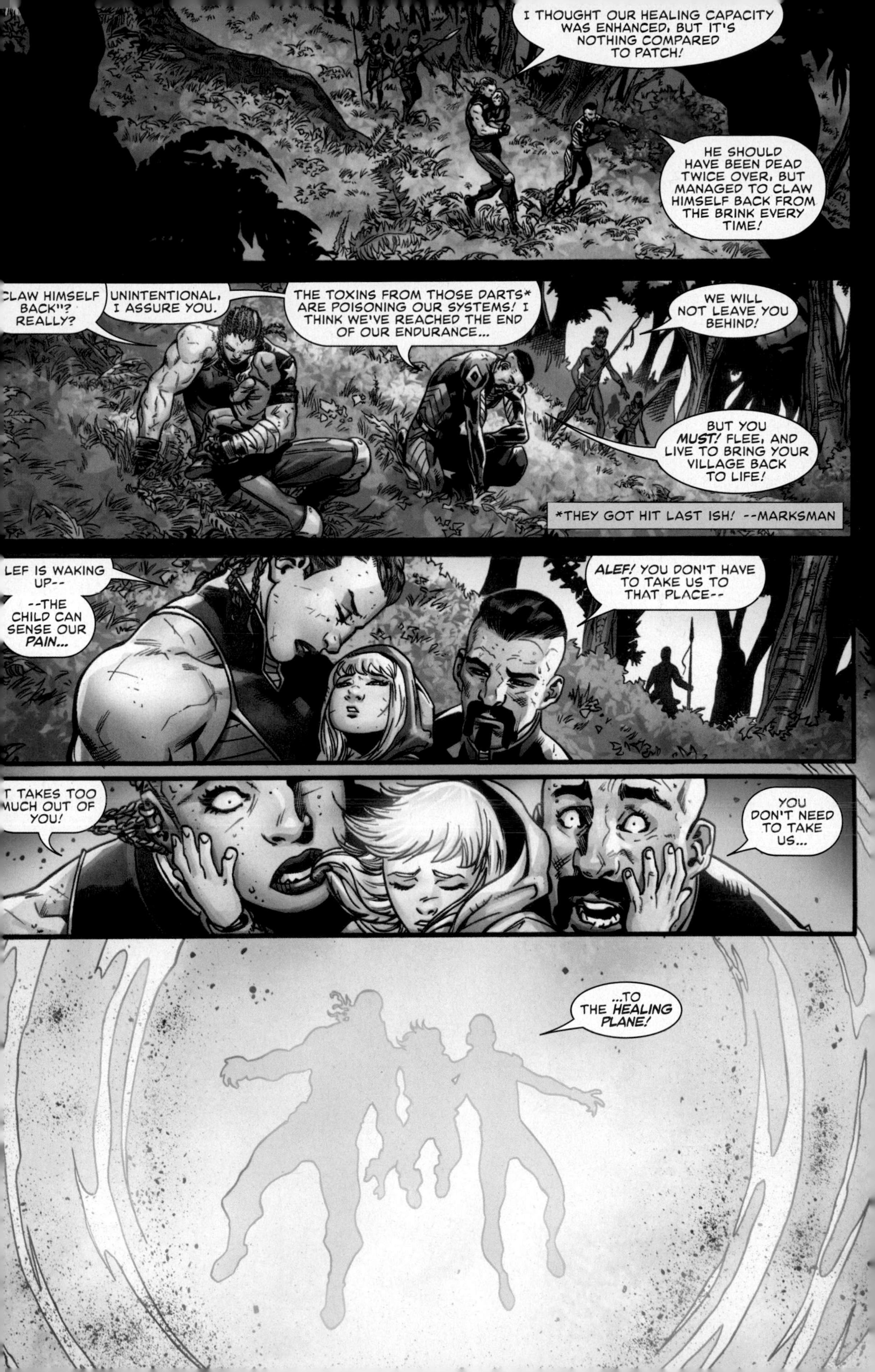
I THOUGHT OUR HEALING CAPACITY WAS ENHANCED, BUT IT'S NOTHING COMPARED TO PATCH!
HE SHOULD HAVE BEEN DEAD TWICE OVER, BUT MANAGED TO CLAW HIMSELF BACK FROM THE BRINK EVERY TIME!
CLAW HIMSELF BACK"? REALLY?
UNINTENTIONAL, I ASSURE YOU.
THE TOXINS FROM THOSE DARTS* ARE POISONING OUR SYSTEMS! I THINK WE'VE REACHED THE END OF OUR ENDURANCE...
WE WILL NOT LEAVE YOU BEHIND!
BUT YOU MUST! FLEE, AND LIVE TO BRING YOUR VILLAGE BACK TO LIFE!
*THEY GOT HIT LAST ISH! --MARKSMAN
LEF IS WAKING UP--
--THE CHILD CAN SENSE OUR PAIN...
ALEF! YOU DON'T HAVE TO TAKE US TO THAT PLACE--
T TAKES TOO MUCH OUT OF YOU!
YOU DON'T NEED TO TAKE US...
...TO THE HEALING PLANE!

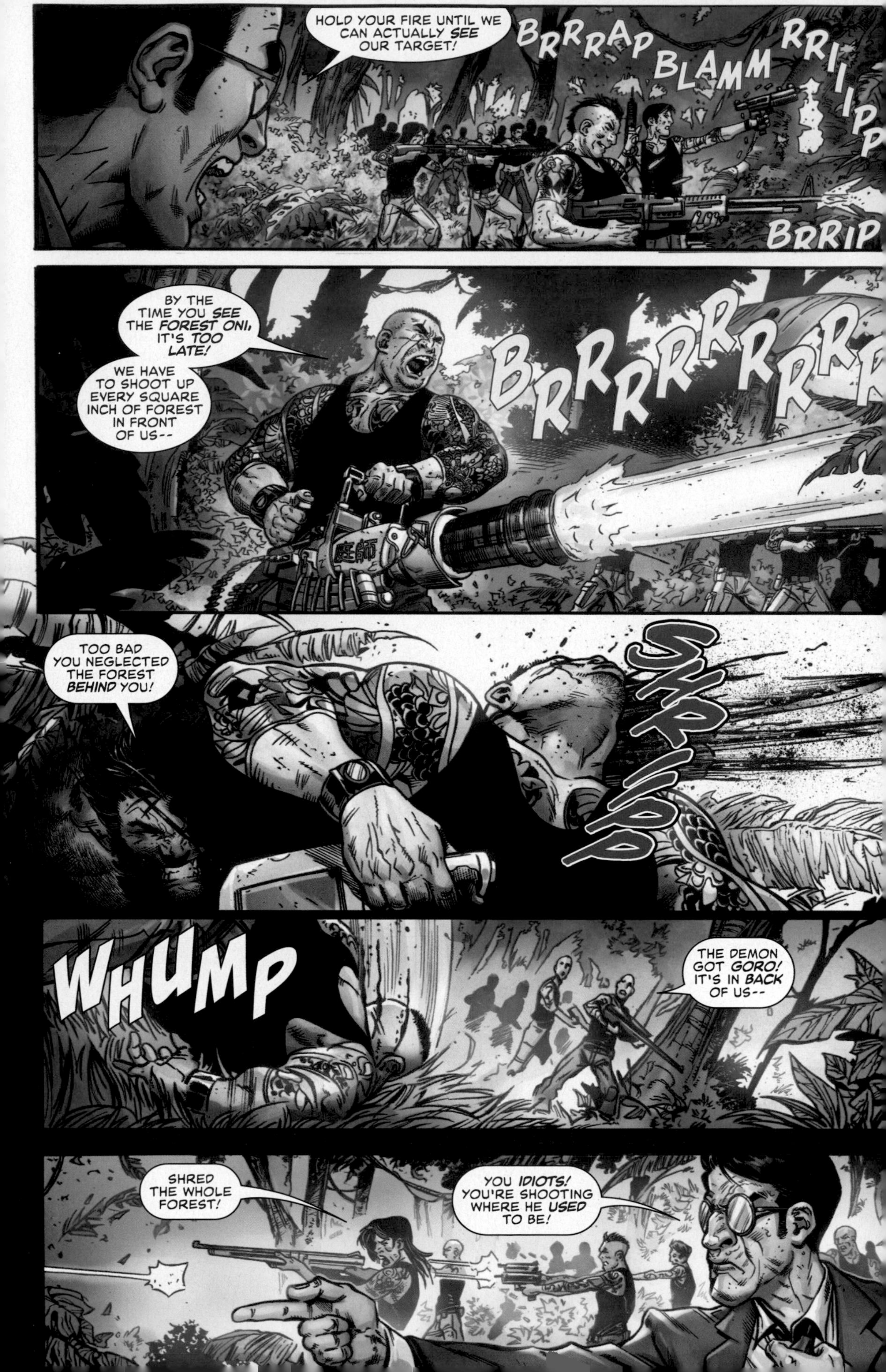
HOLD YOUR FIRE UNTIL WE CAN ACTUALLY SEE OUR TARGET!
BRRRAP
BLAMM
RRIIIPP
BRRIP
BY THE TIME YOU SEE THE FOREST ONI, IT'S TOO LATE!
WE HAVE TO SHOOT UP EVERY SQUARE INCH OF FOREST IN FRONT OF US--
BRRRRRRRRRRR
TOO BAD YOU NEGLECTED THE FOREST BEHIND YOU!
SHRIIPP
WHUMP
THE DEMON GOT GORO! IT'S IN BACK OF US--
SHRED THE WHOLE FOREST!
YOU IDIOTS! YOU'RE SHOOTING WHERE HE USED TO BE!

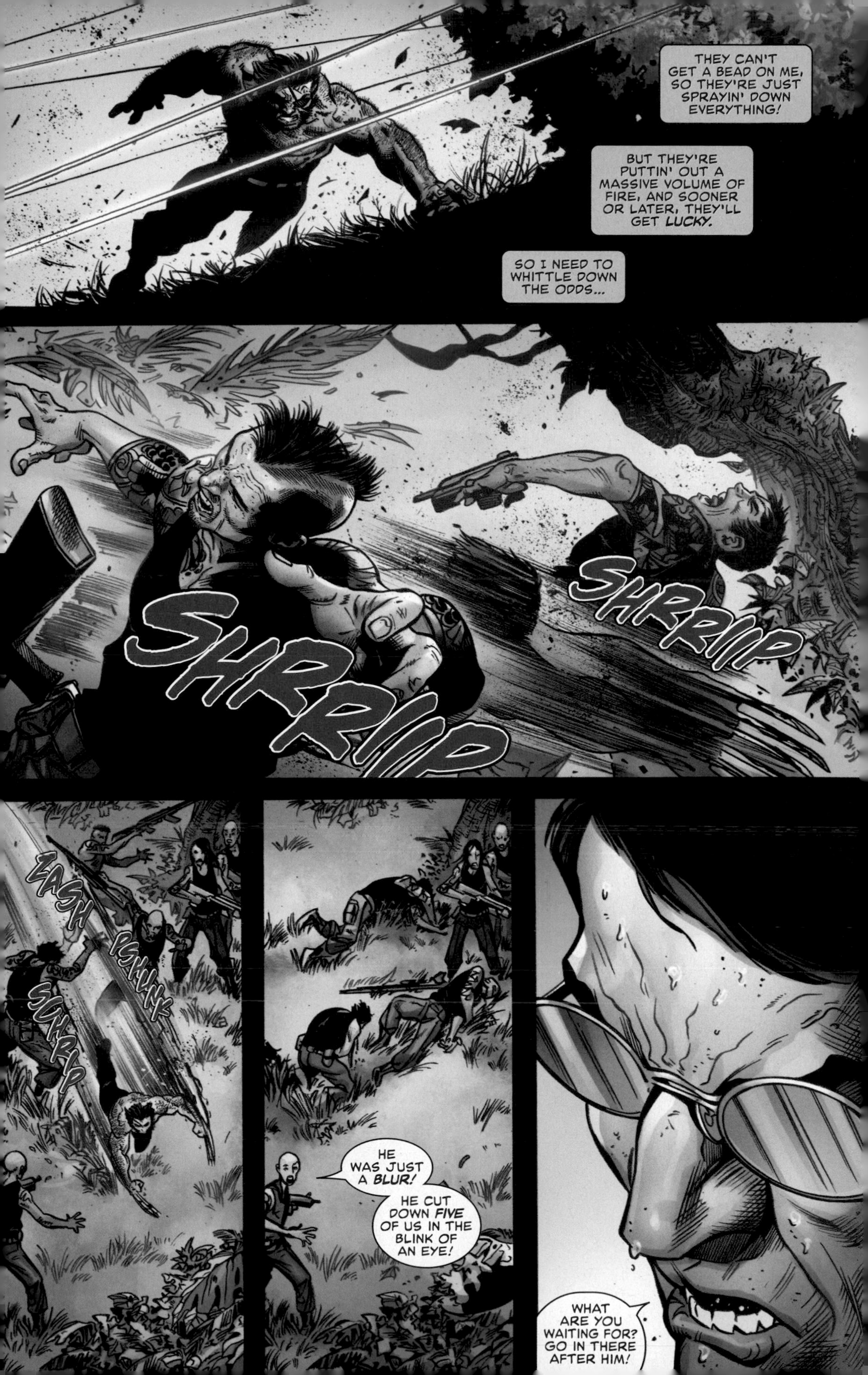
THEY CAN'T GET A BEAD ON ME, SO THEY'RE JUST SPRAYIN' DOWN EVERYTHING!
BUT THEY'RE PUTTIN' OUT A MASSIVE VOLUME OF FIRE, AND SOONER OR LATER, THEY'LL GET LUCKY.
SO I NEED TO WHITTLE DOWN THE ODDS...
SHRRIIP
SHRRIIP
ZASH
PSHUNK
SCHRIP
HE WAS JUST A BLUR!
HE CUT DOWN FIVE OF US IN THE BLINK OF AN EYE!
WHAT ARE YOU WAITING FOR? GO IN THERE AFTER HIM!

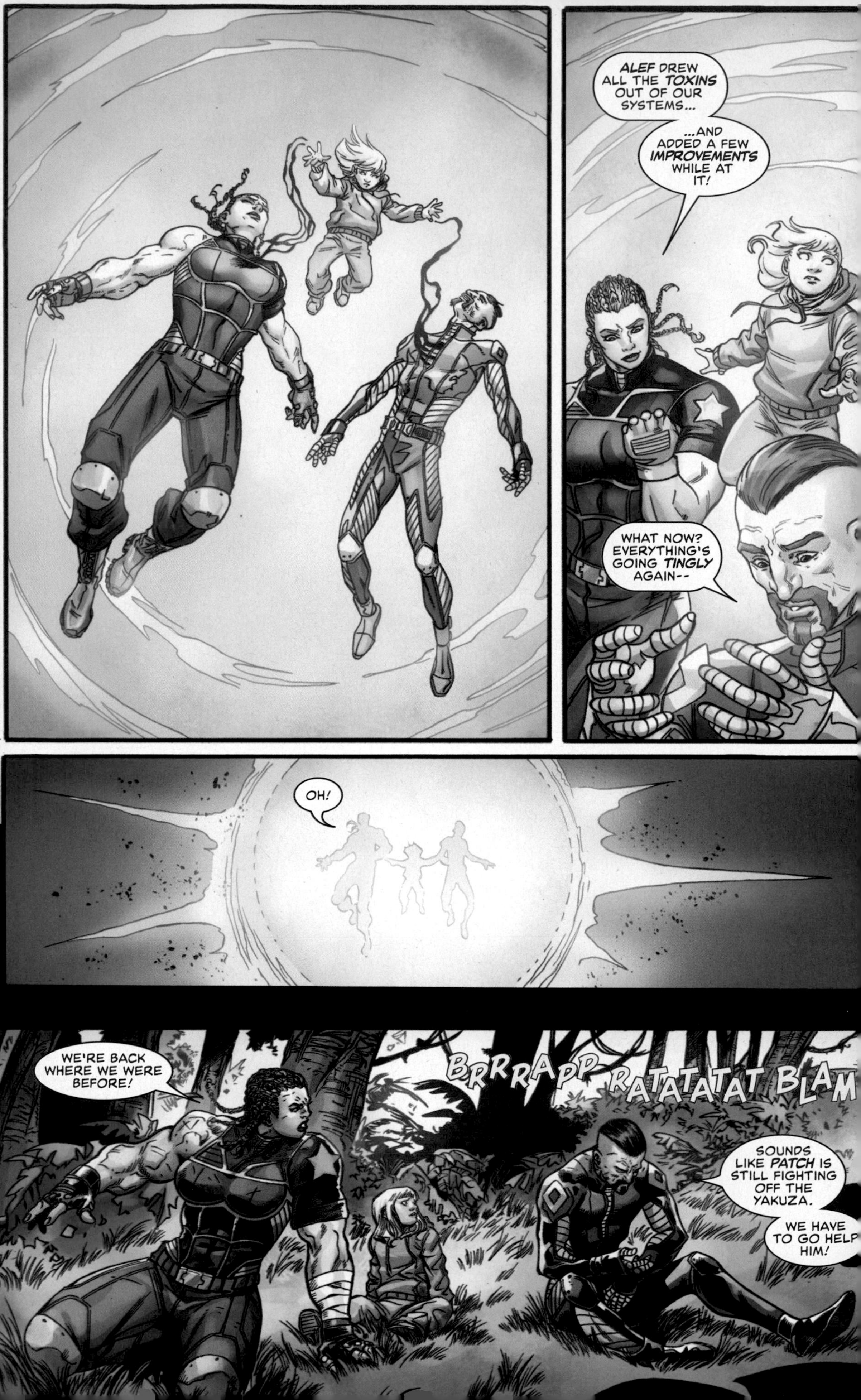
ALEF DREW ALL THE TOXINS OUT OF OUR SYSTEMS...
...AND ADDED A FEW IMPROVEMENTS WHILE AT IT!
WHAT NOW? EVERYTHING'S GOING TINGLY AGAIN--
OH!
WE'RE BACK WHERE WE WERE BEFORE!
BRRRAPP RATATATAT BLAM
SOUNDS LIKE PATCH IS STILL FIGHTING OFF THE YAKUZA.
WE HAVE TO GO HELP HIM!

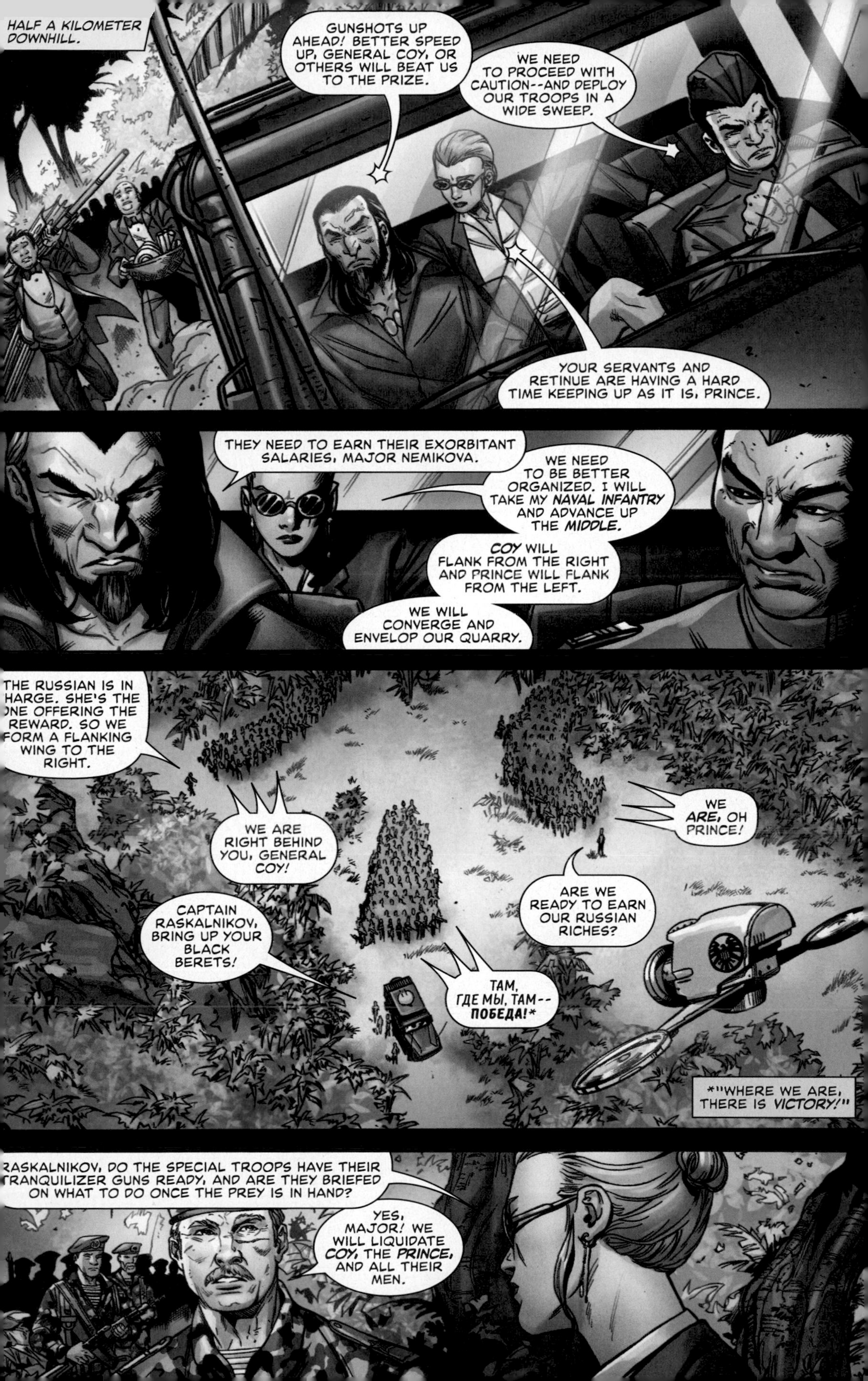
HALF A KILOMETER DOWNHILL.
GUNSHOTS UP AHEAD! BETTER SPEED UP, GENERAL COY, OR OTHERS WILL BEAT US TO THE PRIZE.
WE NEED TO PROCEED WITH CAUTION--AND DEPLOY OUR TROOPS IN A WIDE SWEEP.
YOUR SERVANTS AND RETINUE ARE HAVING A HARD TIME KEEPING UP AS IT IS, PRINCE.
THEY NEED TO EARN THEIR EXORBITANT SALARIES, MAJOR NEMIKOVA.
WE NEED TO BE BETTER ORGANIZED. I WILL TAKE MY NAVAL INFANTRY AND ADVANCE UP THE MIDDLE.
COY WILL FLANK FROM THE RIGHT AND PRINCE WILL FLANK FROM THE LEFT.
WE WILL CONVERGE AND ENVELOP OUR QUARRY.
THE RUSSIAN IS IN HARGE. SHE'S THE ONE OFFERING THE REWARD. SO WE FORM A FLANKING WING TO THE RIGHT.
WE ARE RIGHT BEHIND YOU, GENERAL COY!
WE ARE, OH PRINCE!
ARE WE READY TO EARN OUR RUSSIAN RICHES?
CAPTAIN RASKALNIKOV, BRING UP YOUR BLACK BERETS!
ТАМ, ГДЕ МЫ, ТАМ--ПОБЕДА!*
*"WHERE WE ARE, THERE IS VICTORY!"
RASKALNIKOV, DO THE SPECIAL TROOPS HAVE THEIR TRANQUILIZER GUNS READY, AND ARE THEY BRIEFED ON WHAT TO DO ONCE THE PREY IS IN HAND?
YES, MAJOR! WE WILL LIQUIDATE COY, THE PRINCE, AND ALL THEIR MEN.

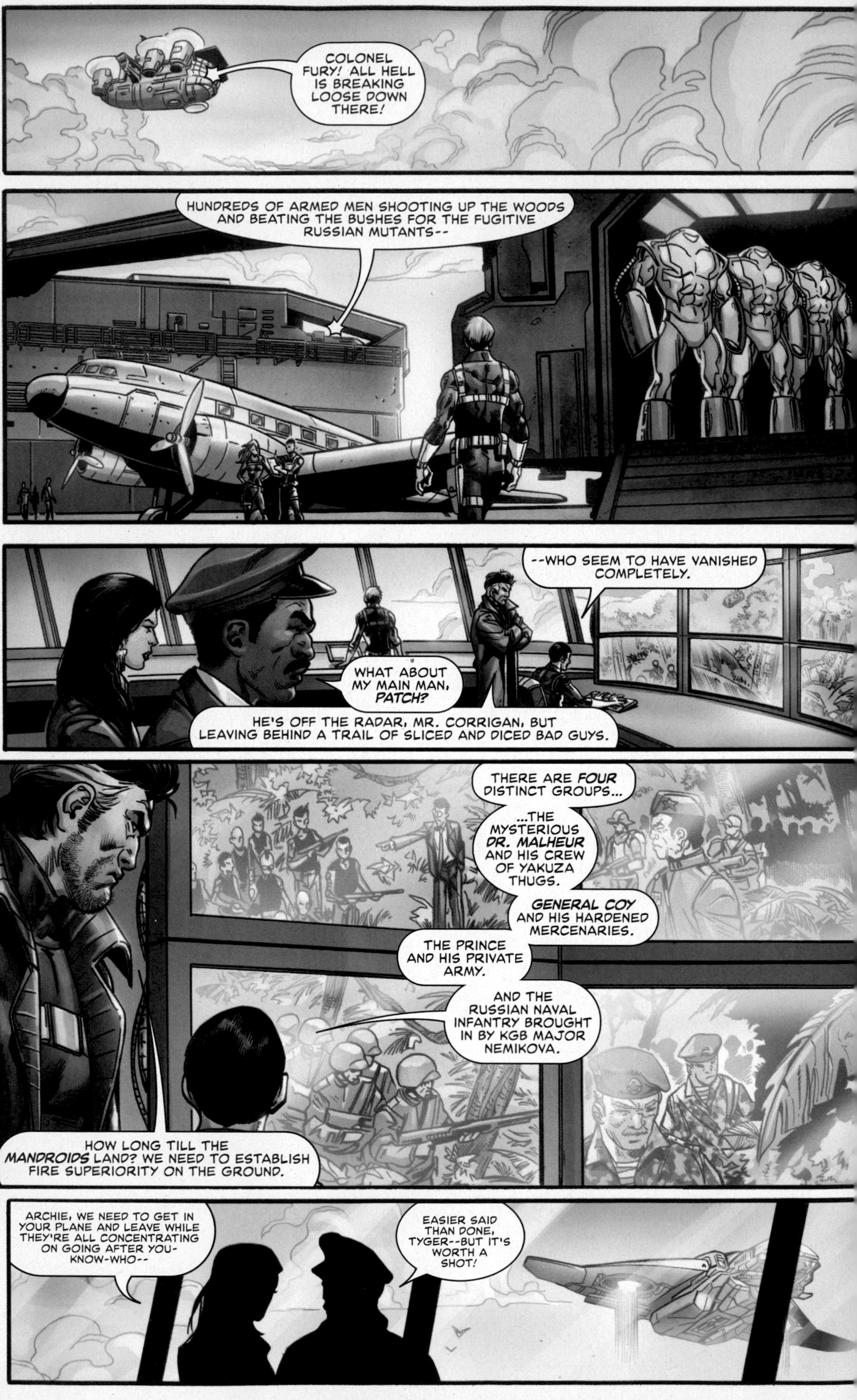
COLONEL FURY! ALL HELL IS BREAKING LOOSE DOWN THERE!
HUNDREDS OF ARMED MEN SHOOTING UP THE WOODS AND BEATING THE BUSHES FOR THE FUGITIVE RUSSIAN MUTANTS--
--WHO SEEM TO HAVE VANISHED COMPLETELY.
WHAT ABOUT MY MAIN MAN, PATCH?
HE'S OFF THE RADAR, MR. CORRIGAN, BUT LEAVING BEHIND A TRAIL OF SLICED AND DICED BAD GUYS.
THERE ARE FOUR DISTINCT GROUPS...
...THE MYSTERIOUS DR. MALHEUR AND HIS CREW OF YAKUZA THUGS.
GENERAL COY AND HIS HARDENED MERCENARIES.
THE PRINCE AND HIS PRIVATE ARMY.
AND THE RUSSIAN NAVAL INFANTRY BROUGHT IN BY KGB MAJOR NEMIKOVA.
HOW LONG TILL THE MANDROIDS LAND? WE NEED TO ESTABLISH FIRE SUPERIORITY ON THE GROUND.
ARCHIE, WE NEED TO GET IN YOUR PLANE AND LEAVE WHILE THEY'RE ALL CONCENTRATING ON GOING AFTER YOU-KNOW-WHO--
EASIER SAID THAN DONE, TYGER--BUT IT'S WORTH A SHOT!

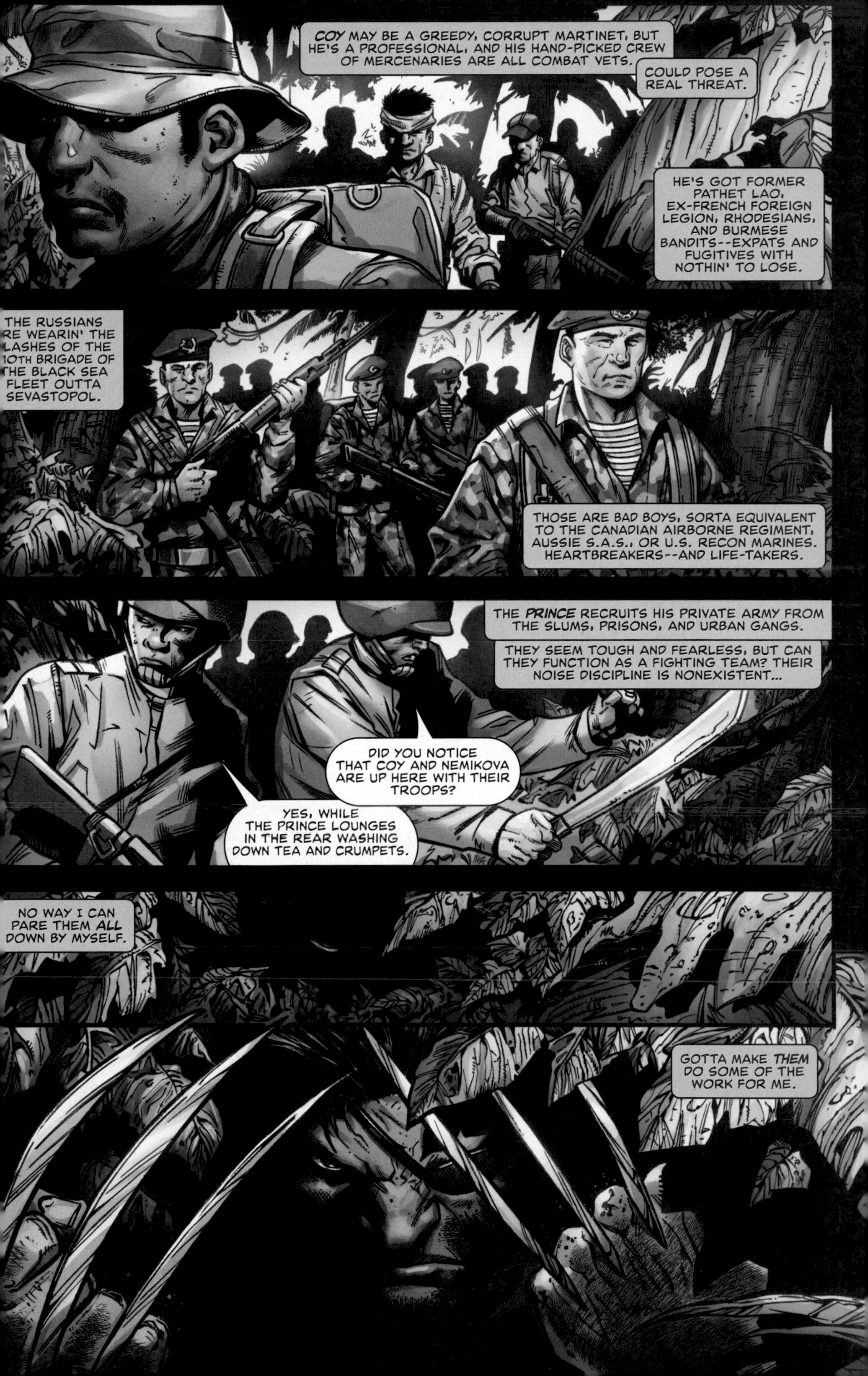
COY MAY BE A GREEDY, CORRUPT MARTINET, BUT HE'S A PROFESSIONAL, AND HIS HAND-PICKED CREW OF MERCENARIES ARE ALL COMBAT VETS.
COULD POSE A REAL THREAT.
HE'S GOT FORMER PATHET LAO, EX-FRENCH FOREIGN LEGION, RHODESIANS, AND BURMESE BANDITS--EXPATS AND FUGITIVES WITH NOTHIN' TO LOSE.
THE RUSSIANS RE WEARIN' THE LASHES OF THE 10TH BRIGADE OF THE BLACK SEA FLEET OUTTA SEVASTOPOL.
THOSE ARE BAD BOYS, SORTA EQUIVALENT TO THE CANADIAN AIRBORNE REGIMENT, AUSSIE S.A.S., OR U.S. RECON MARINES. HEARTBREAKERS--AND LIFE-TAKERS.
THE PRINCE RECRUITS HIS PRIVATE ARMY FROM THE SLUMS, PRISONS, AND URBAN GANGS.
THEY SEEM TOUGH AND FEARLESS, BUT CAN THEY FUNCTION AS A FIGHTING TEAM? THEIR NOISE DISCIPLINE IS NONEXISTENT...
DID YOU NOTICE THAT COY AND NEMIKOVA ARE UP HERE WITH THEIR TROOPS?
YES, WHILE THE PRINCE LOUNGES IN THE REAR WASHING DOWN TEA AND CRUMPETS.
NO WAY I CAN PARE THEM ALL DOWN BY MYSELF.
GOTTA MAKE THEM DO SOME OF THE WORK FOR ME.

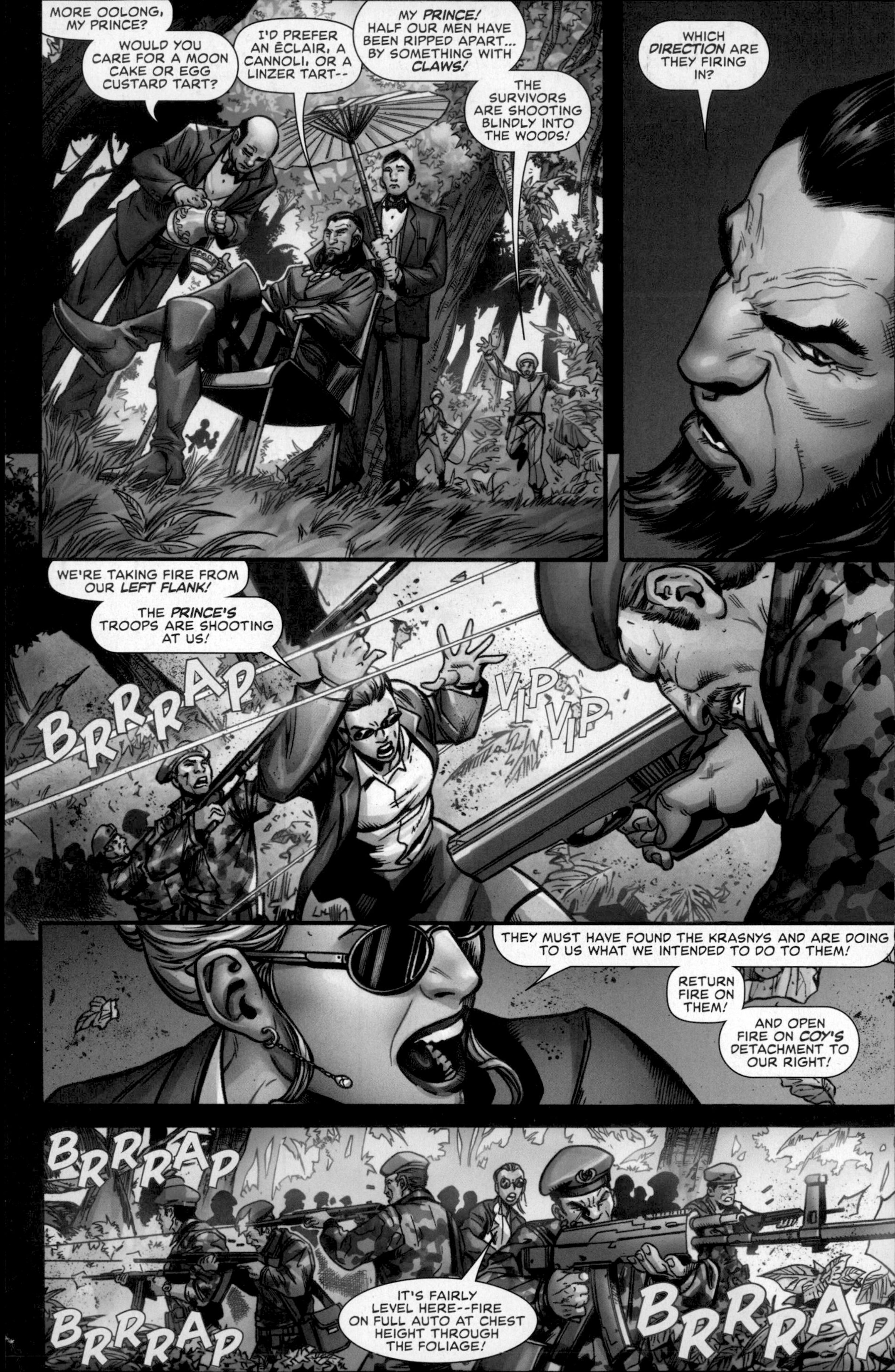

MORE OOLONG, MY PRINCE?
WOULD YOU CARE FOR A MOON CAKE OR EGG CUSTARD TART?
I'D PREFER AN ÉCLAIR, A CANNOLI, OR A LINZER TART--
MY PRINCE! HALF OUR MEN HAVE BEEN RIPPED APART... BY SOMETHING WITH CLAWS!
THE SURVIVORS ARE SHOOTING BLINDLY INTO THE WOODS!
WHICH DIRECTION ARE THEY FIRING IN?
WE'RE TAKING FIRE FROM OUR LEFT FLANK!
THE PRINCE'S TROOPS ARE SHOOTING AT US!
BRRRAP
VIP VIP
THEY MUST HAVE FOUND THE KRASNYS AND ARE DOING TO US WHAT WE INTENDED TO DO TO THEM!
RETURN FIRE ON THEM!
AND OPEN FIRE ON COY'S DETACHMENT TO OUR RIGHT!
BRRRAP
IT'S FAIRLY LEVEL HERE--FIRE ON FULL AUTO AT CHEST HEIGHT THROUGH THE FOLIAGE!
BRRRAP
BRRRRAP

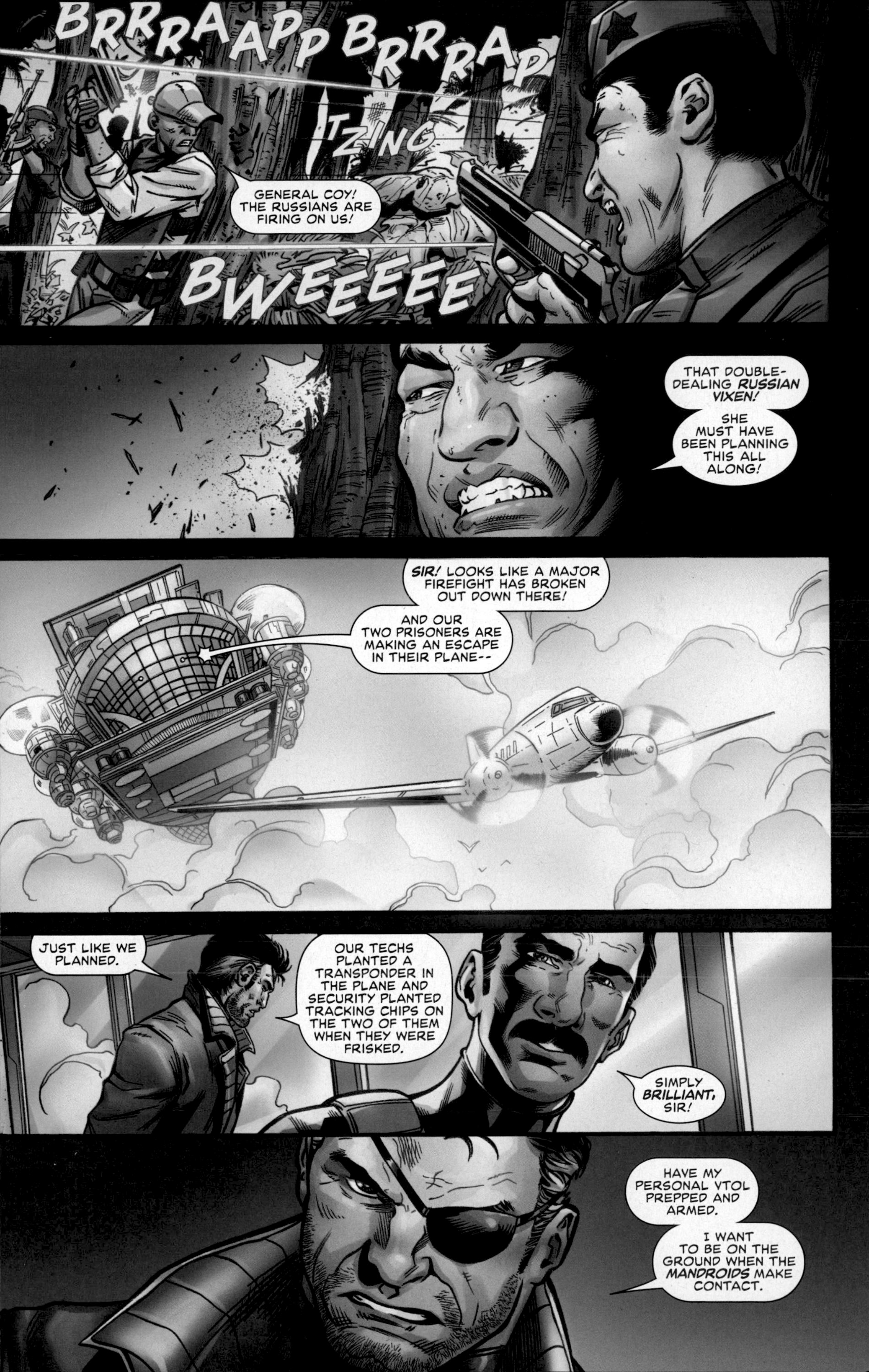
BRRRAAPP BRRRAP
TZING
GENERAL COY! THE RUSSIANS ARE FIRING ON US!
BWEEEEE
THAT DOUBLE-DEALING RUSSIAN VIXEN!
SHE MUST HAVE BEEN PLANNING THIS ALL ALONG!
SIR! LOOKS LIKE A MAJOR FIREFIGHT HAS BROKEN OUT DOWN THERE!
AND OUR TWO PRISONERS ARE MAKING AN ESCAPE IN THEIR PLANE--
JUST LIKE WE PLANNED.
OUR TECHS PLANTED A TRANSPONDER IN THE PLANE AND SECURITY PLANTED TRACKING CHIPS ON THE TWO OF THEM WHEN THEY WERE FRISKED.
SIMPLY BRILLIANT, SIR!
HAVE MY PERSONAL VTOL PREPPED AND ARMED.
I WANT TO BE ON THE GROUND WHEN THE MANDROIDS MAKE CONTACT.

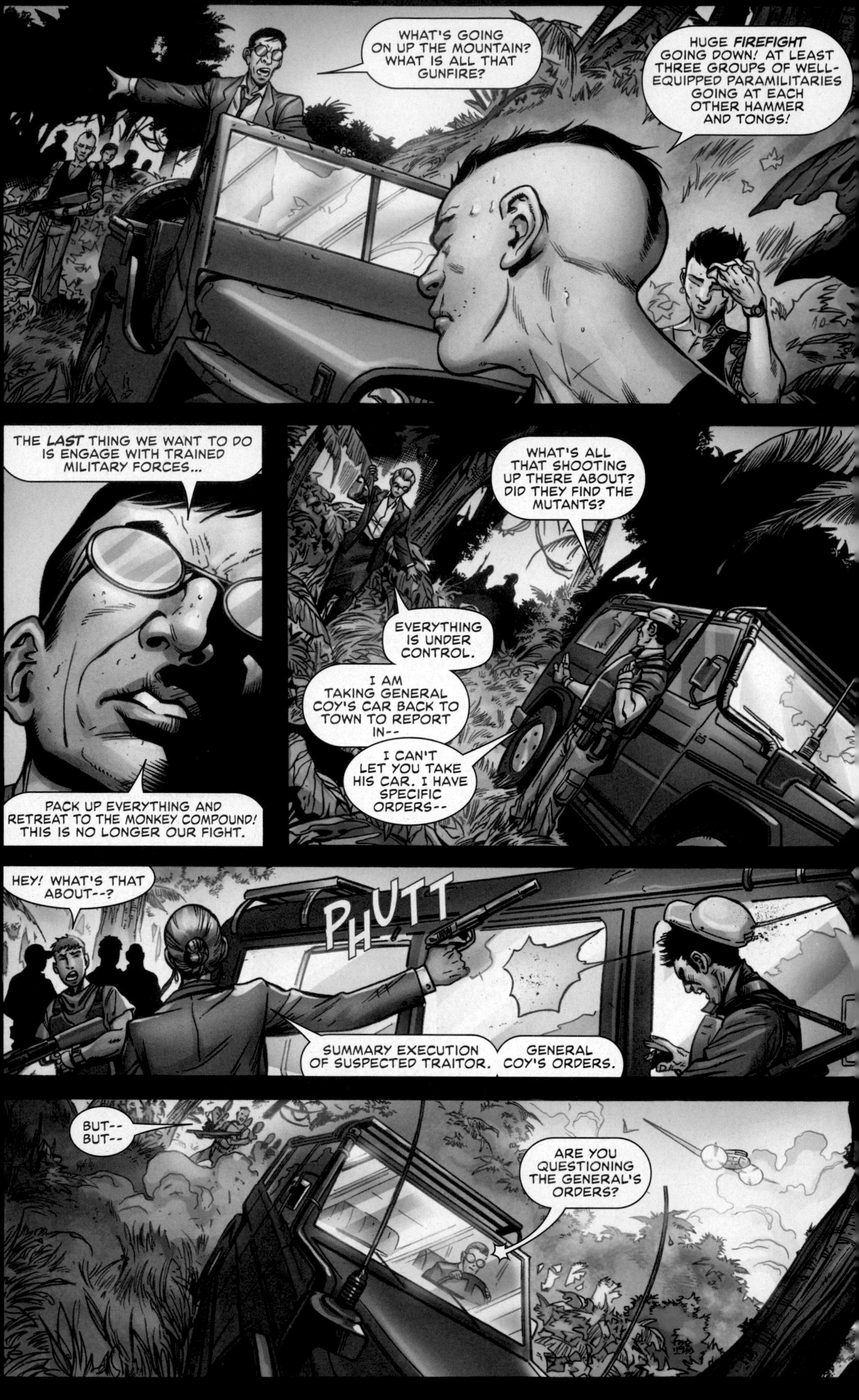
WHAT'S GOING ON UP THE MOUNTAIN? WHAT IS ALL THAT GUNFIRE?
HUGE FIREFIGHT GOING DOWN! AT LEAST THREE GROUPS OF WELL-EQUIPPED PARAMILITARIES GOING AT EACH OTHER HAMMER AND TONGS!
THE LAST THING WE WANT TO DO IS ENGAGE WITH TRAINED MILITARY FORCES...
PACK UP EVERYTHING AND RETREAT TO THE MONKEY COMPOUND! THIS IS NO LONGER OUR FIGHT.
WHAT'S ALL THAT SHOOTING UP THERE ABOUT? DID THEY FIND THE MUTANTS?
EVERYTHING IS UNDER CONTROL.
I AM TAKING GENERAL COY'S CAR BACK TO TOWN TO REPORT IN--
I CAN'T LET YOU TAKE HIS CAR. I HAVE SPECIFIC ORDERS--
HEY! WHAT'S THAT ABOUT--?
PHUTT
SUMMARY EXECUTION OF SUSPECTED TRAITOR.
GENERAL COY'S ORDERS.
BUT-- BUT--
ARE YOU QUESTIONING THE GENERAL'S ORDERS?

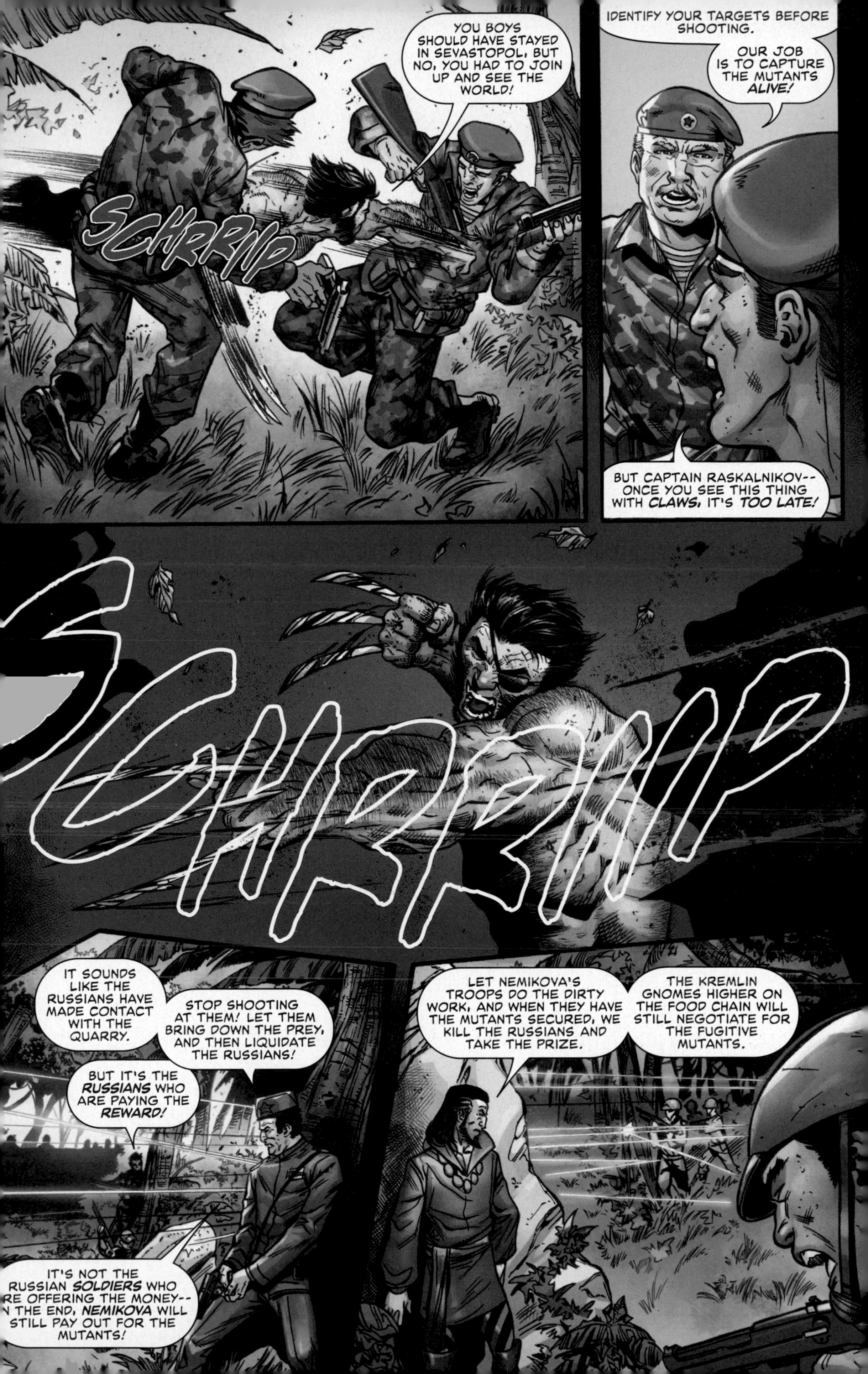
YOU BOYS SHOULD HAVE STAYED IN SEVASTOPOL, BUT NO, YOU HAD TO JOIN UP AND SEE THE WORLD!
SCHRRIIP
IDENTIFY YOUR TARGETS BEFORE SHOOTING.
OUR JOB IS TO CAPTURE THE MUTANTS ALIVE!
BUT CAPTAIN RASKALNIKOV--ONCE YOU SEE THIS THING WITH CLAWS, IT'S TOO LATE!
SCHRRIIP
IT SOUNDS LIKE THE RUSSIANS HAVE MADE CONTACT WITH THE QUARRY.
STOP SHOOTING AT THEM! LET THEM BRING DOWN THE PREY, AND THEN LIQUIDATE THE RUSSIANS!
BUT IT'S THE RUSSIANS WHO ARE PAYING THE REWARD!
IT'S NOT THE RUSSIAN SOLDIERS WHO ARE OFFERING THE MONEY--IN THE END, NEMIKOVA WILL STILL PAY OUT FOR THE MUTANTS!
LET NEMIKOVA'S TROOPS DO THE DIRTY WORK, AND WHEN THEY HAVE THE MUTANTS SECURED, WE KILL THE RUSSIANS AND TAKE THE PRIZE.
THE KREMLIN GNOMES HIGHER ON THE FOOD CHAIN WILL STILL NEGOTIATE FOR THE FUGITIVE MUTANTS.

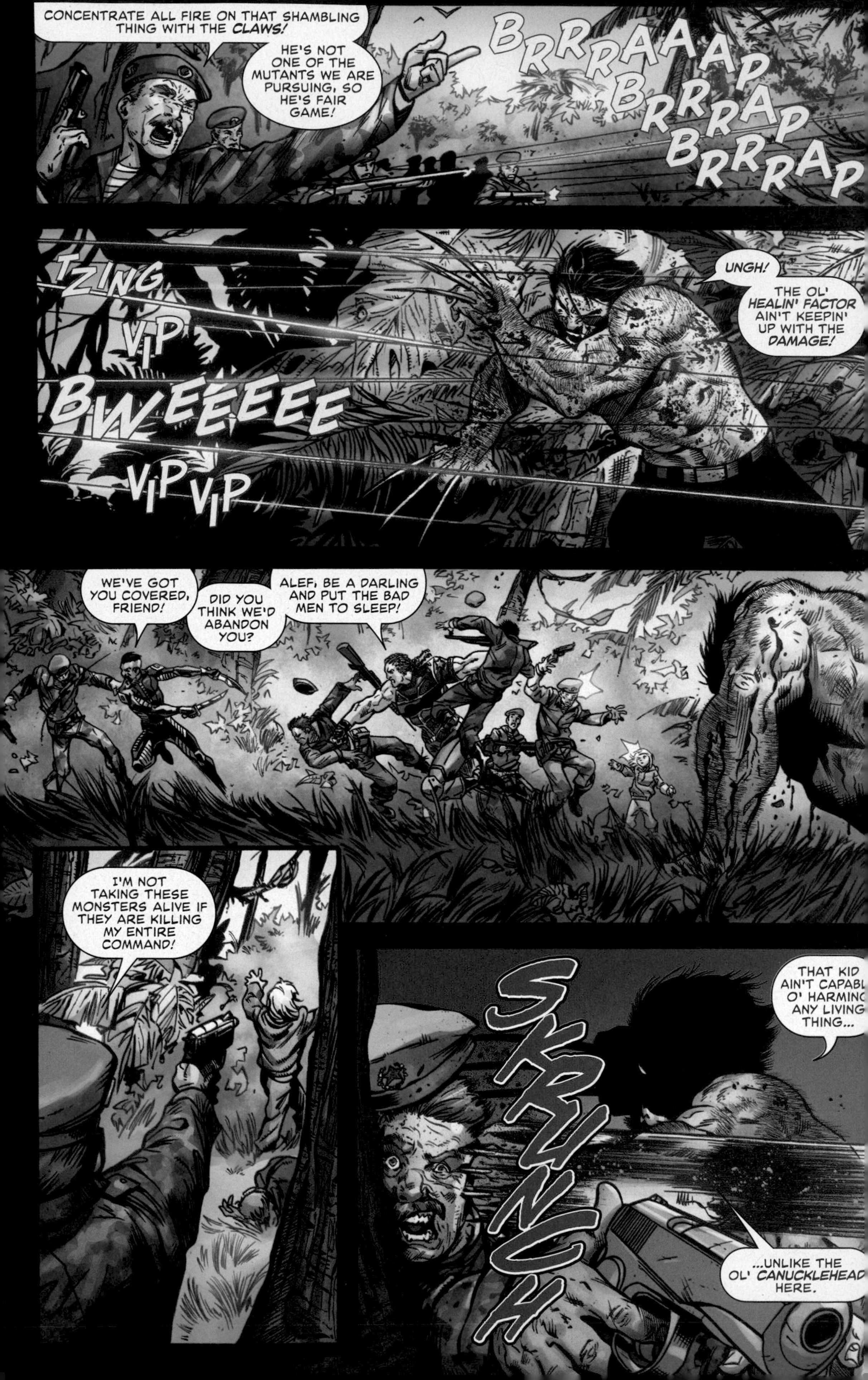
CONCENTRATE ALL FIRE ON THAT SHAMBLING THING WITH THE *CLAWS!*
HE'S NOT ONE OF THE MUTANTS WE ARE PURSUING, SO HE'S FAIR GAME!
BRRRAAAAP
BRRRAP
BRRRAP
BRRRRAP
TZING
VIP
BWEEEEEE
VIP VIP
UNGH!
THE OL' *HEALIN' FACTOR* AIN'T KEEPIN' UP WITH THE *DAMAGE!*
WE'VE GOT YOU COVERED, FRIEND!
DID YOU THINK WE'D ABANDON YOU?
ALEF, BE A DARLING AND PUT THE BAD MEN TO SLEEP!
I'M NOT TAKING THESE MONSTERS ALIVE IF THEY ARE KILLING MY ENTIRE COMMAND!
SKRUNCH
THAT KID AIN'T CAPABL O' HARMINC ANY LIVING THING...
...UNLIKE THE OL' *CANUCKLEHEAD* HERE.

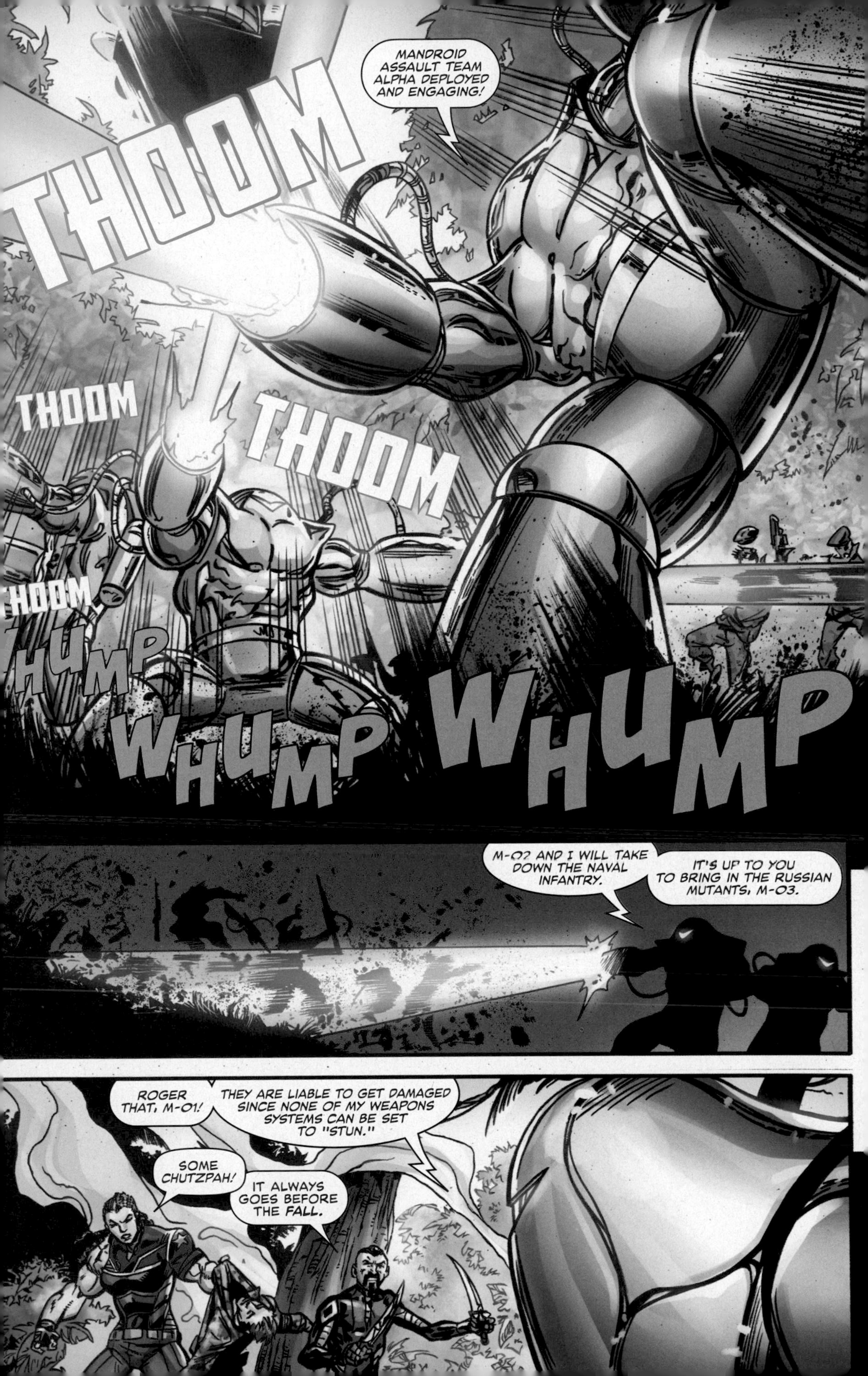
MANDROID ASSAULT TEAM ALPHA DEPLOYED AND ENGAGING!
THOOM
THOOM
THOOM
THOOM
HUMP
WHUMP
WHUMP
M-02 AND I WILL TAKE DOWN THE NAVAL INFANTRY.
IT'S UP TO YOU TO BRING IN THE RUSSIAN MUTANTS, M-03.
ROGER THAT, M-01!
THEY ARE LIABLE TO GET DAMAGED SINCE NONE OF MY WEAPONS SYSTEMS CAN BE SET TO "STUN."
SOME CHUTZPAH!
IT ALWAYS GOES BEFORE THE FALL.

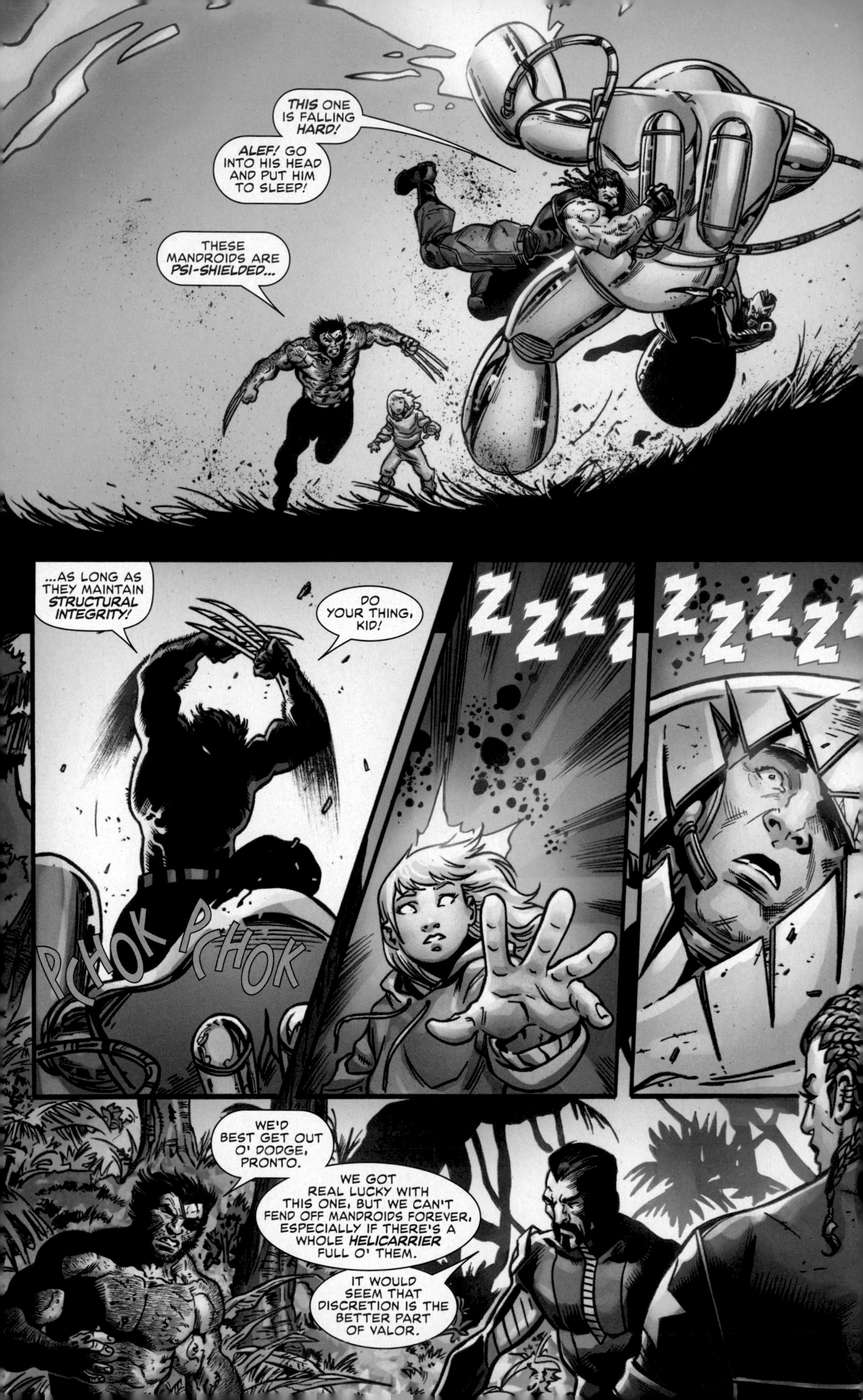

THIS ONE IS FALLING HARD!
ALEF! GO INTO HIS HEAD AND PUT HIM TO SLEEP!
THESE MANDROIDS ARE PSI-SHIELDED...
...AS LONG AS THEY MAINTAIN STRUCTURAL INTEGRITY!
DO YOUR THING, KID!
PCHOK PCHOK
ZZZZ
ZZZZ
WE'D BEST GET OUT O' DODGE, PRONTO.
WE GOT REAL LUCKY WITH THIS ONE, BUT WE CAN'T FEND OFF MANDROIDS FOREVER, ESPECIALLY IF THERE'S A WHOLE HELICARRIER FULL O' THEM.
IT WOULD SEEM THAT DISCRETION IS THE BETTER PART OF VALOR.

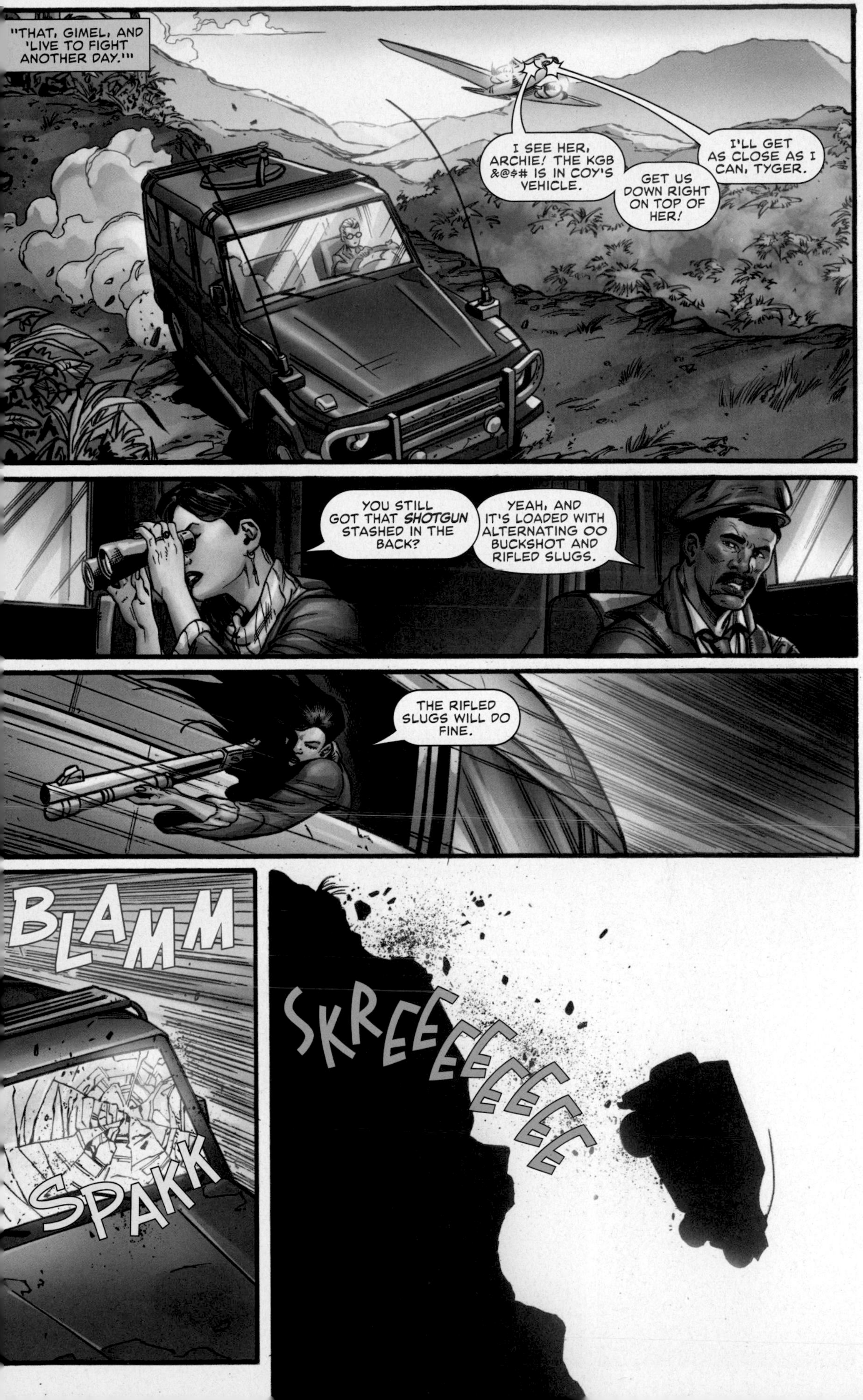
"THAT, GIMEL, AND 'LIVE TO FIGHT ANOTHER DAY.'"
I SEE HER, ARCHIE! THE KGB &@$# IS IN COY'S VEHICLE.
GET US DOWN RIGHT ON TOP OF HER!
I'LL GET AS CLOSE AS I CAN, TYGER.
YOU STILL GOT THAT SHOTGUN STASHED IN THE BACK?
YEAH, AND IT'S LOADED WITH ALTERNATING OO BUCKSHOT AND RIFLED SLUGS.
THE RIFLED SLUGS WILL DO FINE.
BLAMM
SPAKK
SKREEEEEEEEE

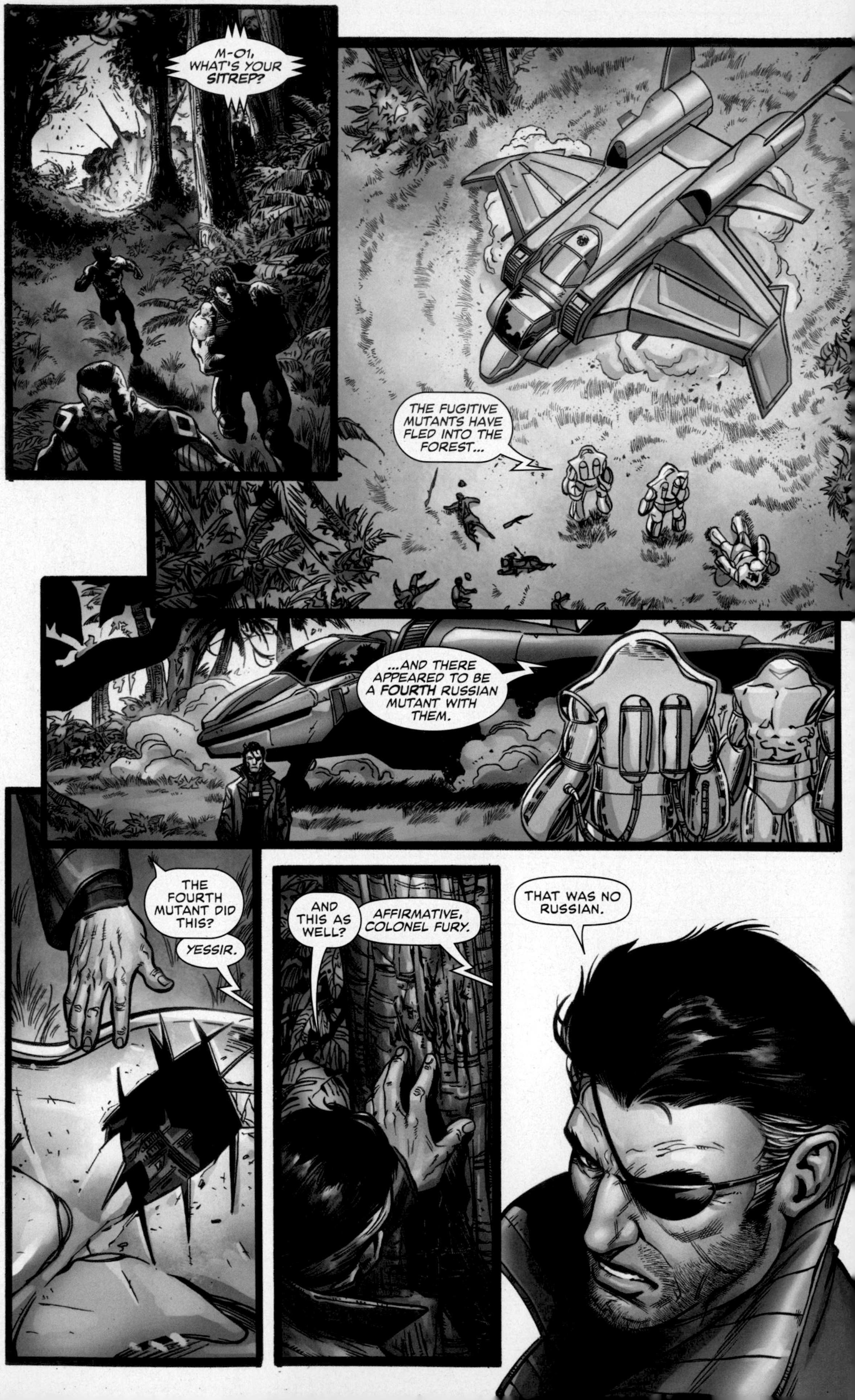

M-01, WHAT'S YOUR SITREP?
THE FUGITIVE MUTANTS HAVE FLED INTO THE FOREST...
...AND THERE APPEARED TO BE A FOURTH RUSSIAN MUTANT WITH THEM.
THE FOURTH MUTANT DID THIS?
YESSIR.
AND THIS AS WELL?
AFFIRMATIVE, COLONEL FURY.
THAT WAS NO RUSSIAN.

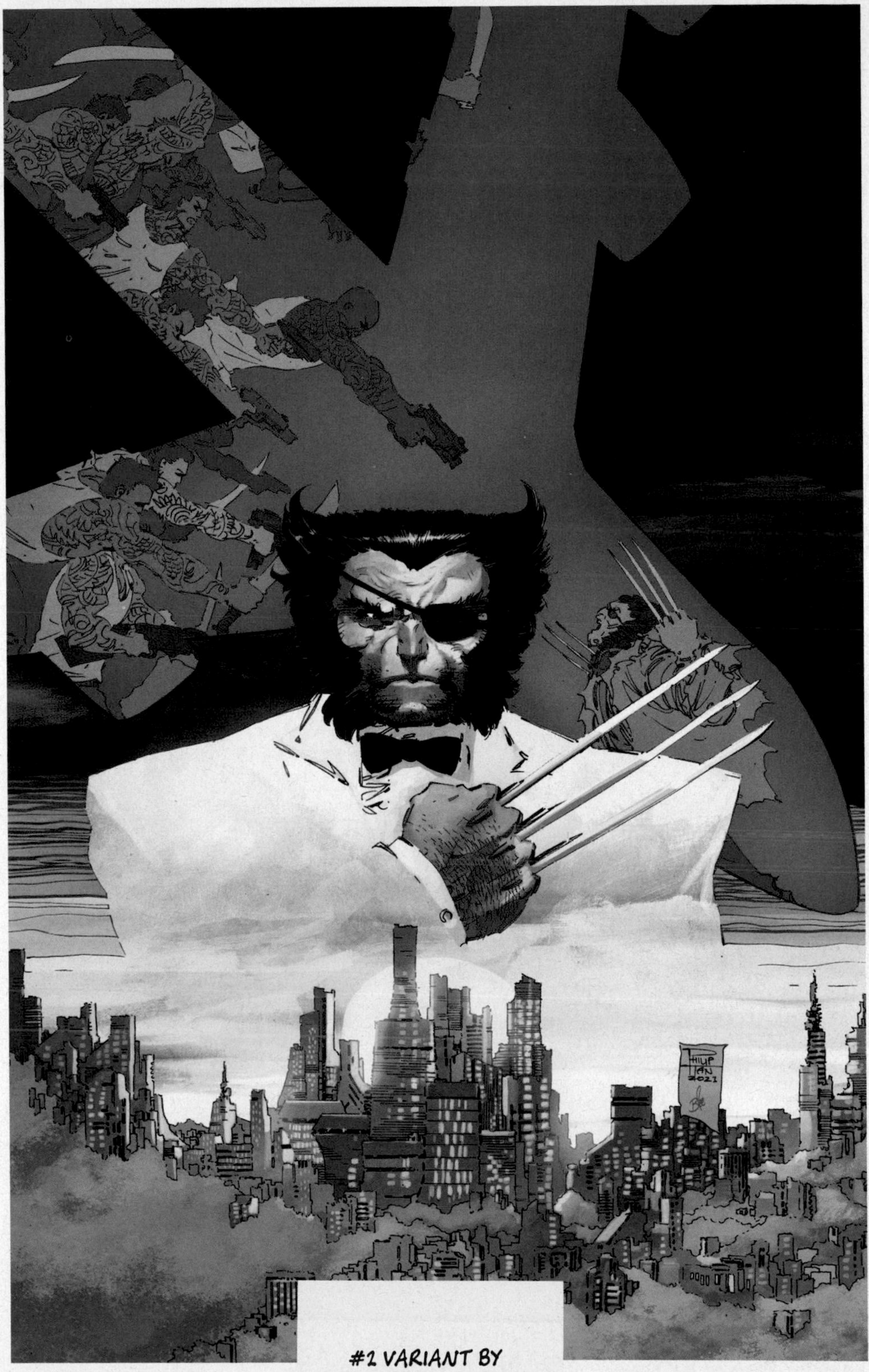

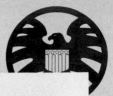

#2 VARIANT BY

PHILIP TAN & FEDERICO BLEE

INTERNAL REVIEW ONLY

#5

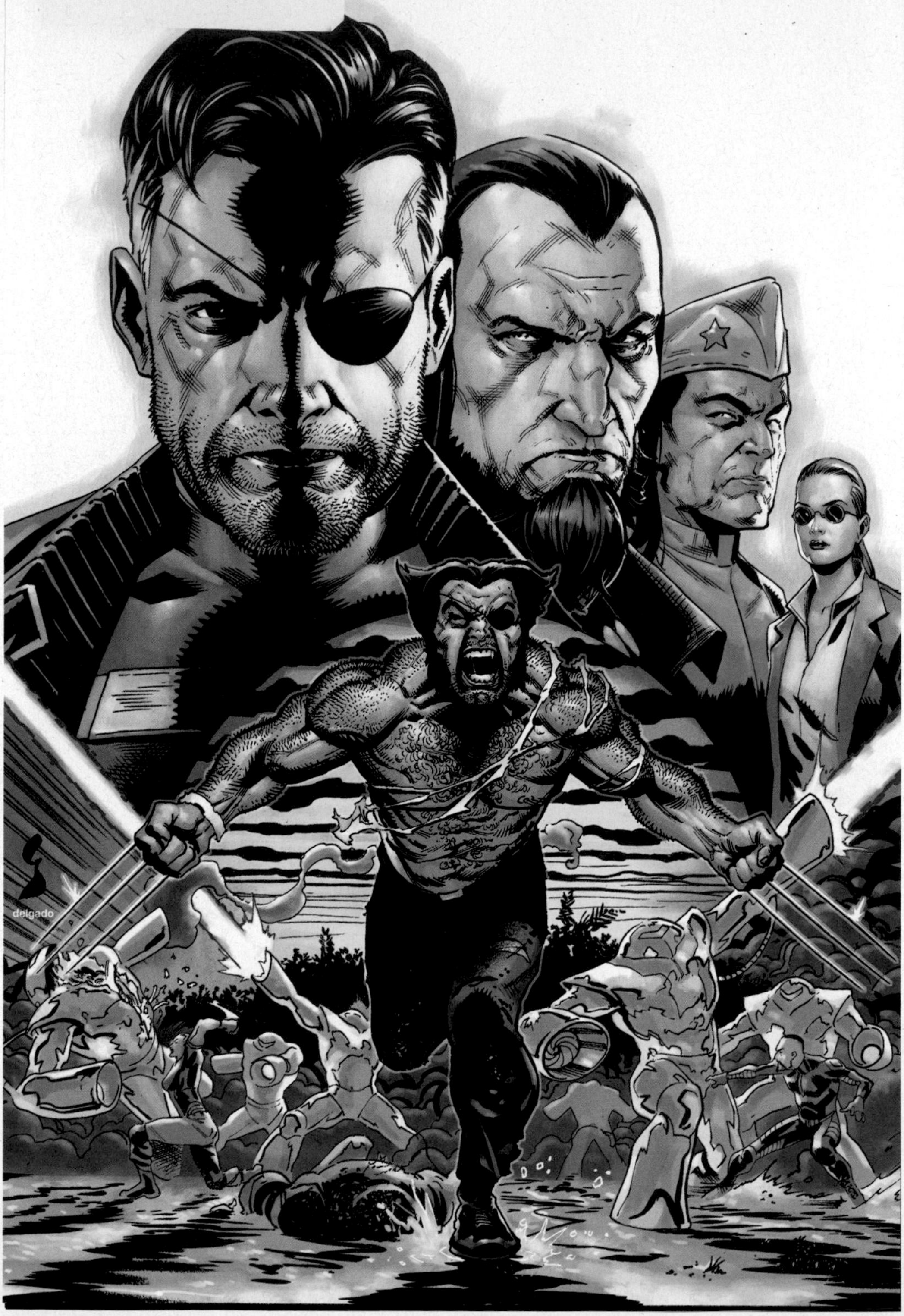
delgado

INTERNAL REVIEW ONLY

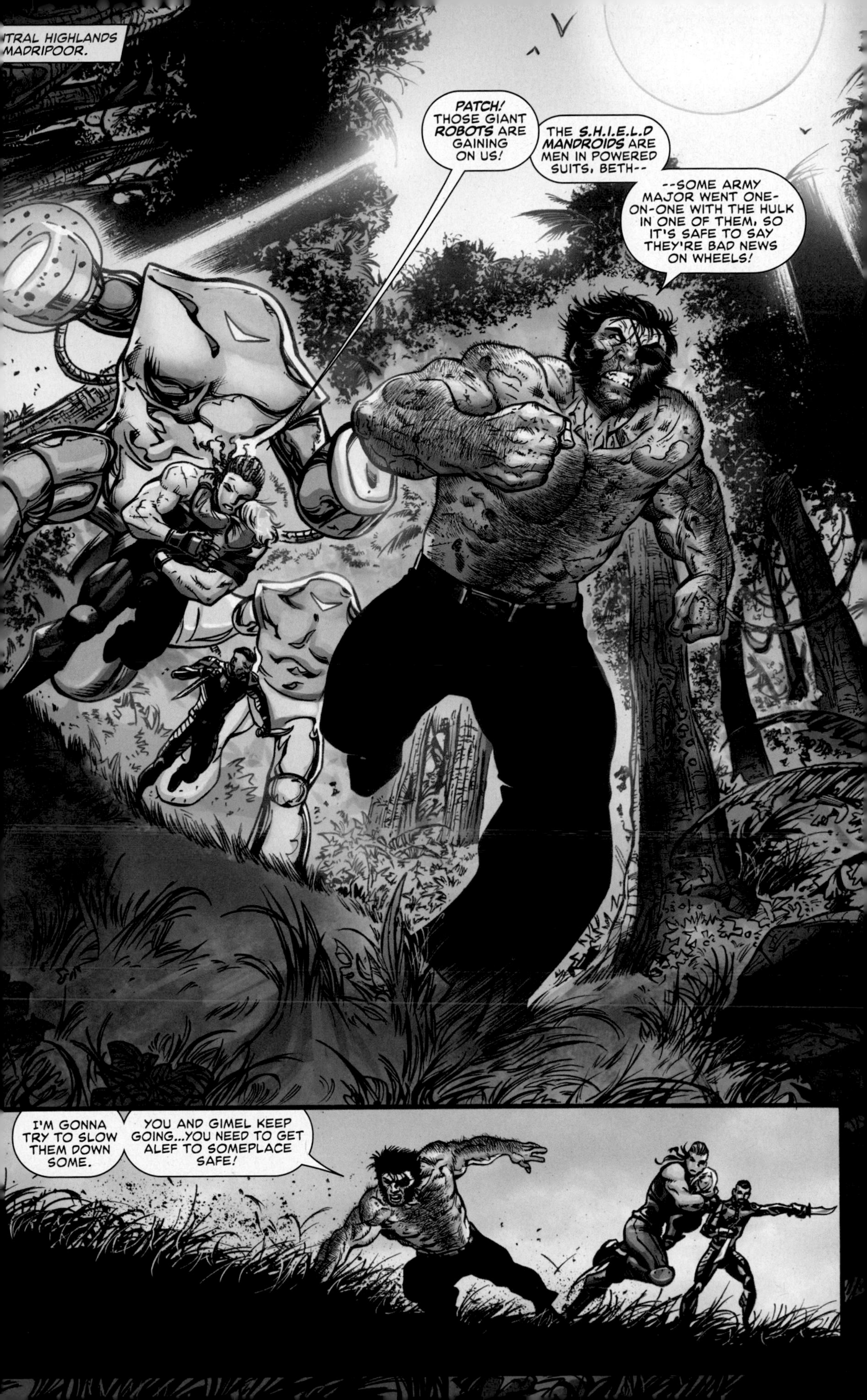

TRAL HIGHLANDS
MADRIPOOR.
PATCH! THOSE GIANT ROBOTS ARE GAINING ON US!
THE S.H.I.E.L.D MANDROIDS ARE MEN IN POWERED SUITS, BETH--
--SOME ARMY MAJOR WENT ONE-ON-ONE WITH THE HULK IN ONE OF THEM, SO IT'S SAFE TO SAY THEY'RE BAD NEWS ON WHEELS!
I'M GONNA TRY TO SLOW THEM DOWN SOME.
YOU AND GIMEL KEEP GOING...YOU NEED TO GET ALEF TO SOMEPLACE SAFE!

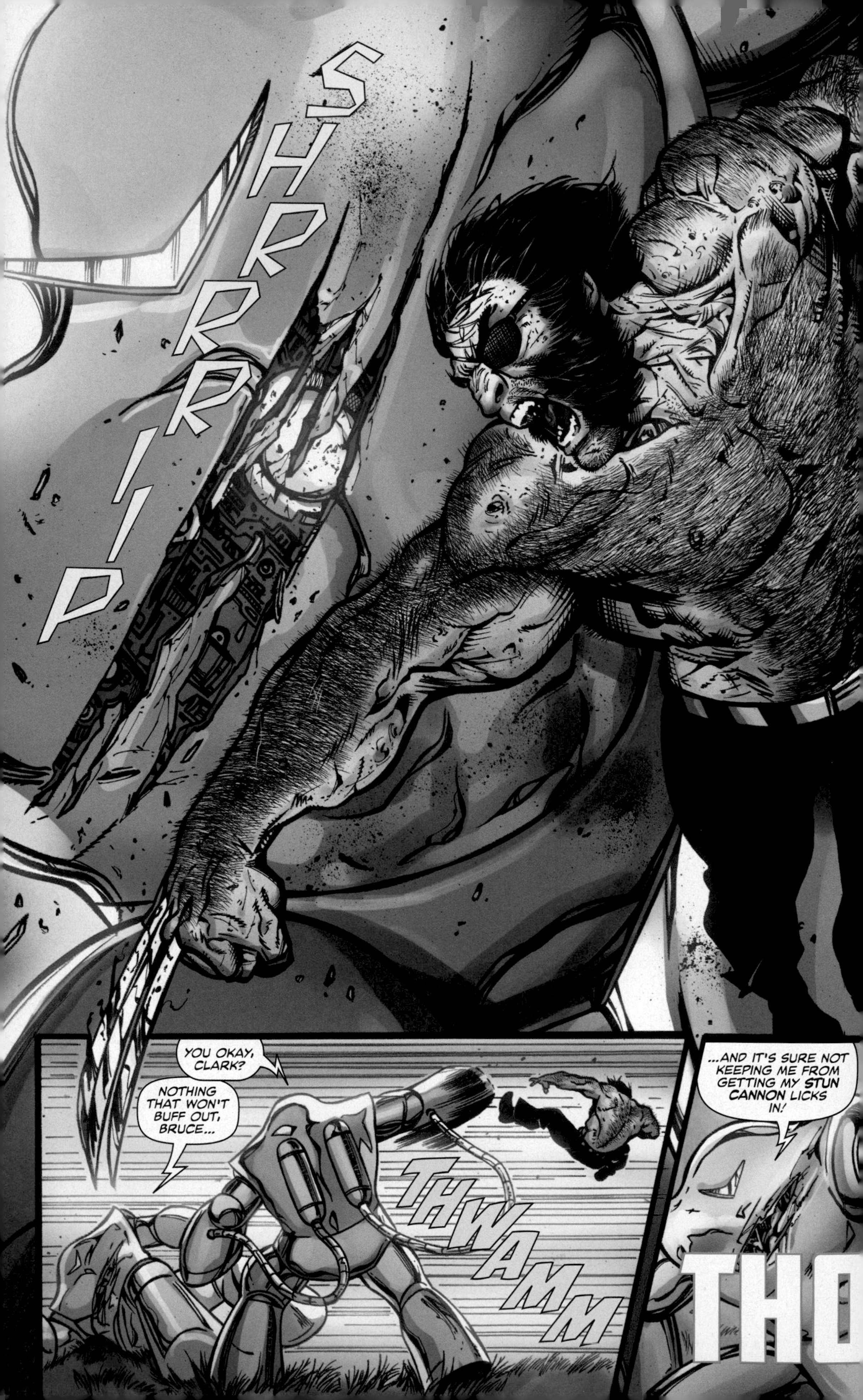
SHRRRIIIP
YOU OKAY, CLARK?
NOTHING THAT WON'T BUFF OUT, BRUCE...
THWAMM
...AND IT'S SURE NOT KEEPING ME FROM GETTING MY STUN CANNON LICKS IN!
THO

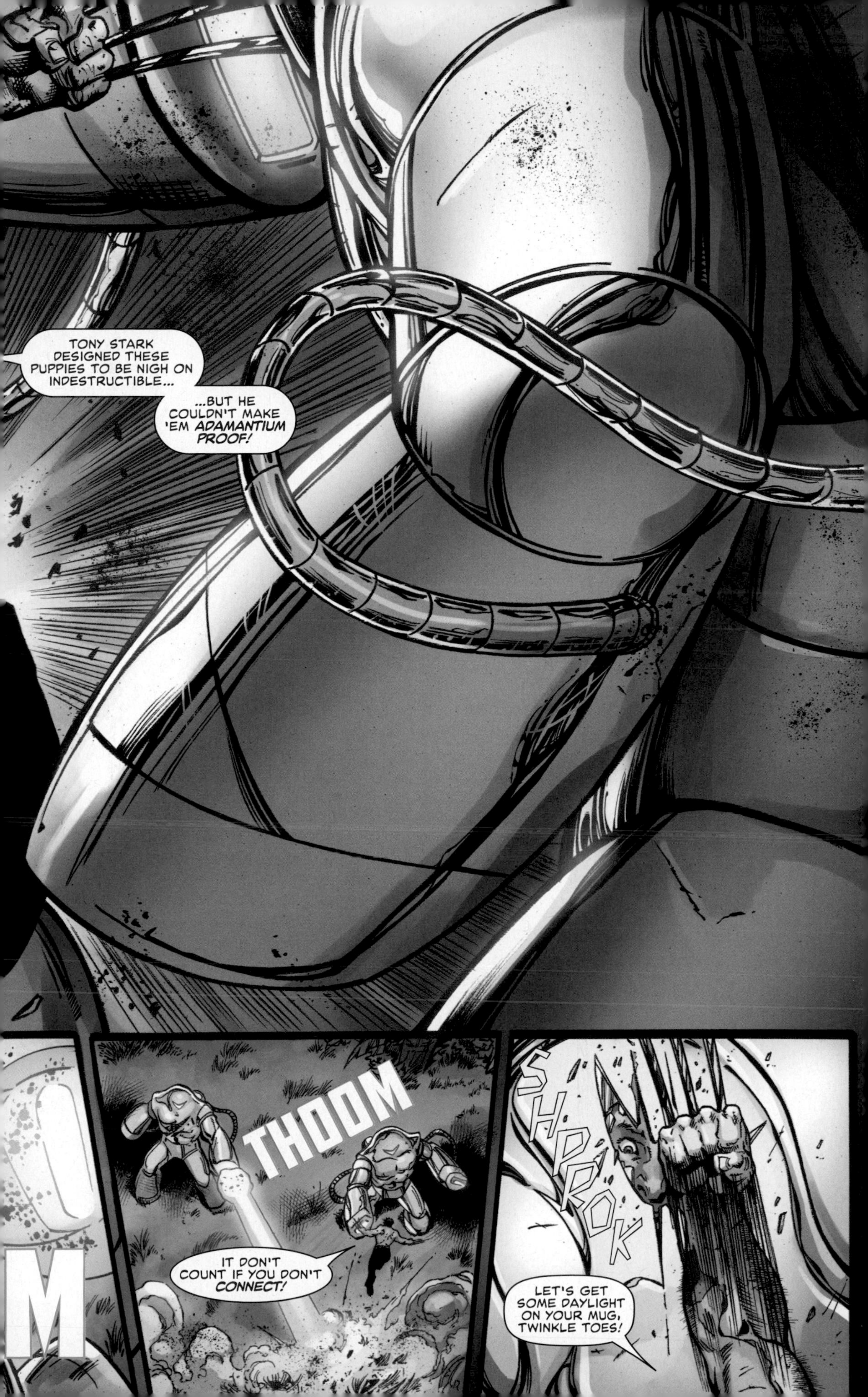
TONY STARK DESIGNED THESE PUPPIES TO BE NIGH ON INDESTRUCTIBLE...
...BUT HE COULDN'T MAKE 'EM *ADAMANTIUM PROOF!*
THOOM
IT DON'T COUNT IF YOU DON'T *CONNECT!*
SHRROK
LET'S GET SOME DAYLIGHT ON YOUR MUG, TWINKLE TOES!

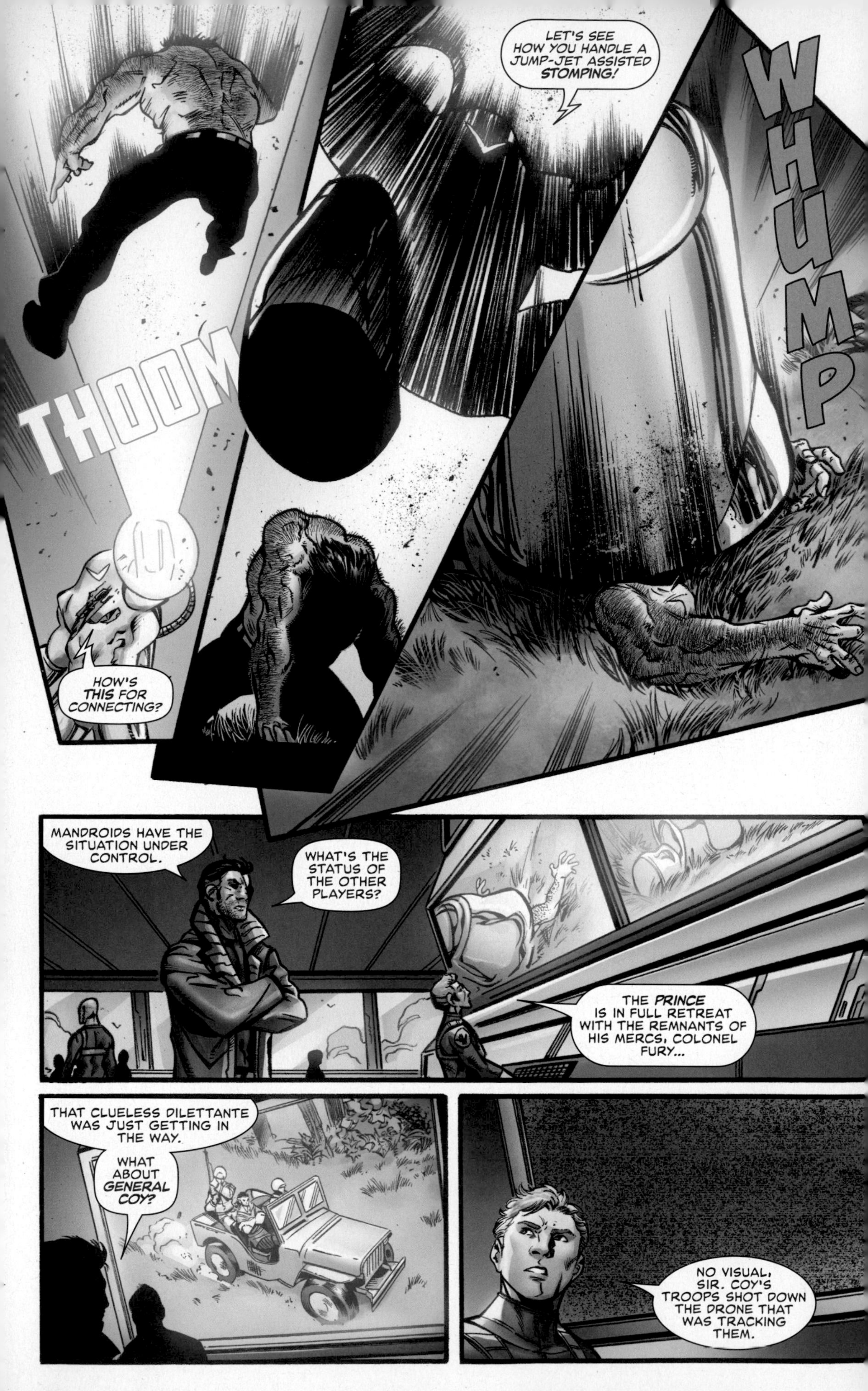
THOOM
HOW'S THIS FOR CONNECTING?
LET'S SEE HOW YOU HANDLE A JUMP-JET ASSISTED STOMPING!
WHUMP
MANDROIDS HAVE THE SITUATION UNDER CONTROL.
WHAT'S THE STATUS OF THE OTHER PLAYERS?
THE PRINCE IS IN FULL RETREAT WITH THE REMNANTS OF HIS MERCS, COLONEL FURY...
THAT CLUELESS DILETTANTE WAS JUST GETTING IN THE WAY.
WHAT ABOUT GENERAL COY?
NO VISUAL, SIR. COY'S TROOPS SHOT DOWN THE DRONE THAT WAS TRACKING THEM.

POINT-BLANK LASER BLAST SHOULD FIX HIS WAGON--

NYET!

LAY OFF HIM, YOU AYZN SCHTARKER!

IS THAT ALL YOU GOT, SHRIMP? I'M GOING TO CRUSH YOU LIKE--

LIKE WHAT?

I CAN'T HEAR YOU, CHAZER!

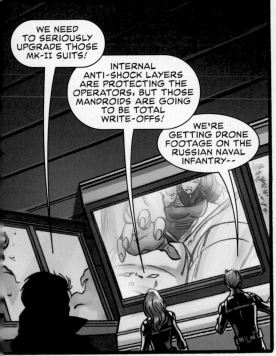

WE NEED TO SERIOUSLY UPGRADE THOSE MK-II SUITS!

INTERNAL ANTI-SHOCK LAYERS ARE PROTECTING THE OPERATORS, BUT THOSE MANDROIDS ARE GOING TO BE TOTAL WRITE-OFFS!

WE'RE GETTING DRONE FOOTAGE ON THE RUSSIAN NAVAL INFANTRY--

THEY'RE CALLING FOR AIR SUPPORT! THE CALLER IDENTIFIED HIMSELF ON THE COMMAND NET AS *CAPTAIN MUSSORGSKY*...

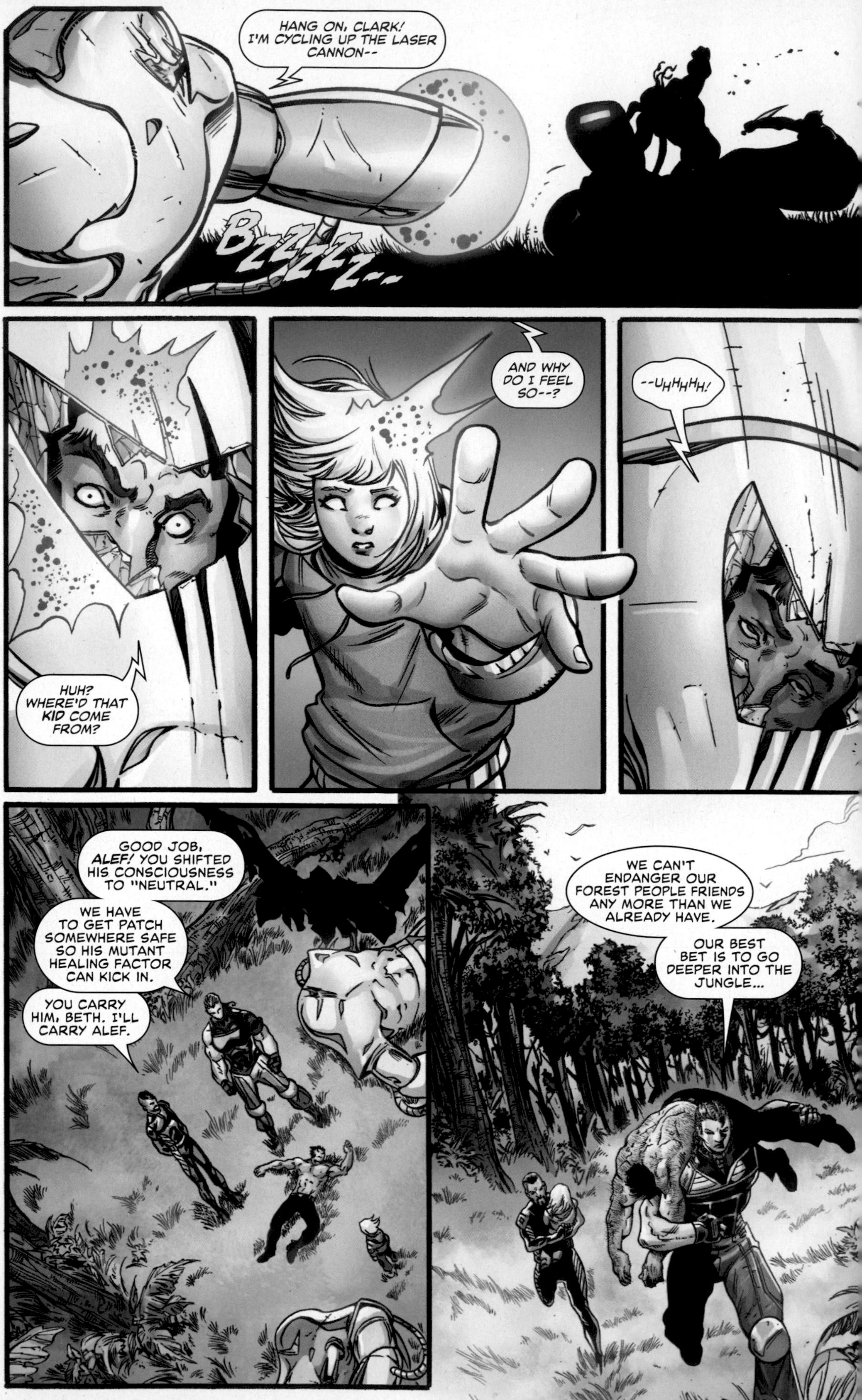
HANG ON, CLARK! I'M CYCLING UP THE LASER CANNON--
BZZZZZZ--
HUH? WHERE'D THAT KID COME FROM?
AND WHY DO I FEEL SO--?
--UHHHHH!
GOOD JOB, ALEF! YOU SHIFTED HIS CONSCIOUSNESS TO "NEUTRAL."
WE HAVE TO GET PATCH SOMEWHERE SAFE SO HIS MUTANT HEALING FACTOR CAN KICK IN.
YOU CARRY HIM, BETH. I'LL CARRY ALEF.
WE CAN'T ENDANGER OUR FOREST PEOPLE FRIENDS ANY MORE THAN WE ALREADY HAVE.
OUR BEST BET IS TO GO DEEPER INTO THE JUNGLE...

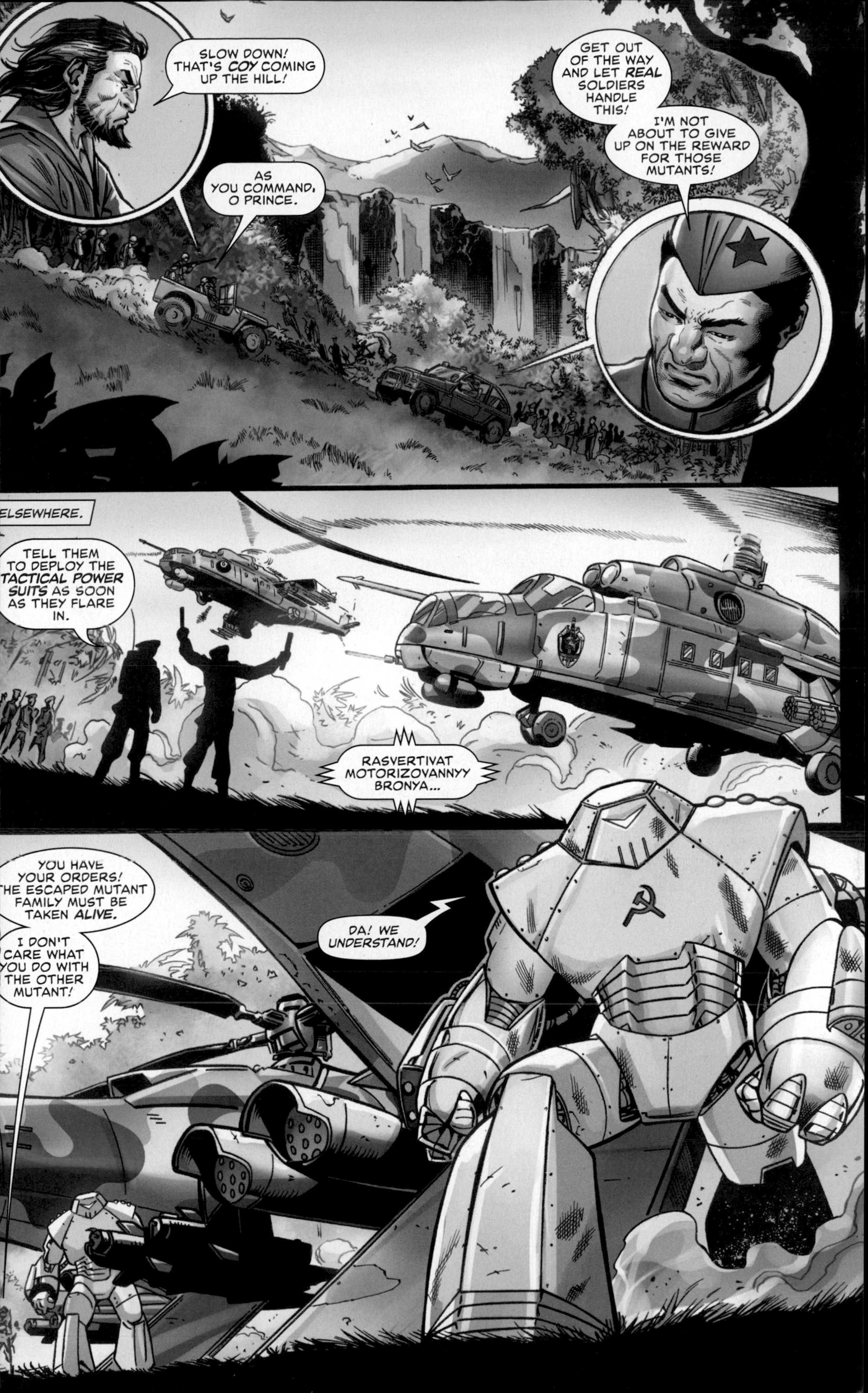
SLOW DOWN! THAT'S COY COMING UP THE HILL!
AS YOU COMMAND, O PRINCE.
GET OUT OF THE WAY AND LET REAL SOLDIERS HANDLE THIS!
I'M NOT ABOUT TO GIVE UP ON THE REWARD FOR THOSE MUTANTS!
ELSEWHERE.
TELL THEM TO DEPLOY THE TACTICAL POWER SUITS AS SOON AS THEY FLARE IN.
RASVERTIVAT MOTORIZOVANNYY BRONYA...
YOU HAVE YOUR ORDERS! THE ESCAPED MUTANT FAMILY MUST BE TAKEN ALIVE.
I DON'T CARE WHAT YOU DO WITH THE OTHER MUTANT!
DA! WE UNDERSTAND!

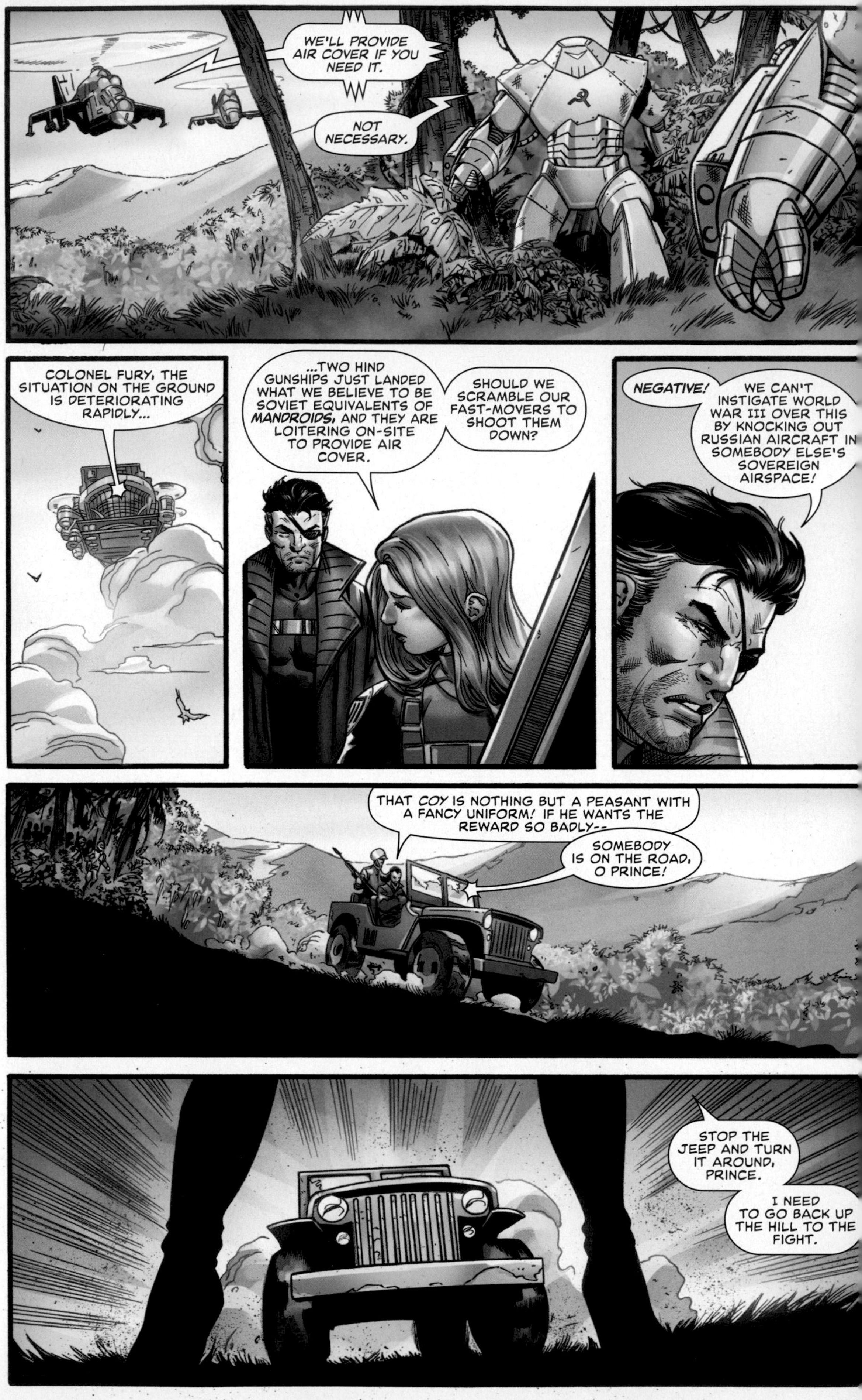

WE'LL PROVIDE AIR COVER IF YOU NEED IT.
NOT NECESSARY.
COLONEL FURY, THE SITUATION ON THE GROUND IS DETERIORATING RAPIDLY...
...TWO HIND GUNSHIPS JUST LANDED WHAT WE BELIEVE TO BE SOVIET EQUIVALENTS OF MANDROIDS, AND THEY ARE LOITERING ON-SITE TO PROVIDE AIR COVER.
SHOULD WE SCRAMBLE OUR FAST-MOVERS TO SHOOT THEM DOWN?
NEGATIVE!
WE CAN'T INSTIGATE WORLD WAR III OVER THIS BY KNOCKING OUT RUSSIAN AIRCRAFT IN SOMEBODY ELSE'S SOVEREIGN AIRSPACE!
THAT COY IS NOTHING BUT A PEASANT WITH A FANCY UNIFORM! IF HE WANTS THE REWARD SO BADLY--
SOMEBODY IS ON THE ROAD, O PRINCE!
STOP THE JEEP AND TURN IT AROUND, PRINCE.
I NEED TO GO BACK UP THE HILL TO THE FIGHT.

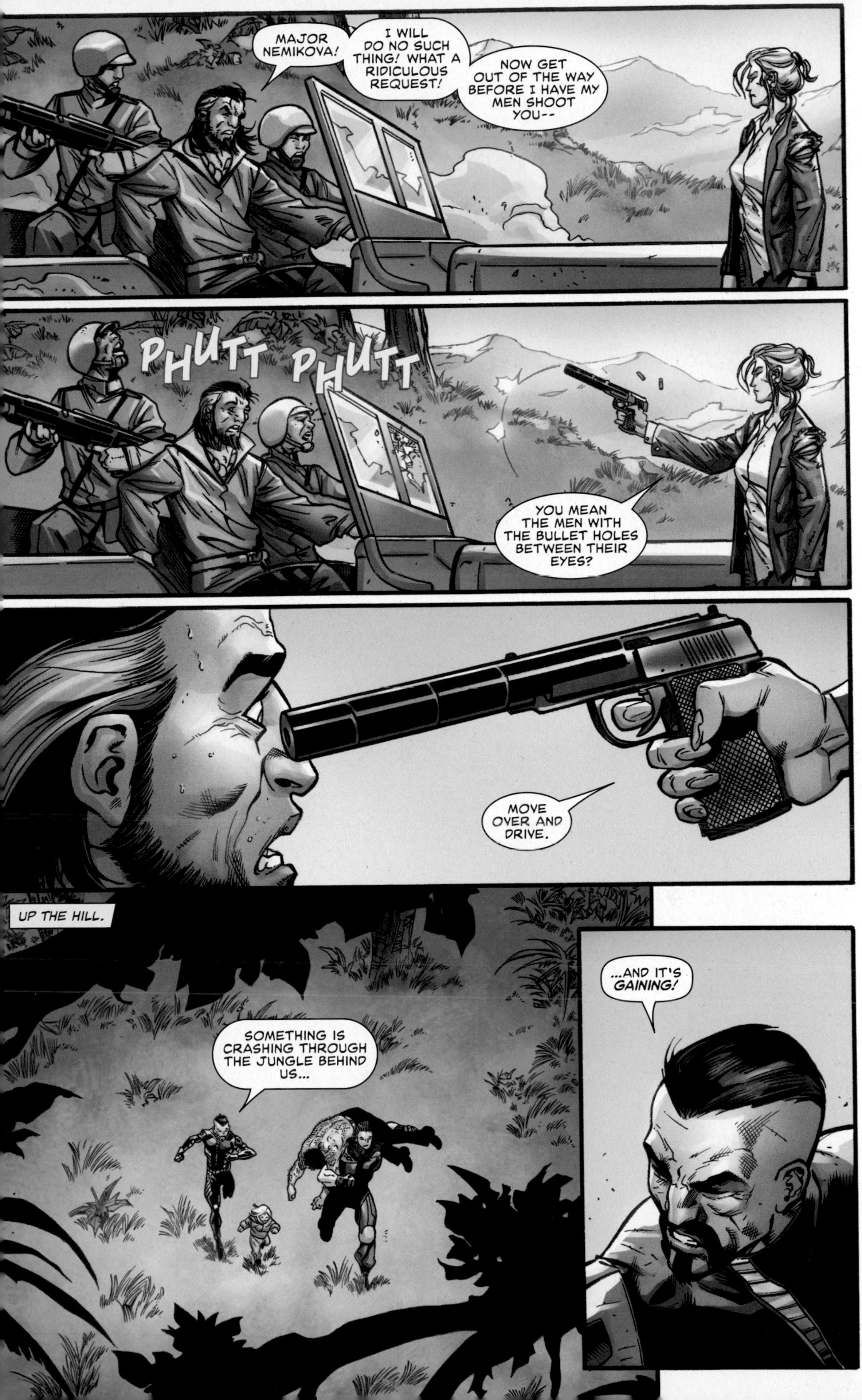
MAJOR NEMIKOVA!
I WILL DO NO SUCH THING! WHAT A RIDICULOUS REQUEST!
NOW GET OUT OF THE WAY BEFORE I HAVE MY MEN SHOOT YOU--
PHUTT PHUTT
YOU MEAN THE MEN WITH THE BULLET HOLES BETWEEN THEIR EYES?
MOVE OVER AND DRIVE.
UP THE HILL.
SOMETHING IS CRASHING THROUGH THE JUNGLE BEHIND US...
...AND IT'S GAINING!

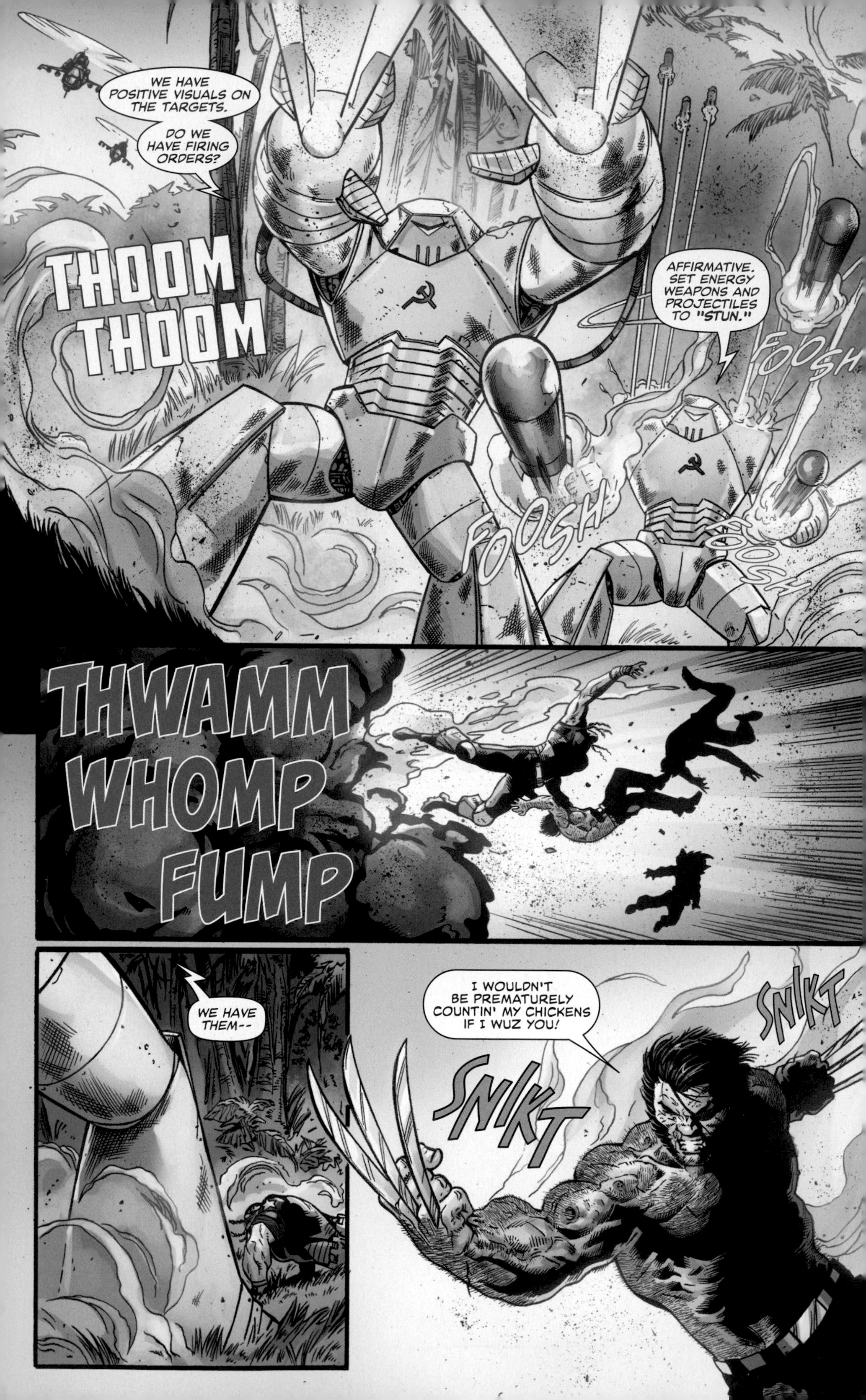
WE HAVE POSITIVE VISUALS ON THE TARGETS.
DO WE HAVE FIRING ORDERS?
THOOM THOOM
AFFIRMATIVE. SET ENERGY WEAPONS AND PROJECTILES TO "STUN."
FOOSH
FOOSH
FOOSH
THWAMM WHOMP FUMP
WE HAVE THEM--
I WOULDN'T BE PREMATURELY COUNTIN' MY CHICKENS IF I WUZ YOU!
SNIKT
SNIKT

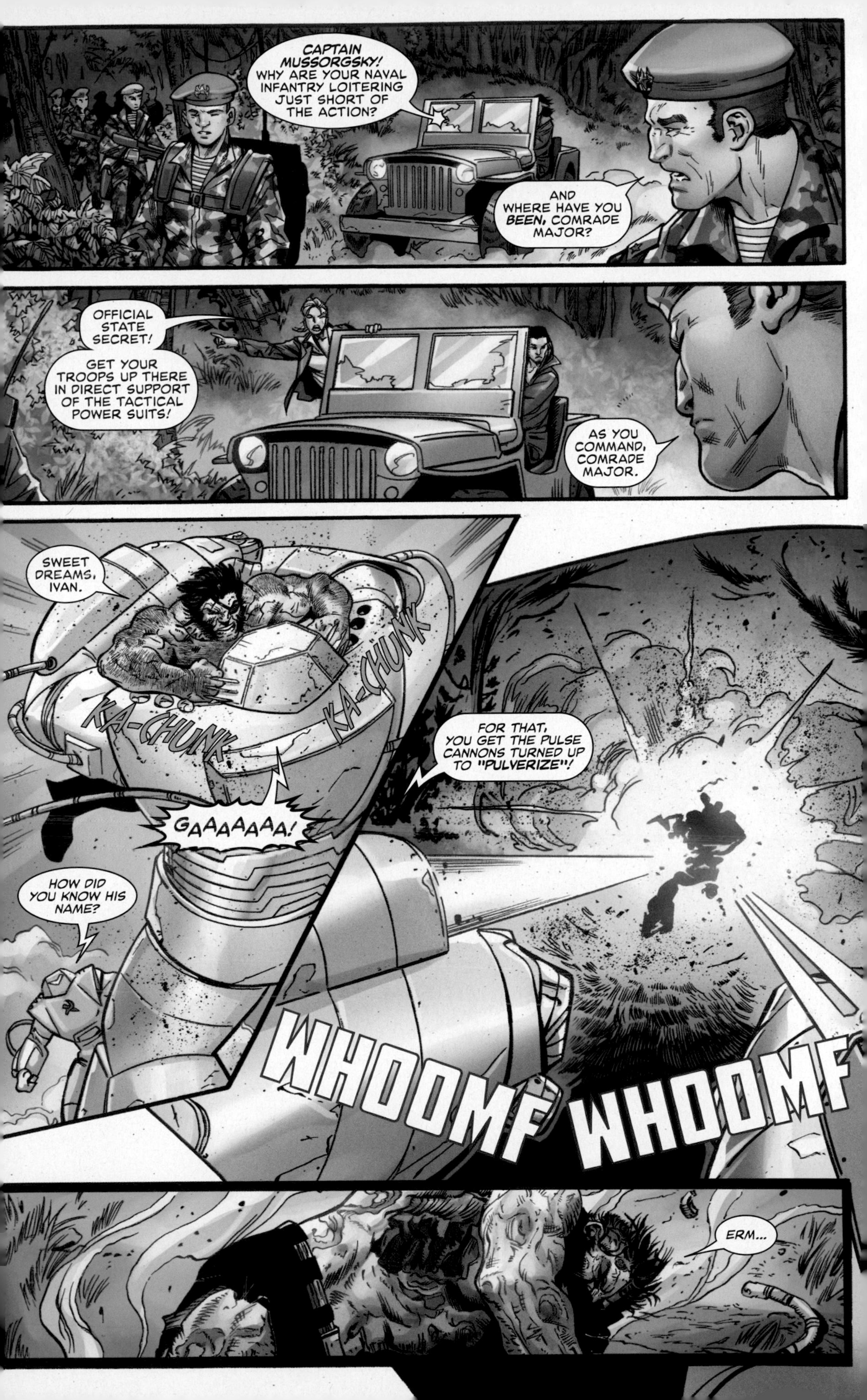
CAPTAIN MUSSORGSKY! WHY ARE YOUR NAVAL INFANTRY LOITERING JUST SHORT OF THE ACTION?
AND WHERE HAVE YOU BEEN, COMRADE MAJOR?
OFFICIAL STATE SECRET!
GET YOUR TROOPS UP THERE IN DIRECT SUPPORT OF THE TACTICAL POWER SUITS!
AS YOU COMMAND, COMRADE MAJOR.
SWEET DREAMS, IVAN.
KA-CHUNK
KA-CHUNK
GAAAAAAA!
FOR THAT, YOU GET THE PULSE CANNONS TURNED UP TO "PULVERIZE"!
HOW DID YOU KNOW HIS NAME?
WHOOMF WHOOMF
ERM...

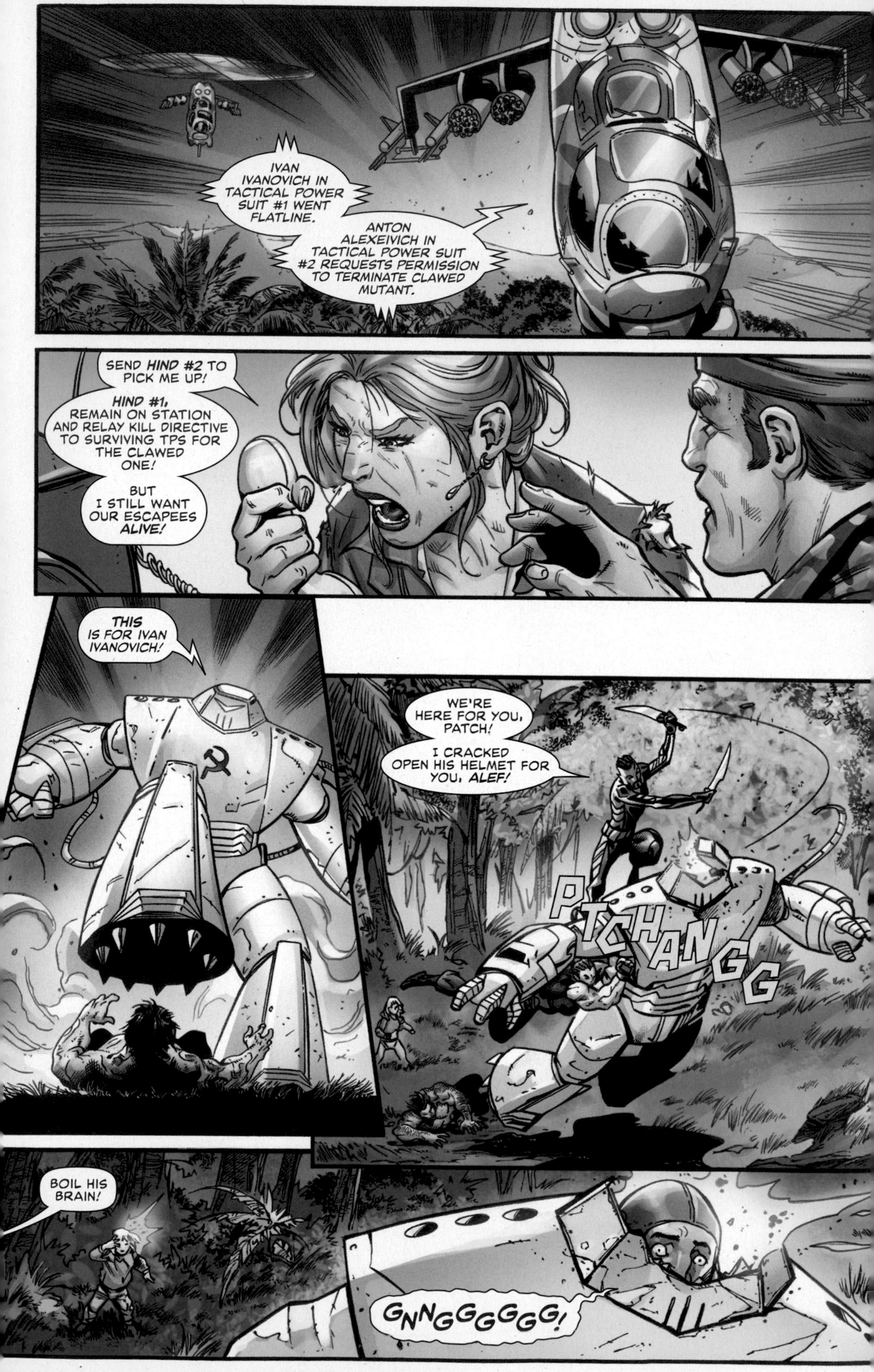
IVAN IVANOVICH IN TACTICAL POWER SUIT #1 WENT FLATLINE.
ANTON ALEXEIVICH IN TACTICAL POWER SUIT #2 REQUESTS PERMISSION TO TERMINATE CLAWED MUTANT.
SEND HIND #2 TO PICK ME UP!
HIND #1, REMAIN ON STATION AND RELAY KILL DIRECTIVE TO SURVIVING TPS FOR THE CLAWED ONE!
BUT I STILL WANT OUR ESCAPEES ALIVE!
THIS IS FOR IVAN IVANOVICH!
WE'RE HERE FOR YOU, PATCH!
I CRACKED OPEN HIS HELMET FOR YOU, ALEF!
PTCHANGG
BOIL HIS BRAIN!
GNNGGGGGG!

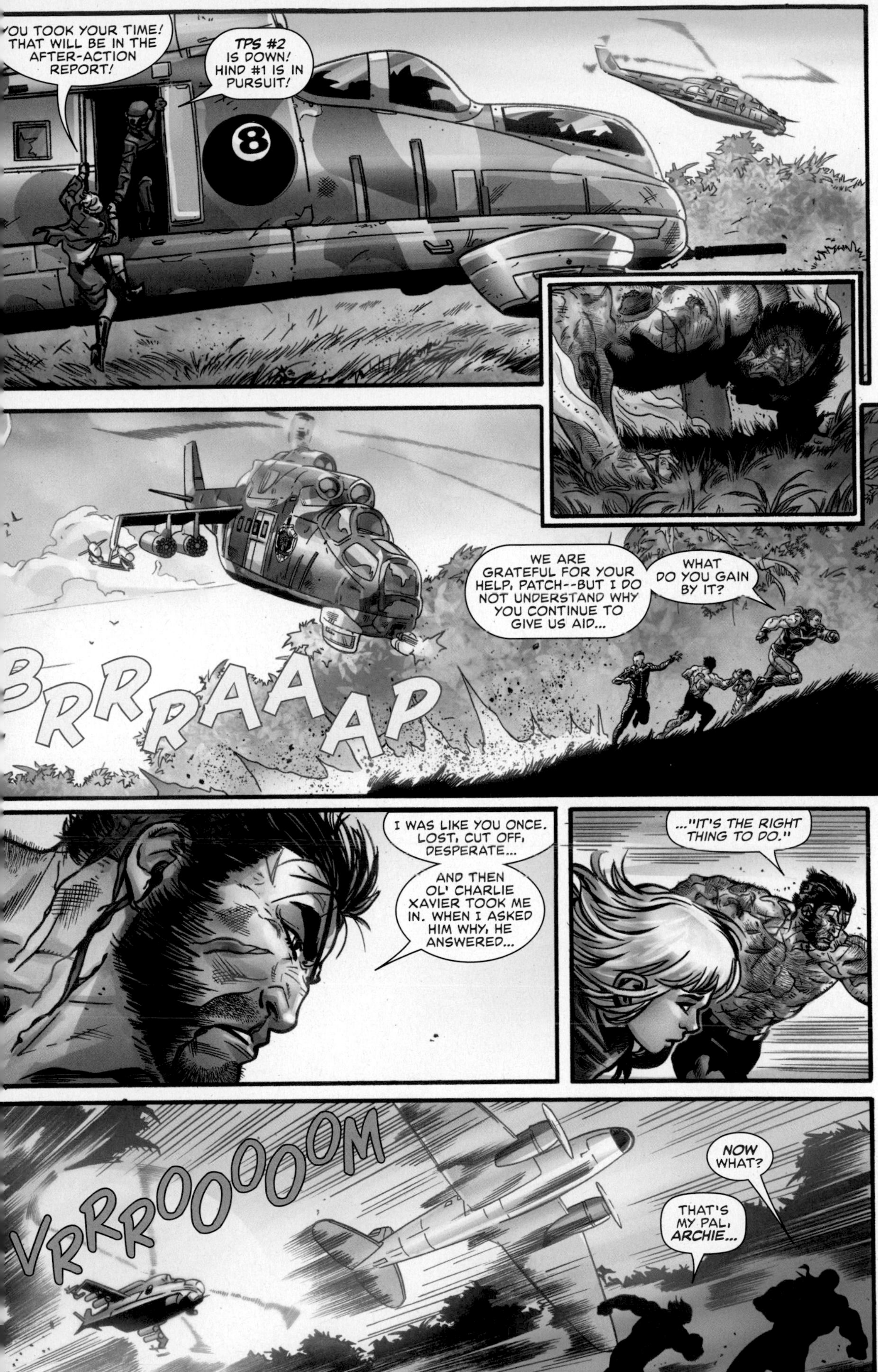

YOU TOOK YOUR TIME! THAT WILL BE IN THE AFTER-ACTION REPORT!
TPS #2 IS DOWN! HIND #1 IS IN PURSUIT!
8
WE ARE GRATEFUL FOR YOUR HELP, PATCH--BUT I DO NOT UNDERSTAND WHY YOU CONTINUE TO GIVE US AID...
WHAT DO YOU GAIN BY IT?
BRRRAAAP
I WAS LIKE YOU ONCE. LOST, CUT OFF, DESPERATE...
AND THEN OL' CHARLIE XAVIER TOOK ME IN. WHEN I ASKED HIM WHY, HE ANSWERED...
..."IT'S THE RIGHT THING TO DO."
VRRROOOOOOM
NOW WHAT?
THAT'S MY PAL, ARCHIE...

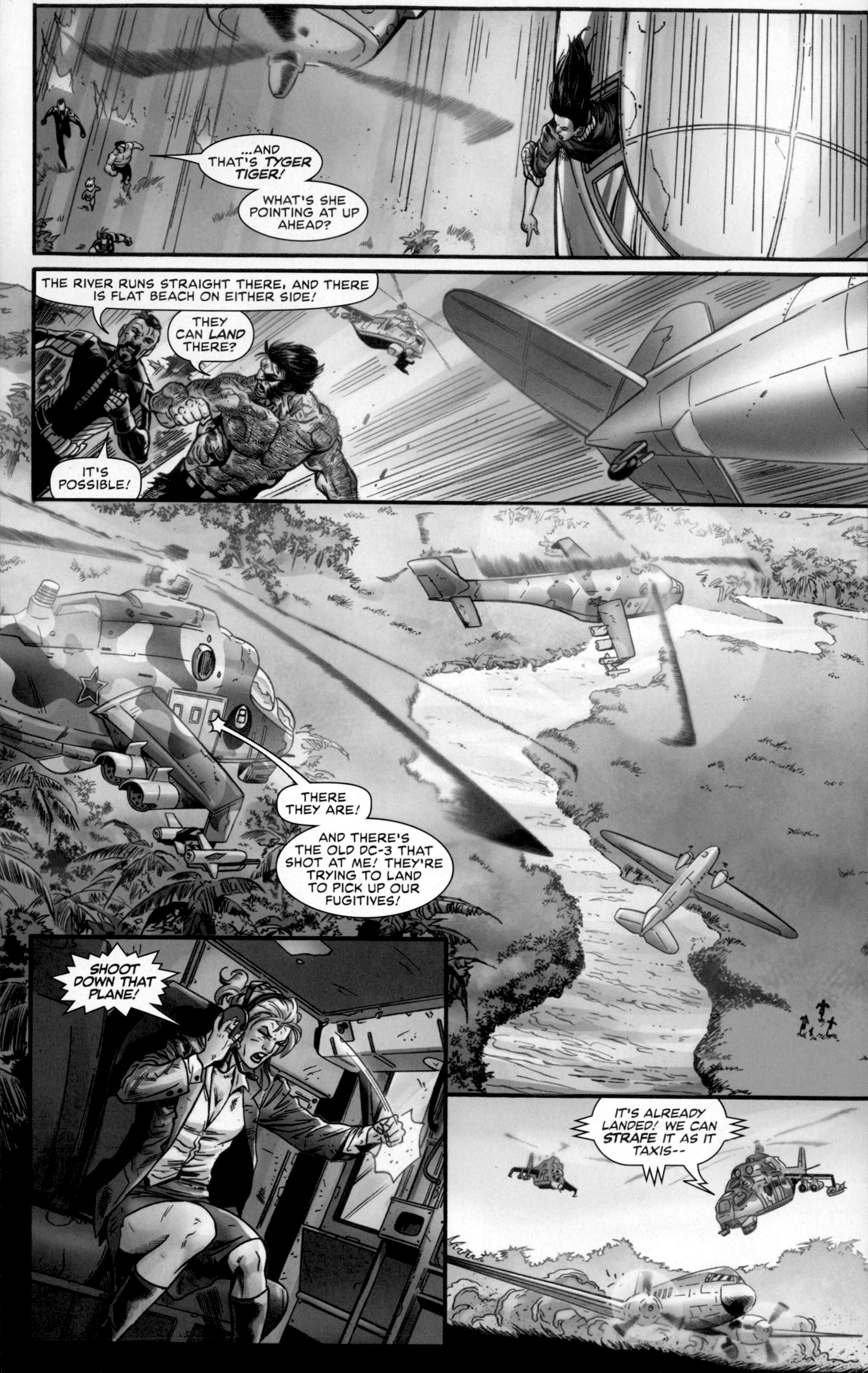
...AND THAT'S TYGER TIGER!
WHAT'S SHE POINTING AT UP AHEAD?
THE RIVER RUNS STRAIGHT THERE, AND THERE IS FLAT BEACH ON EITHER SIDE!
THEY CAN LAND THERE?
IT'S POSSIBLE!
THERE THEY ARE!
AND THERE'S THE OLD DC-3 THAT SHOT AT ME! THEY'RE TRYING TO LAND TO PICK UP OUR FUGITIVES!
SHOOT DOWN THAT PLANE!
IT'S ALREADY LANDED! WE CAN STRAFE IT AS IT TAXIS--

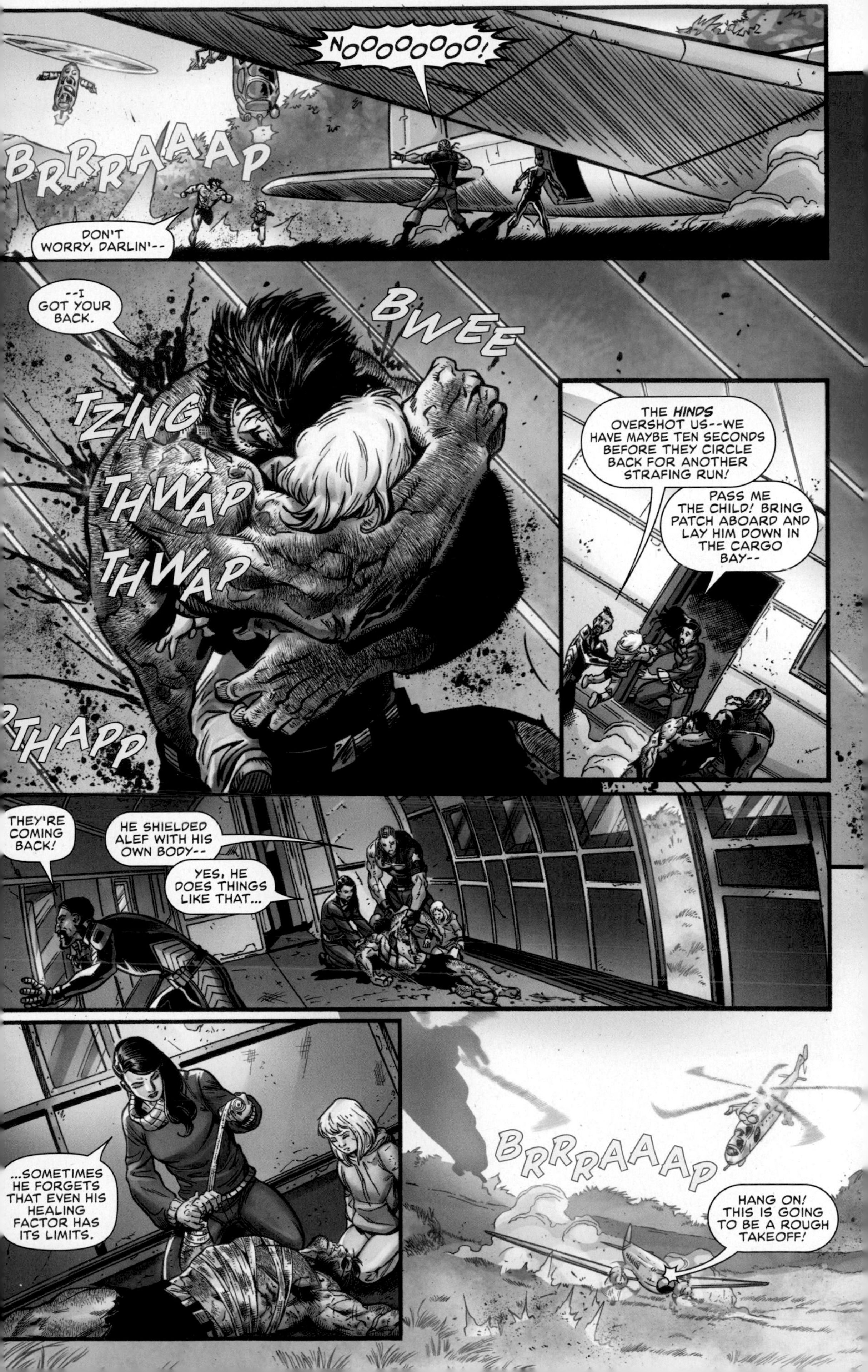
NOOOOOOOO!
BRRRAAAAP
DON'T WORRY, DARLIN'--
--I GOT YOUR BACK.
BWEE
TZING
THWAP
THWAP
THAPP
THE HINDS OVERSHOT US--WE HAVE MAYBE TEN SECONDS BEFORE THEY CIRCLE BACK FOR ANOTHER STRAFING RUN!
PASS ME THE CHILD! BRING PATCH ABOARD AND LAY HIM DOWN IN THE CARGO BAY--
THEY'RE COMING BACK!
HE SHIELDED ALEF WITH HIS OWN BODY--
YES, HE DOES THINGS LIKE THAT...
...SOMETIMES HE FORGETS THAT EVEN HIS HEALING FACTOR HAS ITS LIMITS.
BRRRAAAAP
HANG ON! THIS IS GOING TO BE A ROUGH TAKEOFF!

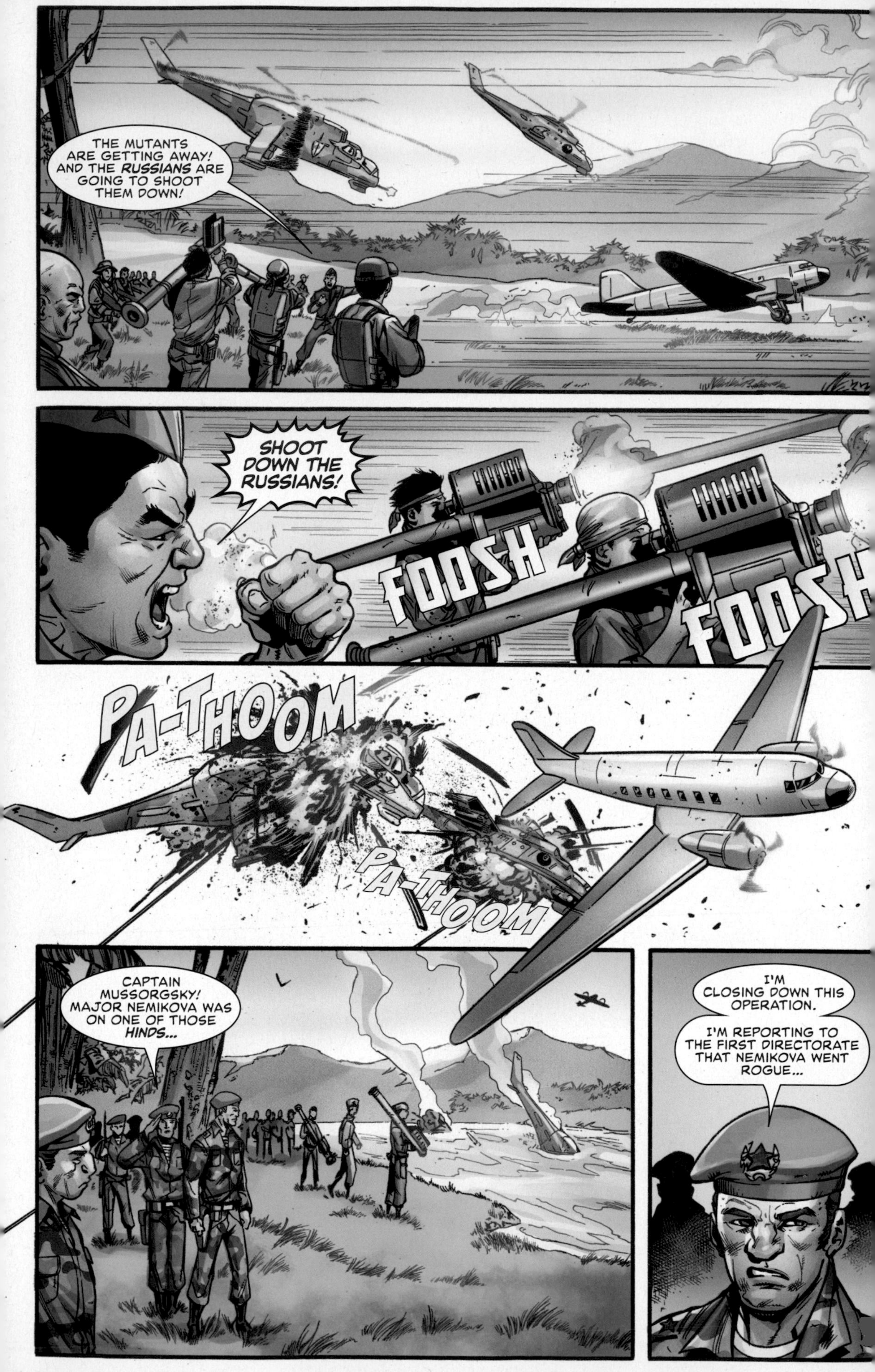
THE MUTANTS ARE GETTING AWAY! AND THE RUSSIANS ARE GOING TO SHOOT THEM DOWN!
SHOOT DOWN THE RUSSIANS!
FOOSH
FOOSH
PA-THOOM
PA-THOOM
CAPTAIN MUSSORGSKY! MAJOR NEMIKOVA WAS ON ONE OF THOSE HINDS...
I'M CLOSING DOWN THIS OPERATION.
I'M REPORTING TO THE FIRST DIRECTORATE THAT NEMIKOVA WENT ROGUE...

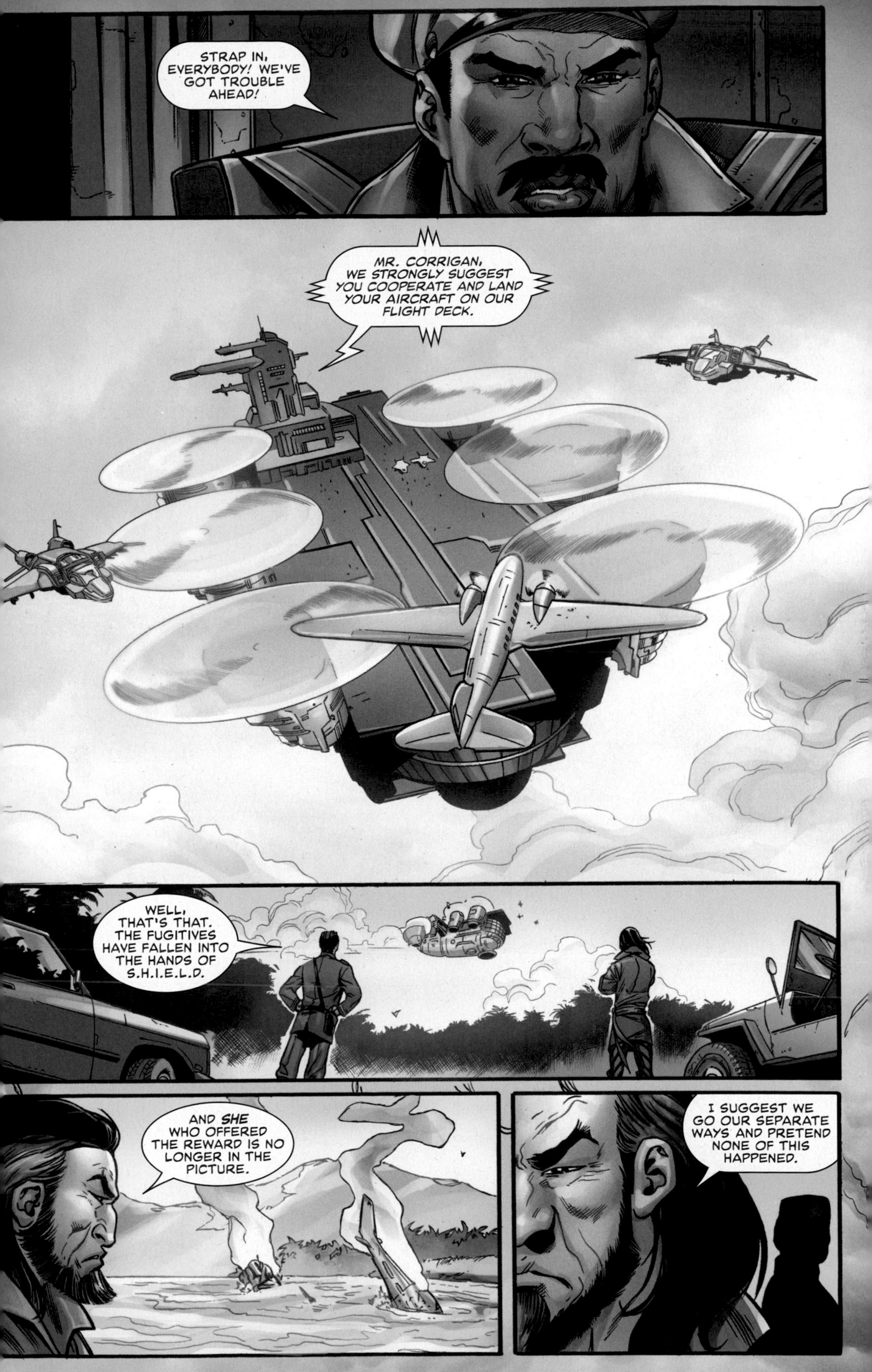
STRAP IN, EVERYBODY! WE'VE GOT TROUBLE AHEAD!
MR. CORRIGAN, WE STRONGLY SUGGEST YOU COOPERATE AND LAND YOUR AIRCRAFT ON OUR FLIGHT DECK.
WELL, THAT'S THAT. THE FUGITIVES HAVE FALLEN INTO THE HANDS OF S.H.I.E.L.D.
AND SHE WHO OFFERED THE REWARD IS NO LONGER IN THE PICTURE.
I SUGGEST WE GO OUR SEPARATE WAYS AND PRETEND NONE OF THIS HAPPENED.

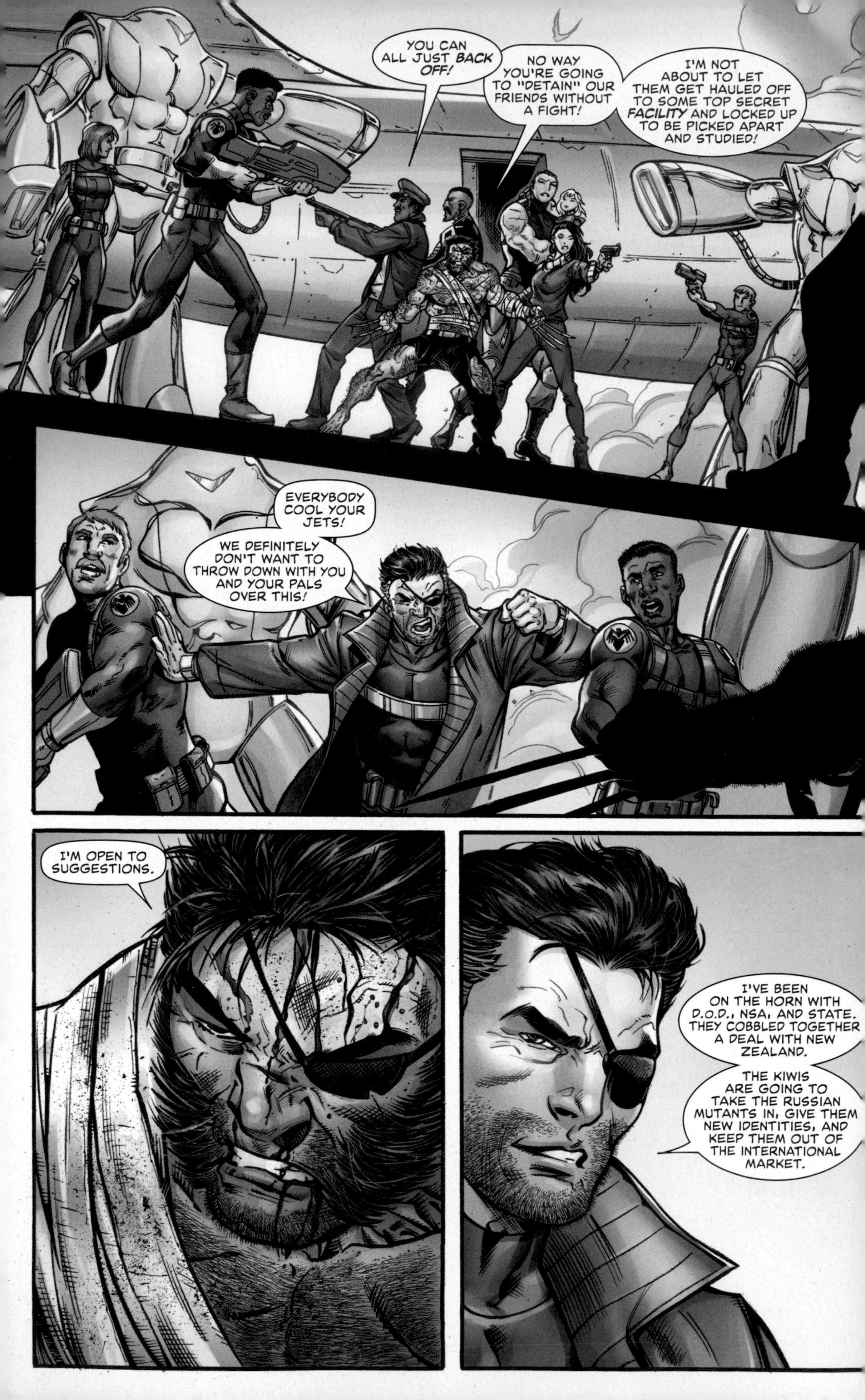
YOU CAN ALL JUST *BACK OFF!*
NO WAY YOU'RE GOING TO "DETAIN" OUR FRIENDS WITHOUT A FIGHT!
I'M NOT ABOUT TO LET THEM GET HAULED OFF TO SOME TOP SECRET *FACILITY* AND LOCKED UP TO BE PICKED APART AND STUDIED!
EVERYBODY COOL YOUR JETS!
WE DEFINITELY DON'T WANT TO THROW DOWN WITH YOU AND YOUR PALS OVER THIS!
I'M OPEN TO SUGGESTIONS.
I'VE BEEN ON THE HORN WITH D.O.D., NSA, AND STATE. THEY COBBLED TOGETHER A DEAL WITH NEW ZEALAND.
THE KIWIS ARE GOING TO TAKE THE RUSSIAN MUTANTS IN, GIVE THEM NEW IDENTITIES, AND KEEP THEM OUT OF THE INTERNATIONAL MARKET.

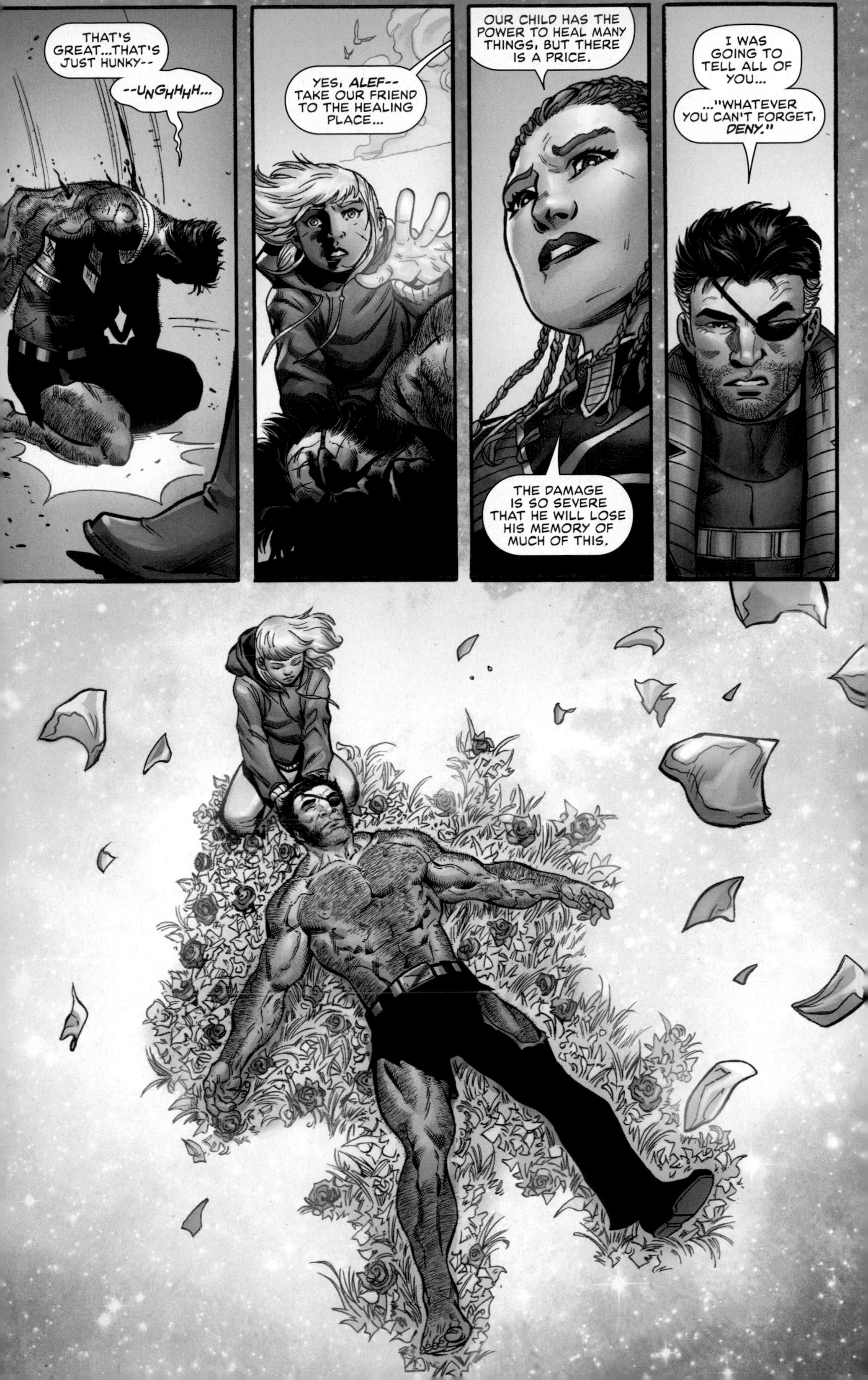
THAT'S GREAT...THAT'S JUST HUNKY--
--UNGHHHH...
YES, ALEF-- TAKE OUR FRIEND TO THE HEALING PLACE...
OUR CHILD HAS THE POWER TO HEAL MANY THINGS, BUT THERE IS A PRICE.
THE DAMAGE IS SO SEVERE THAT HE WILL LOSE HIS MEMORY OF MUCH OF THIS.
I WAS GOING TO TELL ALL OF YOU...
..."WHATEVER YOU CAN'T FORGET, DENY."

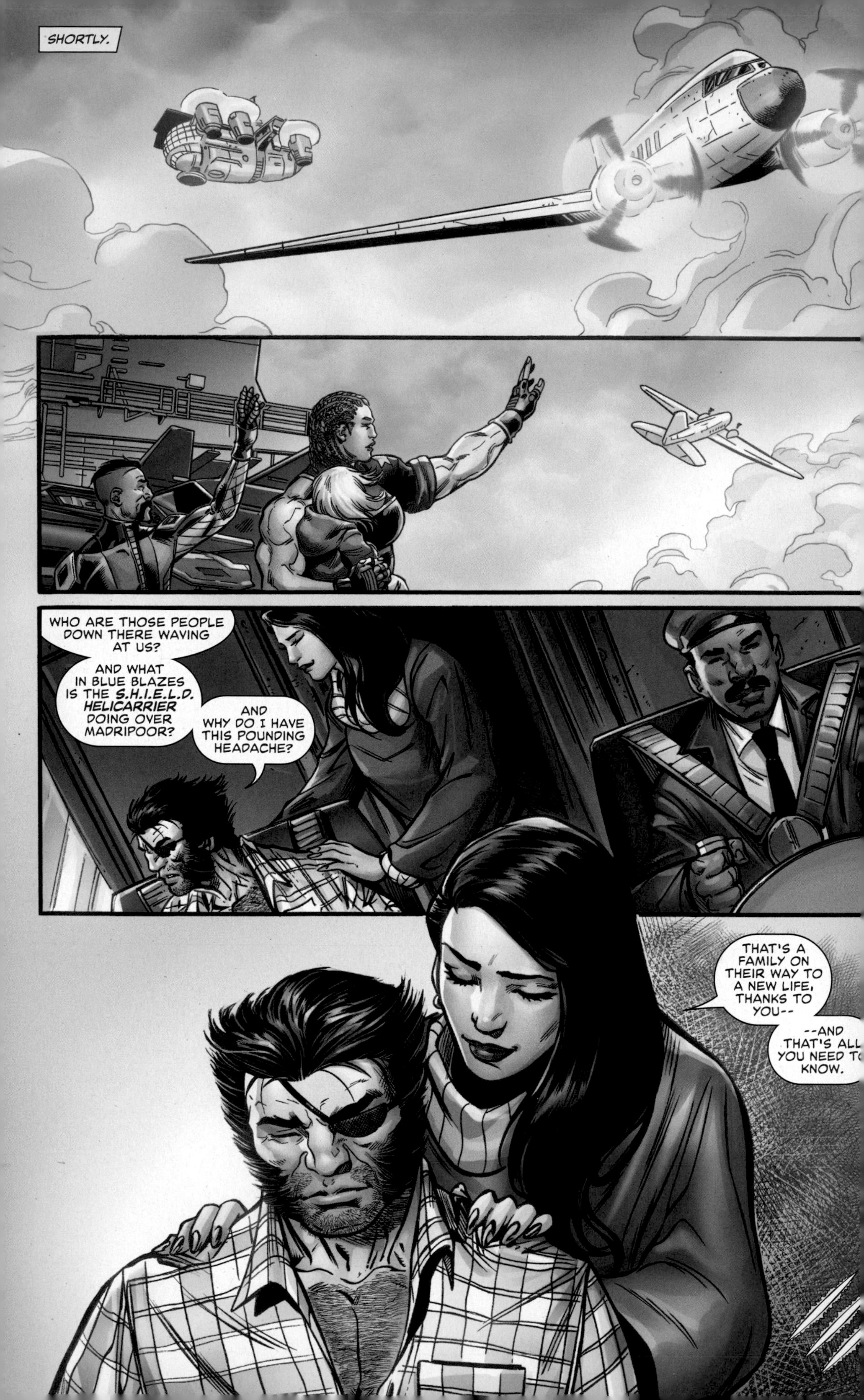
SHORTLY.
WHO ARE THOSE PEOPLE DOWN THERE WAVING AT US?
AND WHAT IN BLUE BLAZES IS THE S.H.I.E.L.D. HELICARRIER DOING OVER MADRIPOOR?
AND WHY DO I HAVE THIS POUNDING HEADACHE?
THAT'S A FAMILY ON THEIR WAY TO A NEW LIFE, THANKS TO YOU--
--AND THAT'S ALL YOU NEED TO KNOW.

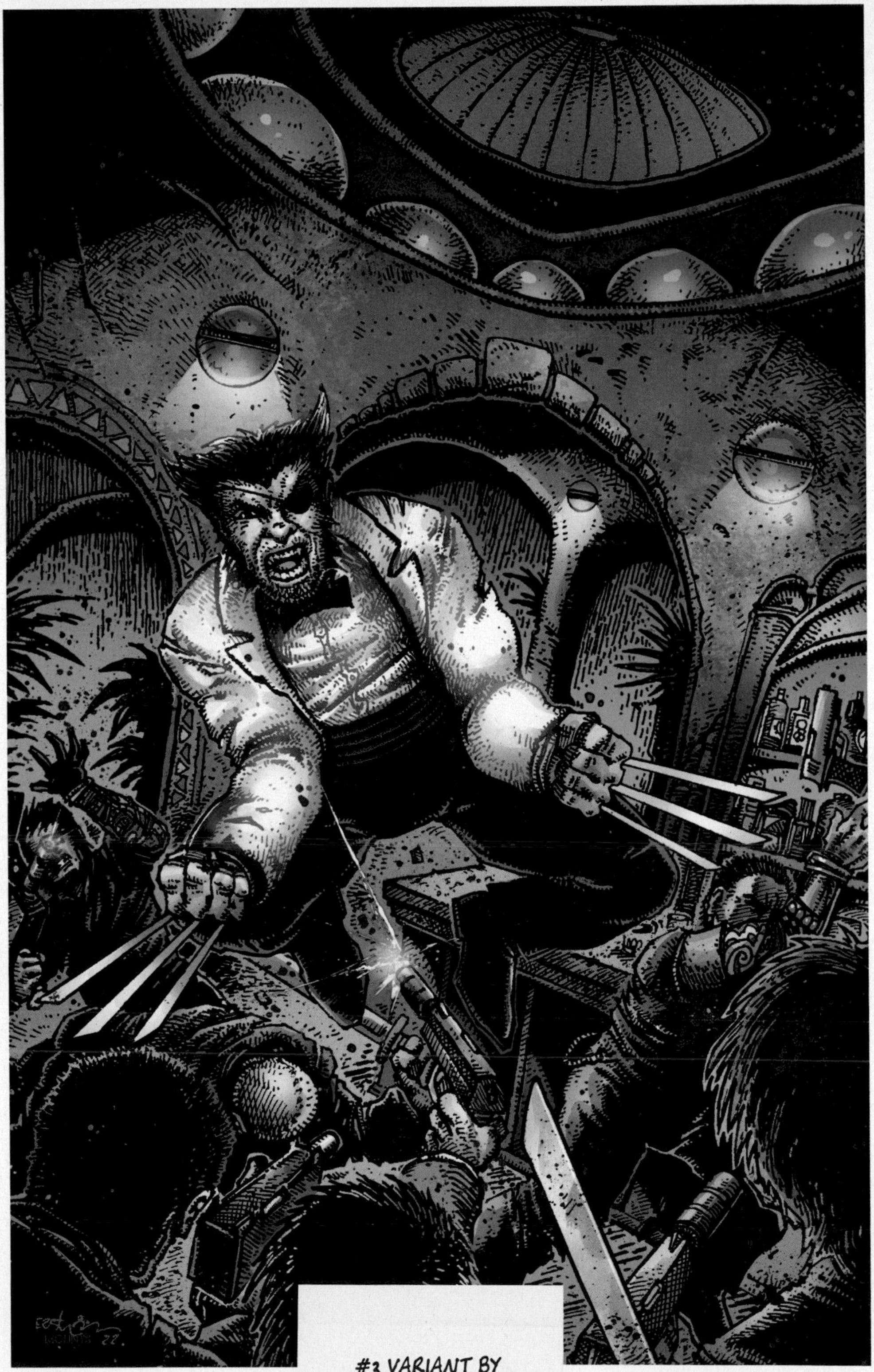

#3 VARIANT BY
KEVIN EASTMAN
& PAUL MOUNTS

INTERNAL REVIEW ONLY

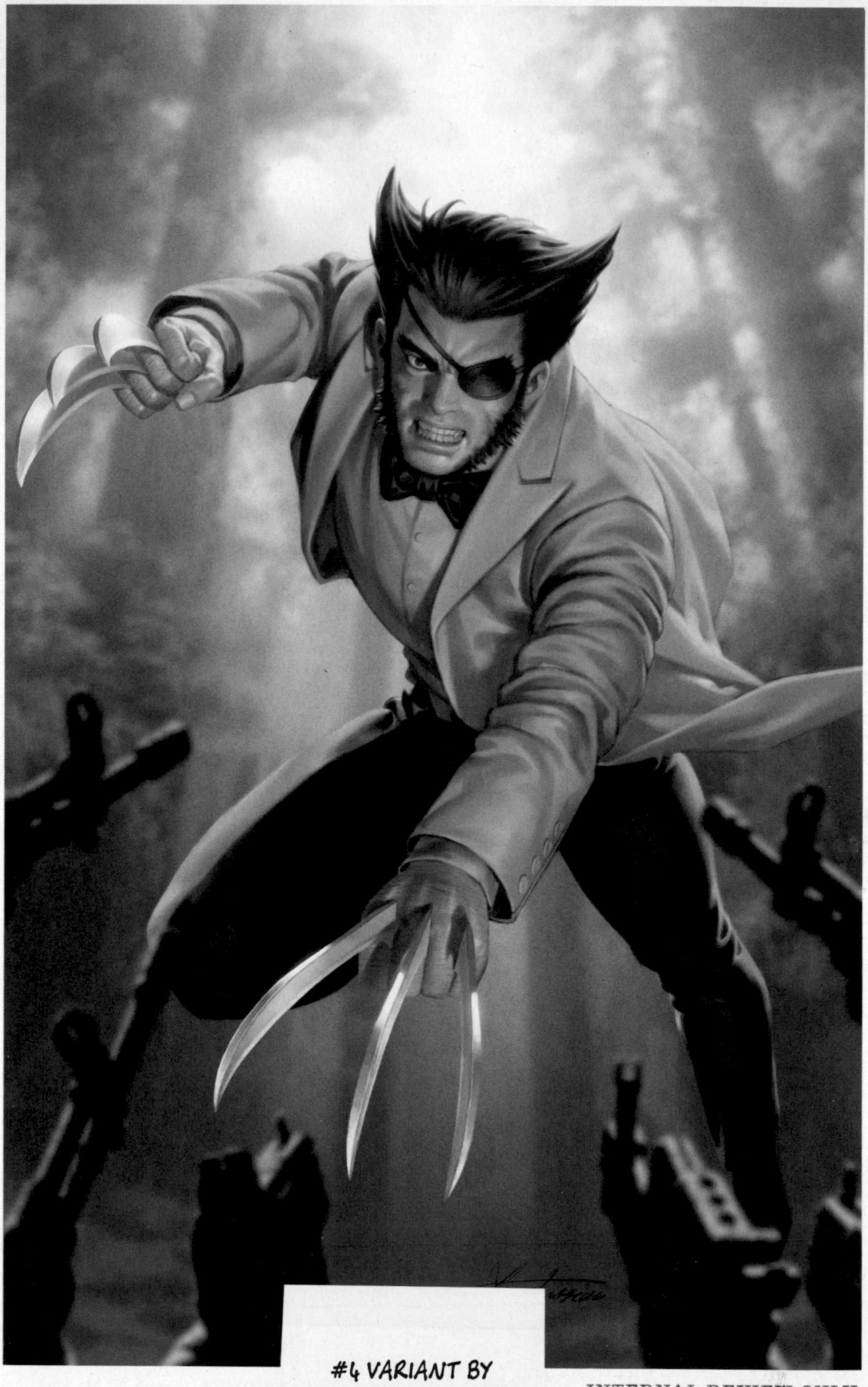

#4 VARIANT BY
JUNGGEUN YOON

INTERNAL REVIEW ONLY

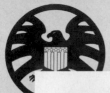